ALL THE QUEEN'S MEN

Albert Snyder

GAY MEN'S PRESS

All the Queen's Men

by Nick Ellwood

First published 1999 by Millivres Ltd,
part of the Millivres Prowler Group,
3 Broadbent Close, London N6 5GG

World Copyright © 1999 Nick Elwood

Nick Elwood has asserted his right to be identified as the author of this work
in accordance with the Copyright, Designs and Patents Act 1988

A CIP catalogue record for this book is available
from the British Library

ISBN 1 902852 03 6

Distributed in Europe by Central Books,
99 Wallis Rd, London E9 5LN

Distributed in North America by InBook/LPC Group,
1436 West Randolph, Chicago, IL 60607

Distributed in Australia by Bulldog Books,
P O Box 300, Beaconsfield, NSW 2014

Printed and bound in the EU by WSOY, Juva, Finland

For my friends:
Kimra, Matt Sterling, Lee Philips,
Lawrence and Jazmin Quill;
my regiment, and Master Georg Soupidis
of the Song Do Kwan, Osnabrück

NULLA VESTIGA RETRORSUM

Prologue

Everything happened fast in my first week as a student at Essex University. My military haircut still hadn't grown out, I'd made new friends, taken drugs, and replaced symbols of rank and regiment with political and sexual badges: 'Ban the Monarchy', 'Give us Your Sons', 'Axe the Poll Tax' and 'Queer as Fuck'. On political demonstrations I joined in the chanting as a chorus of voices bellowed: "Tory Scum!" or "Maggie, Maggie, Maggie, Out! Out! Out!" As a soldier I'd never been encouraged to think, and now that academic topics invaded my head they challenged my parochial world perspective. I'd never been able to be truly open about my sexuality and university provided me with a Lesbian and Gay Society. It was better to be gay than straight at Essex. Being straight was boring and gave no added status.

Within days I found myself involved in student politics, joined the Lesbian and Gay Society and adopted an openly gay identity. Elected secretary, one of my first jobs was writing a sarcastic letter inviting the Queen to attend our Pink Festival. I explained how I'd always been a fan of hers as a Trumpet Major* in the 15th Dragoons. I never expected a reply; it was just an outrageous thing to do.

I had come from the experience of fourteen years in a wilderness, where ideas were rarely untangled or challenged, and mentalities were incapable of forging or developing an argument or idea in all but the crudest manner. Most soldiers, even officers, are mentally crippled, by a claustrophobic institution that espouses uniformity, conformity, masculinity whilst stifling the unique. How could soldiers be anything other than intellectually challenged in such a cultural wasteland?

I had never considered the extent to which the army had conditioned me. This became obvious in habits to which I'd grown accustomed. I polished my shoes regularly, kept baths, toilets and showers clean and washed my cutlery and dishes immediately after use. Such behaviour contrasted with my student flatmates who left their plates to clutter the draining-board, and left communal areas to the cleaners. But there were stranger idiosyncrasies. I avoided walking on grassed areas and took concrete paths to all my destinations. A bar of chocolate or a sweet was never eaten outside. Such traits, which soon faded, amused my student friends. For the first time in my adult

---

* For explanation of all military terms and abbreviations, see the Glossary on p.262.

life I could march out of step and bang my drum in the cracks of the music, and I loved it. And then there were the hairs growing on my thighs; years of wearing cavalry tights had rubbed them bald.

In December 1989, I was crossing a windy campus square when a well-dressed woman called out: "Cpl Elwood!" I didn't recognise her and stood gawking. "You were in the 15th Dragoons, weren't you?"

"Yes."

"In the band?"

"Yes."

"I'm Colonel Naylor's wife, though he's a brigadier now."

"God! Fancy meeting you here. What are you doing, are you a student?"

"Well, I'm taking an art course." Typical, I thought. Art was a suitably pretentious subject to talk about in the Officers' Mess or at bourgeois dinner parties.

"How long have you been out of the regiment?" she asked.

"Oh, over a year. I left in '88 and came straight to university."

"To do what?"

"Sociology."

"I would have thought you'd have followed a music degree – a radical change to sociology, isn't it?"

"Well," I grinned, "I wanted a change, and besides, all the music colleges I applied to wanted keyboard skills which I didn't have; at least not to the level they required."

She looked at her watch. "Look, I'm sorry, I can't stop. My lecture begins in five minutes. We're having a Christmas party in a few weeks. Perhaps you'd like to come along? You don't have to decide now. I'll send you an invitation via the students' pigeonholes."

"Yes, that would be fun," I said. "Give my regards to your husband."

It deflated my ego to discover I'd been invited to a dinner held for the brigadier's servants, their wives and a few junior officers. It was a dinner for the lowly and menial. In a large anteroom covered in luscious carpets we stood sipping sherry. I felt uncomfortable; I had little in common with the servants, less with their wives, and felt I had to censor my conversation with the officers.

"What do you study, then?" asked one baby officer.

"Sociology."

He grimaced. "Oh, bit of an old lefty subject." As if I were a leper, the officer avoided me for the rest of the occasion.

Christmas dinner was served around a great mahogany table in the dining-room. Silver candelabras decorated the table and several large crystal bowls were piled with assorted fruits: pineapples, oranges, tangerines and fresh figs. The place mats I recognised immediately as they were from my regiment. They were colourful historical prints of mounted troopers in ceremonial dress, of a sturdy drum horse, trumpeter or regimental standard. Under each scene, in flowing italics was inscribed the regimental motto, *Forever Onwards*. Besides each mat was a party-popper topped with a small Union Jack. I wanted to tear mine up or set a match to it. Even during a Christmas lunch we were celebrating our nationhood. The brigadier began carving the turkey whilst the servants and officers made deferential jokes and our hosts retorted.

"Are you sure you know how to do that, Brigadier?"

"Don't you know how to use a carving knife, Sir?"

"Better stick to battle strategy," said Cpl B, a house servant. He had a pointy little face and a neat moustache. "You won't make such a mess of that, Sir." The brigadier feigned coyness whilst his wife laughed loudly like a horse.

"Yes," she chuckled. We're rather lost without your expert carving skills, Cpl B."

The officers had this patronising habit of calling the house staff and their wives by their surname's initial. It was an attempt to mask class divisions but served only to highlight them. There was Cpl B and his wife, Mrs B, some W's, O's and two troopers – one an A and the other an E. I was the odd one out, they called me by my first name.

"Oh, Tpr E, do have some more sprouts."

"Thank you, Ma'am," replied Tpr E, politely.

"We grew them ourselves in the garden. Awfully tasteful I must say." Tpr E clumsily lifted individual sprouts to his plate. "And the horse-chestnut sauce," she continued, "Sgt W made with chestnuts we collected around the paddocks."

"How is your horse, Brigadier?" asked Sgt O.

"Oh, Dancing Dragoon, she's fine. She's been performing well this year."

"Nick, do have some more turkey," fussed the brigadier's wife. "Student life is so financially restricting. I suppose most of your meals are rice and pasta, are they?" She pushed a pile of tender turkey onto my plate.

"Yes," I laughed, "it's surprising what you can do with rice and an onion." I avoided calling her Ma'am.

"So, Nick, what are you studying?" asked her husband.

"Sociology."

"Oh," he muttered. "So what do you make of all these homeless

9

people on the streets at the moment?" I felt an uneasiness around the table, almost imperceptibly people stiffened and heads and eyes turned towards me. It was as if raising such a question from amidst our opulent setting was somehow threatening. There was silence and I blushed.

"I suppose I'd have to look at the social conditions which promote inequality."

"All theoretical," snapped a baby officer.

"As is everything else," I retorted.

"They want to bloody well get a job," cawed Mrs O like a parrot. For a moment her head twitched just like an agitated bird. She was a woman of great depth.

"I rather agree with you, Nick," replied the brigadier. "It's all too simplistic, blaming the cause of it on their unwillingness to work. Why, I've known several officers who retired their commissions and spent months looking for work. They found dole a traumatic experience."

"Yes!" spat Mrs O, a speck of turkey flying from her mouth. "But at least they looked for work. They didn't just idle about and accept handouts."

"But these were men with qualifications and pensions. Many people don't have such an advantage," he replied sipping wine from his glass. The table was silent.

"Sounds to me, Brigadier, you're flying the Red Flag," laughed the baby officer.

"We have to be sympathetic," claimed the brigadier.

"Do have some more potatoes, Mrs O," continued his wife. Politics neatly side-stepped, our conversation returned to the mundane.

"My, what lovely chestnut stuffing," someone mumbled.

"Yes, they're made with game sausage, most delightful," boasted the brigadier's wife.

After Christmas pudding, coffee was served and in a strained atmosphere we popped our party-poppers. Streamers of red, white and blue shot into the air and fell to festoon our table in patriotic colours. Later, when we left the house, they wished us each of us a Merry Christmas and gently shook everyone's hand. I kissed her on the cheek. It was what I'd consider a gentlemanly kiss but she didn't like it. I could tell by the way her body stiffened. They only ever kiss within their circle of officer friends, I thought. And then it's that pathetic kissy-kissy palaver which always involves a kiss on both cheeks. For that very reason I kissed her on one cheek only. Outside, on the noisy gravel, my military chauffeur awaited.

Another contact with the army was a letter asking me to rejoin or face possible conscription. Headed by an official crest, it was signed by some brigadier. That week I'd received several phone calls from old comrades. All had been sent similar letters and were worried. Settled into civilian life, with wives, children and mortgages, they had personal reasons to remain civvies, reasons which they cloaked with political and moral arguments whose sincerity failed to convince me. Paul had spent a number of years as a reservist and had attended several exercises for which he'd been paid. His only concern had been the financial reward. I hadn't the least intentions of going to the Gulf and from friends still in the band I learnt they were being deployed as medical orderlies. Suddenly, some band members – notably senior ranks – had developed illnesses or family problems which they used as excuses to avoid a war. I replied to my call to arms:

Dear Brig, regarding your letter dated 18th Dec 1990;
Would you please make a record of the fact that I am gay. I wrote and told you this two years ago and so far you have failed to acknowledge it. I have not the least interest in your businessmen's war. Don't take your soldiers to battle – take them to bed instead. They'll probably have a lot more fun and so might you. On second thoughts, I know a lot of them will be doing it anyway. As for me, I'm having fun sucking 'our boys'' cocks in a toilet outside the local barracks.

Within a week the brigadier phoned me.

"Can I speak to Nick Elwood, please?"

"Speaking."

"It's Brigadier Wharton here. I'm phoning reference your letter in which you claim you're gay."

"Oh. I see. And?"

"Well, we have no reference of your previous letter and naturally we have to ascertain that you are gay. It's become a popular way of avoiding call-up."

"Really, well what am I excepted to do? There's no way I'm being drafted, not unless there's a change in the law."

"Basically, we need proof of your claimed sexuality."

"Well how the hell am I supposed to prove it? Are you going to send me round a sexy soldier or something?"

"Don't be silly, Mr Elwood. This is a serious matter."

"Of course it's silly, you want me to prove I'm gay. It's laughable. I mean, everybody here at university knows. It's my lifestyle."

"What are you studying?"

"Sociology."

"Might have bloody well known. Well can't you get me a letter from a lecturer or principal?"

"Are you serious? A letter from a lecturer?"

"Well we have to be official about this."

"Things haven't changed much since I left, then."

"Or," he paused... "You could submit to a rectal examination."

"No fucking way, sorry. You don't still believe that to be the most foolproof method of ascertaining if someone's gay, do you?"

"I'm only complying with our guidelines on the matter. A rectal examination tends to put soldiers off claiming they're gay."

"Well personally, I'm not into bums so your silly examination wouldn't prove anything. Perhaps I could suck someone off for you?"

"I really don't want to get involved in such a stupid suggestion. I'm far too busy for that."

"Are you going to war then?"

"That's neither here nor there. If you'd kindly arrange to have a letter sent to us, we can adjust our records."

"Fine then, I'll do that."

Several days later I visited the Dean of Students.

"You want me to write and tell them you're gay?" she asked. "I've never had a request like this before. How do I know you're really gay? On what do they expect me to confirm your claim? It all seems rather far-fetched."

"I know. I told them that on the phone but that's the army for you."

"Haven't they heard of equal opportunities?"

"Of course not," I laughed. "It's an institution run exclusively by men. What do you expect?"

"Well what can we tell them?"

"I'm treasurer for the Lesbian and Gay Society and in my first year I was secretary. So I suppose a letter mentioning that is about all I can do to prove it."

Later I received an official document from MRO medically discharging me from future service. The letter claimed I was 'permanently unfit for any form of Army service'.

I hadn't heard from Andreas since I saw him when he returned from America in 1983. Sometime in early 1992, I wrote to him. I inquired what he was doing, that it would be good to hear from him and generally asking after his well-being. I was off to an early morning lecture on 'Foucault and Sexual Histories' when his reply dropped onto my doormat. I stooped down, picked it up and immediately recognised the handwriting. It was postmarked Berlin. Rather than open it in the house where my student flatmates were busy making breakfast, I decided to wait.

At the bus stop frosty cold turned expelled air into gaseous white clouds that floated around my head. I waited until comfortably seated before I prised the envelope apart, withdrew the letter and slowly opened it. It was a boring chronicle of his life over the last eight years. Despite this I read it through several times and later put it somewhere safe.

Eventually, I plucked up the courage to call him. I didn't know why I wanted to speak to him or even why I had written in the first place. Naturally I was inquisitive as to his history but my love for the Andreas of 1982 still invaded the present. I still couldn't listen to ABBA and somewhere amongst the boxes, packages and carrier bags of moving house, I'd lost his ring. I know I put it somewhere safe but its location I forgot. I'm sure I put it inside my sad box alongside a piece of gum, a cigarette stub and various other significant objects but then, maybe I didn't. When I looked in there it was gone; perhaps I'd already thrown it out.

I picked up the phone, sighed and dialled his number. It rang with a distinctive Continental peeping.

"Hallo?" a voice answered.

"Hello, is Andreas Bic there please? I'm calling from the UK and my German isn't fluent."

"Oh, you're English!"

"Yes." It's probably Andreas's boyfriend, I thought.

"Well, darling, he's not in at the moment," he said in perfect English. "But I can give him a message for you?"

"Tell him Nick called."

"Nick?"

"Nick from the army."

"Oh, that Nick. I'll tell him."

"Thanks," I replied. He said goodbye and I put down the phone knowing that I wasn't yet ready to talk to him.

As my relationships with some students developed, I realised that I hardly knew most of my army mates. It was no one's fault; the army had been largely a physical rather than cerebral experience. Since childhood I'd been taught that the best mates you'll ever have in life are the ones you make in military life.

"The best mates you'll ever have," my dad used to tell me. "You can call them up years after and they'll help you out, lend you money, give you a bed for the night or give you advice. Like it or not, they're always there for you." For years I believed him. But gradually, by one means or another, I came to realise that a military career might provide you with 'mates' but not necessarily 'friends'. Occasionally I met old mates and felt distanced from them. Somehow we just couldn't make connections or they were dull or bigoted. Whenever I've met old comrades that's how it is. It's not easy to tell someone they're thick or boring or that they're racist or sexist.

In May 1992, I visited the Cavalry Memorial Parade held annually in Hyde Park. I had played at this event on several occasions. Cavalry regiments each sent a contingent of troops to escort their regimental standards. Cavalry old comrades from the length and breadth of the country paraded with their regimental associations. There were young and old alike. The associations assembled behind their regimental standards in the park whilst the massed bands marched there from Hyde Park Barracks. On the march towards the park there was a point when the band was 'cut off' by the Drum Majors, and an 'eyes left' ordered. Across in the park was a bandstand where seven bandsmen had died in a terrorist attack. It was always a very sombre moment and no doubt many of the tourists who lined the street wondered what they were doing. It didn't matter, as for bandsmen it was a personal tribute. In the park old comrades met up and exchanged handshakes and grins. It was always an exciting moment wondering who you were going to meet from amongst the many that had left or were still serving. And of course bandsmen felt a need to seek out old pals from other regiments.

Parade was sounded by the State Trumpeters and each regiment, in order of seniority, sounded its Regimental Call. Contingents and associations moved into parade positions. On the rousing beat of each regimental band, they set off towards the bandstand where a drumhead church service was held. There, the State Trumpeters were a spectacle. In State ceremonials of intricately intertwined gold thread, knee-high, shiny black boots and silver spurs, they swaggered to the front of the parade. It was a proud, beautiful cavalry swagger. Then they sounded Cavalry Last Post. We made two minutes' silence throughout which I stood to attention, and then with a swish the trumpets swung up, lungs were filled and Cavalry Reveille sounded. The bands played the cavalry hymn, 'Supreme Sacrifice'. Then the regiments dismissed, scuttled back to their distant buses outside the barracks and made their way to their own reunions.

Cavalry Memorial was a class-ridden affair which was listed high in the *Sloane Ranger Handbook*. It always made me sick. Masquerading as a memorial for fallen comrades, it was really a swanky reunion of the officer class. It was immediately obvious what rank someone was – or had been – by their dress. Low ranks wore blazers and slacks, senior ranks wore dark suits, and the officers, three-piece striped suits with bowler hats and black umbrellas. Many old war veterans wore greasy suits or blazers that had seen a lifetime of weddings and funerals. They were tired old suits, worn and slimy, that all looked the same. The lower ranks' columns were swollen with hobbling, bent and ancient men whose medals jangled as they tried to march in step to the beat.

The strange thing about meeting your past is how mates fail to accommodate the fact you've changed; not only as the product of experience but with the passage of time. Mates who had left years before still treated me as I had been in distant days.

"God, Nicky, don't you know not to wear brown shoes with a dark suit?" said one.

"And don't you know how to wear your regimental tie?" said another.

"I'm not really bothered how you wear it properly. What's important is that I'm here." As if I were a little child, he began fixing my tie.

"You're supposed to have the yellow stripe on top, Nicky," he mumbled, pulling at the knot. I could smell his aftershave. "I don't know, still having to dress you after all these years," he complained.

"Who gives a fuck," I replied. "It's only a tie!"

"Still the same old rebel then?"

"Oh no! Much worse. I thought you were supposed to go all right-wing as you get older, I'm doing the opposite."

"You haven't changed, Nicky," he replied. 'You haven't changed' is the most frequent cliché at a reunion.

Ash was now a policeman and had put on a ton of weight. All afternoon he bragged about the arrests he had made and the truncheon bashings he had administered. Then he moaned about anti poll-tax demonstrators and the blacks. He actually knew how many victims he'd arrested to date and what percentage of them were black or unemployed. Someone else bragged about all the women he'd fucked as a driving instructor. Others stood at the bar getting pissed and doing the same as they'd been doing for the last ten years or more. Their cheeks had erupted in tiny ruptured capillaries that flushed away the glow of youth that had once enlivened their faces. Their bellies sagged, their jowls hung and already a few had collapsed onto sofas.

On July 20th, 1992, , the 15th Dragoons were amalgamated with another regiment. Their name changed as did their regimental colours, cap badge and stable belt. Charles King wrote to me asking if I would attend the regiment's final parade, to be held in Paderborn where they were still stationed. I wrote him a scathing attack on the armed forces. Though I never condemned the regiment I was critical of the wall of homophobia that had denied the sexuality of troops past and present. Charles didn't think it was such an important issue. Though I never went to the final 15th Dragoon parade, I felt like a world had been annihilated. Most old comrades feel an affinity with their regiment. They know that it is always there, still adhering to the ancient traditions that have bonded cavalrymen across generations; things like Guard Mount, Cavalry Reveille, a cavalry swagger and mates. Suddenly it's gone and you feel exposed and alone, and a little part of your life, a crucial point of reference changes forever.

An article appeared in a national newspaper about my life as a gay soldier and prompted a spate of phone conversations. Gig and Matt were the only ones that didn't criticise me. Ash ranted for the whole conversation.

"Why did you do it? Why did you open your big mouth? We all protected you. Jim says you're blacklisted from the regimental association for life. Leon thinks you shouldn't have said anything and RSM Wexton wants to kick your head in. You've upset lots of people. I can't understand why you criticised them. I mean, what did you think you were doing? It was illegal. You shouldn't have joined if you didn't like the rules."

"Look, it's either wrong or it isn't. You can't sit on the fence and defend it without suggesting that you agree with such discrimination."

"Well it is wrong. I don't want my kids being taught about homosexuality in schools. God, the whole world could turn gay. What would happen then?"

"Don't be so stupid, human sexuality isn't like that and you're presupposing gays wouldn't want children. Besides, I spent years being conditioned into heterosexuality and the mission failed. I hardly think fair representation of gays will sway people into being gay. Is heterosexuality so weak it's in danger of floundering?"

"No. But we don't want it rammed down our throats."

"Oh, and heterosexuality isn't?"

"No, it's not."

"But most adverts promote it," I suggested. "Almost every film contains the plot of boy meets girl, a little bit of conflict and its resolution in terms of heterosexuality or family. It's the universal theme."

"But that's because ninety percent of the audience are heterosexual. That's what they want!"

"But I'm not straight. Such persistent images exclude me and bore me. I'm not asking for it to stop or for an equal amount of representation. I'm just asking for some representation."

"Well, it's all because you're a minority."

"Ah, so what you're saying is if you're in a minority it's okay to be abused, neglected, denied?"

"Yes! In a nutshell I am." Our argument rambled on to an inconclusive close.

I've since heard that some comrades and soldiers want to give me a bashing. Having tarnished the name of the regiment they say I'd never be welcomed back. Maybe if I'd written about them beating me up and queer-bashing other suspected gays, they could have held their heads high and been proud. Now I can never go to a reunion without being on my physical and intellectual guard and it makes me angry because it's as much my regiment as it is theirs.

I'm looking at a photo of my band taken in Catterick. It's a yellowed, black and white photo which will soon be twenty-five years old. It was taken in the days of flares, kung fu and Brut aftershave. Days of freedom, energy, hope and youth. How young we all looked, how wide-eyed and optimistic. I still have dreams about those days, years after leaving the band. Army dreams are never pleasant and are often almost nightmares. Though I remember so many good times, my dreams are all about being late for parade or not having my instrument or helmet. At other times I'm dressed in the wrong uniform or my boots turn white during an inspection. They are dreams of fear, humiliation and shame. Mates' faces haven't aged and they still look like they did in 1974, 1986 or whatever. Sometimes I see faces I'd forgotten and in the morning I'll remember them and think, 'Oh, that's what they looked like.'

I've rarely worn a red poppy on Armistice Sunday since I left the army. Instead I wear one painted white with correction fluid. I hate the red poppy as it's the poppy of the British, of heterosexuality, of our boys, our shores and our religion. The simple poppy of remembrance is one of imperial proportions and with simmering, waiting, imperial pretensions. If you fail to wear one, especially if you're a state official, dignitary or media personality, it's practically an offence, and if you dare to wear a white poppy this contravenes emotional correctness and becomes an outrage.

I once wore a white poppy to the Colchester war memorial. It was a silly thing to do since not much has changed in that town since the days of Matthew Hopkins, Witchfinder General. In Colchester, Britain's oldest recorded town, boys are boys and girls are girls. Stilettos, Spice power and brash, pushy youths suggest that for Colchester at least, the post-modern disintegration of gender roles is still far in the next millennium. Aware that a white poppy might earn me a lynching, I tempered it with a red one. I pinned both side by side on my jacket. Despite this I was sneered and sniggered at and eventually two police officers asked me to remove it or be arrested for 'breach of the peace'. They weren't willing to argue and so I walked back to university where at least I sensed optimism for the present and future. Perhaps if war involved killing beautiful, youthful women, straight men would be more reticent to pick up the call to arms.

November 11th is my occasion to remember fallen and past comrades. After playing the German, British and Japanese national anthems, which I do loudly to enrage nationalistic neighbours, I play my old band records. Hearing the familiar sounds to which I contributed brings individuals to life. My foot starts tapping and my fingers sometimes flick over imaginary keys as I remember an old march or some shitty, boring musical insignificance; a concert filler like 'Swedish Rhapsody' or 'The Birdie Song'. I spent years listening to their sounds. I don't hear a cornet or trombone but see and sense individuals. In Lee's gentle vibrato I see his spots and greasy complexion and even the little skin tag on the corner of his eye. He was such an ugly kid. I hear his laughter, sense his warm personality and remember decent conversations about music or whether it's possible to prove or disprove magic. In the sweet cornet tones of Tony Shaw, I see fat cheeks and bright eyes. He always reminded me of a hamster or squirrel. I sense his inflated ego and pushy personality. Murray, who conducted, is also present. A face of cheeky grins, pissed stupors, pride and anger. I sense his humour and hear his jokes. I can slate the forces and discredit my cap badge by being out, but in my heart I loved the regiment and still do. I can really do no other since I am a 15th Dragoon and as a Trumpet Major, was part of its history.

The band record plays on and I realise it's a world that has gone or at least aged. Occasionally, I wish I could be back there now, blowing away, making music and experiencing life anew but it can never be relived or recreated. I smell the polishes: the boot and yellow floor polish, the Brasso, Dual and Duraglit. I see scuttling cockroaches, and lurking in my memories are a hundred uniformed Adonai, amongst them a few whose sweet flesh and quivering dicks I managed to sample. Then the beat draws me into a kaleidoscope of memories from across fourteen years and somewhere amongst them I lose myself.

1

24324732 was the very first thing I learnt as a new recruit. I memo-rised it on a train journey from Sutton Coldfield to Catterick in Yorkshire. It was a number I repeated every day for the next fourteen years of army service. Whether leaving the barracks in my spare time, signing for new army clothing, writing my address on a letter or com-pleting an official document, my eight-digit number came even before my name. A military identification number is something you never forget. It remains part of you personally, as a substitute for a name, and physically where it exists printed on official documents in creaky filing cabinets and on whirring computer systems.

My fellow recruits alongside me, each the proud owner of an eight-digit number, are noisy with excitement and anticipation. Some of the passengers sneak us disapproving frowns, their eyes popping out from behind newspapers and over the top of headrests. It's obvi-ous that we are recruits; our animated conversation gives us away as much as our new uniforms. We are young, myself at seventeen being the youngest. Some of us have come from jobs, some from the ranks of the unemployed, and a few, like myself, straight from school.

Together, we had arrived at the Recruit Selection Centre a few days earlier, unsure whether we'd be selected, where we might be posted or in which branch we might be enlisted. Now I'm sitting on a train dressed in an army uniform and on my way to a new future. We wear our combats with awkwardness, our floppy black berets are shapeless and bear no cap badge and our dull boots are painfully stiff. Already they are beginning to gnaw the skin off the back of my heels. Other than where we come from, how old we are or what we did before enlisting, our animated conversation ignores our experiences as civilians. Instead, we boisterously discuss what life might be like at the training depot and test each other to ensure we have memorised our correct identification numbers. All the while eyes are nosily pok-ing and peering in our direction.

I began to learn, in a rudimentary way, what the army really entailed. I'd read all the glossy magazines that recruiting officers are keen to show a potential recruit. They portrayed an army career as an endless round of eating fine food, playing sports, having Wednesday afternoons off, firing guns and travelling. I realise now that such maga-zines largely ignore what it means to be a soldier. Fun, food and fitness mask the reality of death, mutilation, discomfort and subjugation.

The recruit films we watched at the selection centre further consolidated the facade of a glamorous lifestyle. Their appeal, as intended, seduced me and for better or worse manacled me to an official contract for the next nine years. Before I signed up the only desire I expressed was to be a military musician. When I applied to the local army recruitment office, they thrust me a colourful brochure entitled 'Military Music'. I eagerly fingered through the photos of sport, food, music and travel to find a photo of a bandmaster sat at a desk writing out music. He wore a dark blue uniform that bore chain-mail shoulder epaulettes. A row of medals hung from his chest. He was a handsome man with greying sideburns and a proud, straight posture; the sort of man who suits a uniform. The photo swayed me. This was the uniform I wanted to wear and subsequently I was attached to the Royal Armoured Corps, under which tank regiments are subsumed.

Two of the recruits in our group are enthusiastically discussing military life. There is something in their appearance that separates them from the rest of us. It isn't just that they are older, probably in their mid twenties, but rather in the way they wear their uniforms. Their anonymous berets fit their cropped heads snugly and their boots certainly aren't new. Etched into the soft, creased leather are scuff marks which boot polish fails to hide. Both are former Territorial Reserves. They use all sorts of terms which I am unfamiliar with, terms such as SMG, guards, NBC warfare and pokey drill. The glossy magazines failed to mention such activities.

"Pokey drill," someone asks, "what's that?" Geordie, who is now our military affairs expert, explains it's a form of arm-strengthening exercise in which you use your personal weapon like a dumbbell. It is, he claims, particularly painful. We had an instant respect for Geordie. He was a real soldier. Whilst we spoke of guns, he spoke of a personal weapon, or SMG, which he proudly explained was a submachine gun. There are many different types of uniform, Geordie told us: No2 dress, denims, barrack dress and Noddy suits. He talked about bulling, bumpering, PFAs and beret shaping and told us that the uniforms we we wearing, with their distinctive brown, black, green and sandy camouflage pattern, were combats. He told us many things the recruitment magazines did not.

If there's one thing a military recruit hates, it's being reminded that he's a recruit. Arriving at Darlington station, a large blackboard by the ticket barrier read: 'All recruits for the RAC to wait in the car park'. The lowly status conferred by the word 'recruits' clothed me in shame. It was a status that no doubt all of us would be quick to dump. In the station car park, a large green lorry arrives. Geordie calls it a three-tonner. We clamber, recruit-like, up and over the tail-board whilst a small congregation of civilians pause to watch. Some passing teenagers begin shouting: "Look! It's the new boys."

"Hey, hello, new boys. Welcome to Darlington."

"What nice uniforms, lads. All lovely and new. Where d'you buy them?"

"Raw recruits!"

Again I feel a stab of shame. Me, I think. Me, I'm a raw recruit, a total nobody. Shamefully, I hang my head.

"Fucking civvies," shouts Geordie. By the end of the long journey I'd added to my military lessons that if there's one thing lower than a raw recruit, it's a civilian.

Bolton Barracks, the training centre for the RAC, was where we began our basic training. It lay on the moors several miles from the quaint old town of Richmond. The barrack buildings were all modern and in the bright summer afternoon the camp looked pleasant. On the vast rolling moor which surrounded the camp, yellow and orange gorse bushes burned in the sun. Here and there were rocky outcrops and patches of windswept conifers.

In my naivety, I hadn't considered what miles upon miles of desolate moor meant to a military establishment. It was a moor to be manoeuvred across, crawled through and run over. Past the camp perimeter, beyond the small wooden fence was the mud, dirt and pollution of nature whilst within its confines was order. Here barrack rooms were spotless. All those shining porcelain showers and urinals, the windows void of even a fingerprint and the highly polished stone tile floors, had never seen the care of a civilian cleaner. Cleaning, polishing, scrubbing and dusting, all in the prescribed military fashion, were to become a regular part of my life.

My first week at Bolton Barracks was an orientation week during which we familiarised ourselves with the barracks and the routine of army life. De-civilianisation occurred on our first morning. This consisted of a haircut that left us with a uniform half a centimetre of hair. It was the quickest haircut I've ever had. A swift to and fro with the electric clippers and the barber was finished. On his floor lay shorn our civilian locks. We didn't object, as our shoulder-length hair highlighted our lowly status. Even Geordie was made to have a haircut and though no hair fell from his head, the barber continued. Though we couldn't yet march and still didn't have our uniforms, at least from a distance we looked military.

After the ritual haircut we formed up into a squad and set off marching to the MRO. Geordie looked smart and could march properly. He held his head high, back straight and swung his arms in synchronisation with his legs. In comparison, the rest of us lurched through the barracks. Passing recruits or soldiers stared at us with contempt and though I wanted to lower my head towards the floor our Squad Cpl vigorously encouraged us not to.

"Get yer fucking heads up! Common, get in step! Left, right, left, right, left, right, l-e-f-t. Swing those arms shoulder high!" He screamed the commands at us and abused anyone who appeared to be slacking.

"You! You fucking lanky wanker in the back row."

The 'lanky wanker' looked across at the Cpl who screamed even louder.

"Face the fucking front, sprogg, and bloody well get in step!"

The more we tried to march the more ridiculously we lurched. Several marched with the same leg going forward as their arm. Their bodies swung awkwardly at the hip in a clumsy manner. Others found it difficult to co-ordinate the swing of their arms with the pace of their step. They marched like mad clockwork toys. Our whole squad thrashed along like a giant, floundering octopus. The Cpl kept on shouting but our style didn't improve.

At the MRO we were badged to a regiment within the RAC. I had the choice of two regiments that required trumpet players, but told that the 15th Dragoons were due a posting to Cyprus, I chose them without a second thought. A sunny location seemed to fit the lifestyle I'd seen in those glossy magazines.

From the MRO we marched to the RQMS stores to collect and sign for our military clothing. A storeman piled various uniforms in front of us on the broad counter which divided us from the racks of clothing. Uniforms for the tank park, a parade uniform, PT kit, barrack dress, combats, NBC suits, socks, T-shirts, underpants and khakis. Mechanically he threw a suitcase and regimental forage cap on top of each pile. Forage caps identify regiments and when dressed carry regimental cap badges and buttons. Some were white and black, some red, some patterned with black and yellow zigzags, and others green and yellow. All were peaked in shiny black plastic. Into each cap the storeman placed the appropriate badges and buttons. Finally, with our uniforms piled before us, we signed for each piece of clothing. Next to our name we wrote our military ID, name, rank and signature. Those who didn't know their correct eight-digit number fumbled in their pockets for temporary ID cards. With my suitcase and hold-all stuffed with uniforms I struggled up the hill to our barrack block past sniggering soldiers and recruits.

That afternoon our barrack room was like a fashion show as we tried on uniforms, making sure items fitted and that we knew what to wear with what. Geordie, our mentor, gave advice and criticism freely. We paraded ourselves in front of him anxiously. Between appearances we fitted our gas masks and attached buttons and badges to various uniforms. Throughout the show we goaded or praised one another. In parade uniform, officially known as a No2 dress, one recruit looked like a traffic warden. Someone else's bright red forage cap earned them the nickname Cherry Head. Another lad was named Milkman; his cap was cream-coloured. Mine was green with a yellow band around the centre.

Geordie taught us how to shape our berets so they didn't flop down one side of your head. By rinsing them alternately in hot and cold water they shrank to the desired size. In locker and ablution mirrors we adjusted their shape and in corridors we checked the fit of our boots. I overheard Geordie telling his neighbour that your boots are your most important possession. They needed breaking in just like a new horse. Geordie took his into the toilet, found a mop bucket, pissed in it and after adding tap water submerged them. There they remained until late evening. This was the quickest way to soften the hard leather, he claimed, and a method practised by the Foreign Legion. It was a peculiar sight as underclad bodies, most wearing berets and boots, tried on uniforms and gas masks. Even as I went to bed I wore my damp beret until the very moment I lay down to sleep. Then I carefully placed it on my bedside table to dry.

In the evenings we bulled our boots. Most soldiers occupy a substantial percentage of their military lives engaged in boot bulling – rubbing little rings of polish onto the toe cap until a reflection develops. Geordie had his own way of bulling and told us it becomes an individual art. Some people learnt to bull with a duster, others with their fingers. In the evening, recruits returned from the NAAFI and recounted the techniques of soldiers in other intakes. We all knew who the best bullers were. Bulling brought out a true professionalism and if we heard of a new technique the chances are we experimented with it. Within a few weeks there was a diversity of techniques employed by the twelve soldiers who shared my room. Some used nothing but black polish and others polish that had been melted. Some bulled with cotton wool under running water or softened the toe cap with a red-hot teaspoon before they began. A few applied an initial base of bees' wax whilst some alternated applications of brown and black polish or used Duraglit. There were those who spat onto the boot and worked it in with the polish. Those who huffed their breath onto leather and those who dipped their rag into water. Though the variations were endless the objective was the same – boots that shone like a mirror. When put away at the end of an evening they were placed in a corner of your locker protected by a clean yellow duster. To a recruit, best boots became a most cherished possession, the degree of shine denoting whether he'd just begun initial training or was about to finish. Right until the day I passed out as a fully fledged soldier, and indeed for much of army life, my index finger was stained yellow from the dye in my bulling duster.

In our block hallway hung a notice board on which were posted regimental and squadron Orders. It's part of army law to read them every evening. Returning from the gym one afternoon we read that our intake was due a 'Short Arm Inspection' at 0930 the following day. Geordie, our mentor, had made a detour to the NAAFI and wasn't available to answer our queries.

"Not another weapon inspection."

"Fuck, that's the third in a week."

"Well, it sure beats PT or drill," I mumbled.

A recruit from the intake shortly due to pass out stopped to read the board over our shoulders. He began chuckling to himself. "Intake 17/23 will have a fun day tomorrow," he laughed. "Nothing like a short arm inspection to start the day."

"We're 17/23!"

"Oh, well! Better get cleaning lads," he replied. A suspicious grin stretched across his face as he left the building.

The following morning we paraded in the corridor in alphabetical order. It was almost 0925 and as yet we hadn't been detailed to collect our SMGs.

"Hey Geordie, did you read Orders last night?"

"Of course, I read them every night."

"Well what the fuck is a short arm inspection?"

"An inspection of your tackle," he replied.

"Tackle?" someone asked quietly. A few stony expressions in our line began to drain of colour.

"Tell me it's not what I'm fucking thinking?" asked a worried voice.

"Fuck!" gasped another.

"What d'you mean by tackle?" I asked but a response was cut short by our squad Cpl's bellow. He was in the corridor banging his NCO's baton on the wall.

"Come on you fuckers! Get in a straight line." We shuffled against the corridor wall. "Right! Now to wheedle out the boys from the men." He thwacked his stick on the wall and then spun it between his fingers. "If any of you have a dribbley willy, sore knob end, or even little black crawly things in your pubes, then step straight to the front of the line... Please," he added, sarcastically. No one moved.

The Cpl waited. "Just as I thought, virgins. Right, then, belts undone and start filing in." We began moving towards the NCO's office and with every step I took I felt my dick rapidly shrinking.

"Okay boys, let's have the first five of you in," the Cpl ordered. I was sixth in line. I felt like running away rather than having to submit to such an ordeal. The cruel taunts from the NCOs could be heard in the corridor. A few seconds after each comment a red- or white-faced recruit stepped from the office doing up his trousers. In a heavy silence we empathised with our embarrassed comrades. No one was spared a comment.

"Call that a prick, Tpr? I've seen more prick on a pin head."

"You a fucking Jew boy or you had a fight with a razor?"

"Ginger pubes! Fucking rank!"

"Elwood! Get your arse in line in here!" a voice ordered.

"Yes, Sir!" I turned the corner into the office. Two recruits separated me from the seated Cpl. The intake Sgt sat behind his desk in the corner of the room. He held a pen in his hand. Seated at the side of his desk was the Cpl. On the radiator in front of the windowsill perched the intake L/Cpl. The intake Cpl probed away at the recruit at the front of our short queue. He was using his baton to search out venereal disease and crabs.

"Foreskin back, lad. Come on! We haven't got all day!" His stick began prodding. "My God! I hope you don't let any ladies suck that thing? It's disgusting. You're in the army, that's army equipment. Get it washed!"

"Yes, Cpl!"

"Right, next!" The recruit in front of me stepped forward. He was the smallest in our intake. He was a thin lad with a soft baby face and big brown eyes. There was a touch of femininity in his features that gave him an androgynous appearance. His trousers fell about his ankles revealing his skinny legs. Yanking his pants down to his knees, his arse quivered as the Cpl's prodding began. For a moment I felt a twinge in my dick and began to panic in case I got an erection. I concentrated on the view out of the window.

"Fuckin' hell, Daniels! That thing's a monster. You need a licence before you go using that!" the Cpl shouted. His stick waggled around as if fencing with Daniel's monster cock. Meanwhile, Daniel's bum cheeks spasmed. The L/Cpl on the windowsill grinned as if enjoying a joke. "Right, get it back!" Outside, almost on the horizon, a flame yellow patch of gorse caught my eye. It was bright yellow amidst a collage of dull greens and brown. Daniels fumbled with himself.

"Can't Cpl. It won't go back."

"Right, Donkey Dick needs a circumcision. Get down to the MO now."

"Yes, Cpl!" replied Daniels, his voice trembling. He turned around whilst pulling up his pants. His dick was tiny, barely that of a pubescent boy's. I stepped forward.

"Get 'em down, Elwood!" I let my denim trousers fall to the floor and tugged down my pants. Looking straight ahead I concentrated. It was a sunny day with a little haze over the moor. In one corner of the horizon, tanks churned their way along the brow of a hill, their turrets and barrels silhouetted against the blue sky. A billowing trail of dust followed them. The Cpl shoved his stick under my balls and they twitched in shock. He began scrutinising them at close range.

"Foreskin back!" he ordered. As if unattached to my body my hand obeyed. The row of tanks in the distance looked like a column of daleks. I felt him lift my dick, the prod of his baton so much more invasive than a clinical hand. I tried hard to focus my mind and smother out the assault. Overhead a murder of crows floated across the blue sky.

"I hope you can use that better than you can shoot, Elwood," he said, giving my dick a final nudge with the cold, brass-ended stick. "Okay, pull 'em up!" That was the first and last time I ever underwent a short arm inspection. They were unheard of in regimental life yet stories about such inspections seemed commonplace amongst soldiers and recruits from training regiments and Junior Leaders depots. Several days later Daniels disappeared for a circumcision. When he next showered with us after gym he was secretly the centre of attraction. The story of his huge dick had spread. Faces were quietly shocked when they saw his bruised little willy.

Every morning, except Sunday, the intake Cpl woke us. He was a real soldier serving with the host training regiment. He woke us at 0530 by whipping his NCO's baton on furniture or, if you weren't quick enough out of bed, on your arse. His baton, carried by all JNCOs in his regiment, was about 60cm long, black and tipped with a brass cap. NCOs developed a distinctive swagger whilst carrying them.

After washing we spent half an hour cleaning the barrack rooms, hallway, toilets and bathrooms. This included learning another military discipline, one that I'd heard Geordie term bumpering. Although we lived in the age of electricity we were denied access to electric floor polishers. Instead we used hand bumpers. These were heavy iron blocks the size of a house brick. Short, hard bristles covered one side. Attached to the iron block was a broom handle. The bumpering routine consisted of several recruits rubbing polish onto the floor which was then bumpered over by four or five bumperers. They pushed the iron bristle brush up and down the floor until it began to shine. That this procedure was potentially hazardous, especially if your feet were wet, was immaterial. Just like best boots the floor had to produce a deep, reflective shine.

There wasn't one thing in the barrack room that didn't have a designated military place. Other than a few personal effects that went in the tiny personal drawer in your locker every item of clothing had its assigned position. Underpants, green, military, placed in one space; socks, green, military, in another. We folded every item of clothing in the prescribed manner and laid them in the correct location within our lockers.

On the odd evening when I was free, and chose not to bull my boots, I went out running along the bank of a river that meandered across the moor. I'd never been a particularly sporty person and was aware that I needed to improve my stamina. The river ran along the side of our camp. Our barrack block, the last in the row, stood at the edge of the moor. The distinction between moor and camp was stark. Our windows looked over the final piece of tamed land beyond which the wildness of the moor began. A fence divided military property, with all its neatness and order, from the anarchy of nature. I ran down to the edge of the fence, climbed over and began jogging towards the river. It was a refreshing experience to be away from other recruits, away from the eagle eyes of training Sgts and Cpls, away from the strict order and discipline of military life.

The river was beautiful, its attraction born from its very disorder, its unkempt wildness. It twisted and turned through rocky outcrops and wooded glades. The gentle sounds of nature surrounded me, the chirping of birds and the various noises of the river, sometimes gurgling and bubbling, then crashing.

I must have run a good two miles from the barracks when an opening in the undergrowth on my right-hand side provided me a clear view of the moors. For as far as I could see there was nothing but gently rolling plains which met the sky at a distant point. The view was a patchwork of colours, the flame yellow of the gorse bushes, the miscellaneous shades of green and the criss-cross brown scars of tank tracks. Across this terrain the tanks manoeuvred, their pathways viciously churned into the landscape. I stopped to enjoy the expansive view and varied disorder of nature. Then, before my heart calmed itself, I continued running along the embankment. Just another half mile, I thought, and I'll turn back.

The bank rose steeply and then dropped down into a gully at the bottom of which lay a small shingle shore. I leapt down the side of the slope and stumbled onto my backside. Suddenly, in the bushes, a

dark figure moved. The brighter light in the small clearing momentarily blinded me. Gradually, my eyes accustomed themselves. A rifle
was pointing at me.

"Don't shoot! Don't shoot!" I panted in panic.

"Hey, calm down! I've got a compressor fitted." The rifle lowered and the dark figure stepped away from the bushes. It was a soldier
dressed in full combats, his face and hands smeared with black and
green camouflage paint. In the piece of scrim netting covering his combat helmet small twigs and leaves were attached.

"You've got a what fitted?" I asked, standing up and brushing the
dirt from my knees and arse.

"A compressor," he repeated, motioning towards the yellow at-
tachment at the end of his rifle. He could see I looked bewildered.

"The yellow cylinder on the end of the barrel, it's a compressor.
It allows the rifle to re-cock itself when firing blanks."

"Blanks! I thought it might be lives."

"Fuck, no. A compressor stops bits of cartridge paper flying out.
Who are you with?"

"The 15th Dragoons." I paused a moment. "Well, to be honest
I've only been with them a few weeks – I'm a recruit."

"Same as me then, I'm in my second month of training."

"You really don't look like a recruit."

"Thanks, but neither do you."

"Are you in Bolton Barracks?"

"No. I'm with an infantry training regiment in the next barracks
along. I'm here with my squad – training. The other five are around
somewhere." Up on the opposite bank the bushes stirred. We looked
in the direction of the movement.

"That'll be one of my squad," he said. "I'd best get on, I've fallen
behind." He started moving away. "My name's Collings, perhaps I'll
see you in the Shield Club sometime."

"Maybe." I replied. "Except I won't recognise you."

"Yeah, but I'll recognise you," he grinned. His teeth were pure
white against his dark, camouflaged cheeks.

"Bye," I called meekly, but he didn't hear me.

My ability and determination in all forms of physical activity surprised me. Though I didn't consider myself fit I managed to push
myself through all the gruelling activities. Further, my ability to work
and socialise in an all-male, highly macho environment was likewise a
surprise.

I still have no idea what made me join the army. I'd been a quiet
boy at school and spent most of my spare time either listening to

records of Mahler and Bruckner or playing the trumpet. I knew at thirteen I was queer. In the street where my parents lived I'd had my hand down every boy's pants, but this seemed normal since they had their hands down mine. We all knew that this was something you didn't talk about but also realised it was enjoyable. I spent time in both the Scouts and Sea Cadets. It was generally the case that under canvas or in dorms somebody could be found to wank you off. It took years for me to realise that all those pubescent and adolescent fumblings were sexual. It wasn't until I began to develop intense feelings for other boys and felt drawn to them and their bodies that I started to perceive myself as different.

Perhaps joining the army had been an unconscious attempt to escape the true nature of my sexuality. Perhaps here I might find an escape from years of beating off at the altar of manhood. Perhaps, by joining the ultimate male world, I too would become pure, real male and be cleansed by the objects of my desires. After a few weeks' basic training I began to believe that I was 'normal'. I hadn't thought about boys for weeks and had stopped wanking. It just wasn't possible in the barracks, not without arousing derision. Besides, I was always too tired.

We spent the final weeks almost entirely on the square, marching up and down in slow and quick time and presenting arms with our SMGs. The only interruption to drill was for regular gym sessions where we were beasted through a variety of exercises. Eventually, four months later, our big day came and I passed out to the accompaniment of the host regimental band. Parents and relatives watched the spectacle and some big-wig was invited to take the salute and inspection. He was late arriving but I'd soon learn that dignitaries are always late. We put on our boots with great care and walked to the parade ground as if on hot coals. By the time we'd been inspected, finished our march past and been subject to a rousing speech, most of us were left with toe caps that had shattered or disintegrated. All those weeks of bulling scattered over the parade ground. Months of work reduced to tiny black specks on the tarmac. But at least we were fully fledged soldiers and no longer recruits.

In all those years since I passed out I've kept a photo of our intake. Looking at it I wonder what happened to all those young soldiers. Perhaps some are still serving, possibly senior NCOs in their regiments. I lived and socialised with all those men yet never really got to know one of them. I don't think we even swapped addresses or promised to keep in touch. We were all eager to get to our regiments and practise what we'd been trained to do. Recruit camp wasn't about making friends. It was about getting through each day with the minimum number of press-ups. About getting things done in such a manner that minimised the rifting that we always got anyway, no matter how hard we tried. It was about learning to be shouted at and humiliated, about doing things with vigour and zeal. There were too many military things you had to do in a day before you could get to know someone. By that time you were either too tired or just wanted to idle away a few moments before doing something else, like bulling your boots, bumpering a corridor or going to bed.

As I waited at Darlington station for the train to take me on leave, loaded with all my possessions in four bags, I went into the platform toilet for a piss. A young infantry soldier followed me to the urinals. Like me, he wore full uniform, No2 dress, but his insignia denoted an infantry regiment. I looked down and swung my hips to piss on a lump of chewing gum bobbling in the river of urine and blue toilet fresheners. From the corner of my eye I noticed his head tilted towards me. I looked up and our eyes met. Neither of us said anything. There was something familiar about him but I couldn't recall where I'd seen him. We stood pissing just a moment longer than usual and in this instant an immense sense of fear and excitement passed through me. In my deepest recesses, it was a feeling for which I'd secretly been waiting.

"You don't recognise me, do you?" he asked. I began tucking my dick away.

"No, I don't."

"Last time I met you I had my personal weapon trained on you," he said giving his dick a good shake. "I was in camouflage along the river and you were out running."

"Oh, yes, Collings," I stuttered, embarrassed that I should have remembered his name all these months after such a brief encounter. My breathing became laboured and erratic; I blushed. Though I was aware of staring at him I couldn't help myself. Somehow it felt the right thing to do. Suddenly I had gas-mask vision. All I saw were his uniform, his innocent young face and a cock sticking out of his trousers, green, military.

"The cubicle's empty," he said, motioning to the row of toilets. His voice quivered nervously.

"The what?"

"The cubicle, we could go in the cubicle."

"What for?" I asked. He'd moved so close that I could feel his breath on my neck. I remained anchored to the floor wanting to turn and flee yet compelled to stay.

"A bit of drill... a bit of pokey drill with our personal weapons, like, perhaps a bit of bumpering. How about it?" he whispered into my ear. Our forage caps knocked together with a gentle clinking sound as collar badges jostled against metal, regimental buttons. He slid an arm round my back and began caressing my buttocks. His breath was hot and spasmodic. It caused my neck muscles to spasm in a sensation that was both pleasant and irritating. I remained still. I felt as if I were going to burst and had to force my hand to the front of his crotch. My fingers slipped through his open fly and found him rigidly at attention. His fervent advances pushed me towards an empty cubicle. Our lips met, knocking my forage cap onto the floor. Blindly, my foot kicked it aside. We kissed between gasps of air as his other hand undid my jacket. Sliding through jacket buttons he squeezed his hand into my shirt and onto my chest. Against his pants I felt the heat of his dick. His cheeks were smooth and exciting with the faintest stubble on his chin. For seconds that seemed minutes we kissed frantically as we were drawn into a maelstrom of energetic passion. In my nostrils the smell of his aftershave mingled with that of a grotty gents' toilet. We just about made it to the cubicle when I gently pushed him away. Suddenly there was a distance between us. My lips wet from his sweet, minty saliva. I licked them as I regained my breath.

"Look, I'm sorry," I said, "but I can't do this, besides, my bags are outside." We stood staring at each other. He was beautiful, his forage cap crooked and his uniform dishevelled. He was a picture frozen in my mind. His eyes sparkled, he was tall and lean, his hair recently cut so that he had a chiselled, living Praxiteles appearance. His cap slanted at an angle and a white bulge poked out through his trousers. His dishevelled dress gave him an air of appealing, innocent devilishness. Bending down he picked up my forage cap and handed it to me. I straightened my uniform. My cap was soiled from the grimy, wet toilet floor. I looked at it and casually brushed the muck of it.

"Sorry," he said, apologetically as he buttoned up his flies.

"Me too," I replied. He straightened his cap and then pulling himself up straight gave a me a smart salute. Without thinking, I clipped my heels to attention and saluted in return. It was the ultimate respect that one soldier could pay another and paradoxically, in this situation, the greatest insult to the Queen's uniform. It was the first salute I'd ever executed that was invested with emotion. All those I'd performed on the parade square and around the barracks had been void of emotional content. They'd been the programmed actions of a mere automaton. For a moment we stared at each other across the few feet that separated us in a dingy station toilet. Then I turned to leave.

"Good luck," he said. I looked back over my shoulder.

"You look fucking great," I whispered, and I meant it.

"You too."

Then I turned and left.

Settling down on the train, I picked up a newspaper. Bruce Lee had just died. I read the article but couldn't concentrate. I'd only sat reading the paper to help compose myself on the busy train. I felt pangs of shame at my encounter with Collings, yet it had been exciting. I had come all this way in my basic training to tarnish myself on the day I left my training regiment. I looked down at my forage cap and saw a visible stain from the wet toilet floor. I'd shamed my regiment, I thought. But what was more disturbing was that I'd found his uniform, his military bearing, even his double entendres, sexually arousing. In the space of a few minutes I'd realised how sexually stimulating uniforms and soldiers are. Not only had I failed to escape my sexuality but the very symbols that I thought would cleanse me, those symbols of hyper, military masculinity, developed the potential to arouse me. As much as I felt disturbed, I also felt a sense of fulfilment. It was though I'd arrived somewhere important but wasn't quite sure of the destination. The little clink of our shiny collar badges had been the sigh of long-awaited orgasm.

2

After a three-week leave I was posted to my regiment in the garrison town of Münster, West Germany. I arrived on a bright afternoon in September after flying to RAF Gütersloh and taking a military bus to Münster. Bhurtpore barracks lay at the end of a main road fronted by several rows of grey-faced buildings. The bus dropped me at the camp entrance where the sentry stood at his post by the traffic barrier. He wore a yellow and green forage cap and an SMG hung on a sling from his shoulder. A large yellow and green sign identified the occupants of the barracks: The 15th Regiment of Dragoons. Nervously, I reported to the guardroom, anticipating a telling off; perhaps my hair was too long, my sideburns not short enough, or I wasn't walking in a military manner. Behind the desk the RP Cpl surveyed me. He smiled. I was shocked. The last thing I expected was a smile.

"Welcome. You a new lad?"

I placed my heavy bags on the gleaming tiled floor.

"Yes, Cpl."

"From Catterick or Junior Leaders?"

"From Catterick, Cpl."

"And who have you been attached to?"

"The band."

"Ah. I see. A bandsman?" The manner in which he inflected the word 'bandsman' suggested derision.

"Yes," I replied. My red palms were sore from carrying heavy bags. I looked down at them, blisters had begun to form.

"That'll be the baby bandsman hands you've got."

"Yes, Cpl," I agreed.

He busied himself amongst paperwork on his desk. He wore No2 dress trousers and a neatly pressed cotton shirt. Sharp creases traversed the top of his back and down the sides of his shortened sleeves. The creases interested me since they dissected his chevrons with precision. Above his chevrons and mounted on dark green felt, were the letters 'RP'. They were made of brass and highly polished. Straining my eyes, I was able to see the crease dissecting the felt symmetrically in two. Suddenly, turning around, he shouted into the back of the guardroom.

"Oi! Rushton. Get yer arse out here."

It was a large, spacious guardroom. An enormous blackboard hung from one wall whilst a row of chained SMGs, in a rack, were filed against another. In one corner of the room stood an object that looked out of place. For a moment I was conscious of dragging a memory from deep within my mind. It was a shiny silver object that at first might be mistaken for a vacuum cleaner. When I realised what it was a tiny smile flicked across my mouth. It was an electric floor bumper. The object said much about my new regiment. During the last five months the repetitive action of pushing hand bumpers up and down corridors every day had obliterated the existence of an electric bumper from memory. Perhaps the lonely electric polisher was a symbol of modernity.

From the back of the guardroom, Rushton appeared. He accompanied me to my unit and even carried one of my bags.

A large sign marked the band quarters. It was also formatted in yellow and green stripes and headed by the regimental crest, a portcullis under which was the regimental motto, *Forever Onwards*. Below the motto in bold black letters was spelled the building's occupants: 'S. Troop, 15th Dragoons'. The barrack block was one of those with which most BAOR troops are well acquainted. An old German-style barracks, very long, three floors high and with a spacious cellar and attic. The roof was steep, tiled and interrupted by small windows that jutted out at regular intervals. Such buildings housed a labyrinth of corridors and store rooms in the basement. Opposite the front of the block was the regimental square. Inside the building the familiar smell of bumpering polish welcomed me. The white-walled corridor was large and tall. Rushton carried my bag up the concrete staircase, our heavy footsteps amplified by the bare, solid walls. At the top, on the attic floor, we found the band bar and practice rooms. My guide led me to an office where he introduced me to the BSM. Then he turned on his heels and returned to his duties at the guardroom.

My bunk, on the ground floor, I shared with three other bandsmen. It was a big room with a high ceiling. Situated in the far corner was my bed, a squeaky old iron one. Above this a window looked out onto the back road of the barracks. I was issued the standard barrack furnishings of a mattress, mattress cover, three blankets, sheets, a counterpane, a bedside locker and a small blue carpet. As usual I signed for each item individually. My room mates were Tony Shaw, who'd arrived at the band earlier in the day from JLR, an army institution that trains soldiers too young to join the adult basic training programme. The same age as myself, he'd been in military training since the age of sixteen. Tony, like me, was a cornet player. Then there was Charles King, a clarinettist and saxophonist. He was a bubbly character with dark black curly hair. Finally, in the bed adjacent was Brian Star, a short man built like a bulldog.

The corridor on which my room was situated housed the unmarried bandsmen. In military colloquialisms, an unmarried soldier was known as a 'singlie'. Down the far end of the corridor were the showers and toilets, officially referred to as 'ablutions'. Beyond the toilets were the single rooms that housed the band's JNCOs. That afternoon I spent an hour trying to locate where I could sign out my horse. One of the band Cpls, named AJ, ordered me to find the stables and sign one out.

"A horse!" I exclaimed.

"Well, what do you expect in a cavalry regiment?"

"No one told me that I had to ride a horse. Will I get lessons?"

"Oh, yes. There's a riding school which you'll be attached to for six weeks. It'll be good fun." He gave me directions and I set off on my search. At the back of the barracks, behind the accommodation that bordered the main square, was the tank park. There were several rows of enormous hangars in which stood Chieftain tanks. Some were parked outside hangar entrances where soldiers, clad in oily green overalls, worked on their engines. I'd never seen a tank at close quarters and was surprised by their size. Cold and immense, they looked as if carved out of a single block of iron. Captivated, I walked past the parked vehicles. Suddenly, a tank at the far end of the road fired its motor and in a thick wall of sound the concrete road vibrated. Dense fumes blew from the vehicle's exhaust. In Bolton Barracks I'd seen distant tanks on the moors and had heard their high-pitched whine from miles away. However, when the tank in front of me pulled forward my ears were pierced with the most intense and painful screech. It was a frightening sound of screaming, grating and whining. The sound tore through the air as if a hundred giant hands of sharpened nails were scratching an amplified blackboard. It was the sound of a multitude of solid metal cogs crushing against iron tank tracks. Although its tracks halted, the enormous weight of its body bobbed forward when it stopped. The screech momentarily ceased and suddenly its motor seemed quiet. Then, with several revs which spewed thick fumes into the air, it jerked backwards and the screeching resumed.

Eventually, behind the tank hangars and football pitches I found the stables. Some troopers were busy mucking out and with them I noticed a Sgt. He wore khaki jodhpurs and black riding boots. He saw me approaching and walked towards me.

"Can I help you?"

"I'm from the band, Sgt."

"Well that doesn't help a lot," he said. "What can I do for you? We don't get many bandsmen down this part of the barracks."

"I thought you'd be excepting me. I've come to sign out my horse."

"Oh! I see. Who sent you?"

"L/Cpl AJ." I paused a moment. "Actually, Sgt, I don't know his surname."

"That'll be L/Cpl Reed and no doubt you'll be wanting a tin of elbow grease as well?"

"Pardon, Sgt?" I asked, puzzled.

"You'll be needing a tin of elbow grease to clean the horse's tackle."

"He didn't mention that to me. He just said to sign out a horse."

"Sonny," he said, placing his palm on my shoulder in a paternal manner. "We haven't been a mounted regiment since 1937."

"Really? So we don't ride horses?"

"L/Cpl AJ Reed is winding you up. Playing a joke."

I began to blush. "I see," I mumbled under my breath.

Later that evening the ground floor emptied. Apart from myself, everyone had been invited to a party that had been organised weeks beforehand. I occupied my time arranging my locker, unpacking my bags, sorting out my uniforms and arranging my bed space. My locker was identical to the one I owned at Catterick. Into it I placed all my clothes, boots and personal effects in exactly the same manner as dictated by my training. It wasn't until I left the room to go to the toilet that I saw inside one of my room-mate's lockers. Laundry spilled out from the boot space at the bottom. Clothes of every description, both military and civilian, were jammed into the various compartments. Nothing was folded. I was transfixed; nowhere in army life had I seen such a mess. I doubted he'd even be able to close the doors. Beside his bed, on the tin bedside locker, lay a half-eaten portion of chicken. On his blue bedside carpet stood an open can of lager, with a couple of cold, abandoned chips beside it.

It was years later that a passing comment by Tony threw the evening into a wider context. I wasn't invited to the party as I looked like a 'boring square'. Apparently, the Cpls had debated whether I should be invited, but decided to leave me behind. Their decision was partly based on my style of clothes. I had arrived at the barracks in crimplene trousers, a fluorescent green shirt and a checked blazer that was to become known affectionately as my teacher's jacket. I'd been too excited by my new surroundings to wonder why I was the only person left on our floor of the building.

I quickly settled into the band routine which was easy compared to life in my training regiment. The summer season had finished several weeks previously and so the band were having a lazy time. Weekday routine consisted of individual practice in the first half of the morning followed by full band after morning NAAFI break. Individual consisted of practising either on our own or in pairs. It was customary during individual to practise a variety of exercises such as scales, chords and taxing passages of music. NAAFI break was the official term for a mid-morning break during which time we could visit the NAAFI for refreshments. There was also a small shop which sold newspapers, magazines, canned drinks and books. NAAFI shops also sold a wide selection of war comics with titles such as *Commando* and *Battle*. Squaddies were avid readers of these small comics and referred to them as training manuals. After NAAFI break, we assembled for full band where our entire ensemble rehearsed together. In the afternoons we played sport or formed jazz bands or pop groups. On many afternoons we did as we pleased though we were excepted to be discreet.

Within the band I sat at the bottom of the third cornet stand. Military bands usually have three sets of cornet players. The solo cornets play the difficult parts and always play the tune, whereas the second and third cornets play harmony and support. Playing third cornet was a boring job since in march music you spent most of your time playing offbeats. You rarely faced anything of a challenge. This arrangement was because poor and inexperienced instrumentalists progressed up through the stands. The clarinets, horns and trombones were divided into stands in the same way as the cornets. Tony, however, was the exception to the stand progression. His ability as a soloist secured him the position of second player on the first stand.

My solitary lifestyle was complicated by my interest in the kung fu novels and television series which were popular at the time. The Buddhist philosophy of peace, tranquillity, oneness with nature appealed to me but served to consolidate my alienation. Charles King, one of my room-mates, asked me why I didn't socialise more.

"I don't need to, I see all sorts of things going on in the world without needing to socialise."

"Such as what?" he asked, shocked by my pompous reply.

"I know where these spiders' webs hang... you've passed there every day this week but you've never even noticed them. I know where there's a mouse nest, where there's a wasps' nest. There is more to life than just humans." My reply was straight from one of my kung fu novels.

It was shortly after this incident that I decided to carve a crucifix on my chest. Perhaps it was a cry for help. I knew I was homosexual but as yet hadn't fully acknowledged the fact. When I was thirteen, I'd tried to confess to my father but lost courage at the last moment. I had fallen in love for the first time. Craig was in my class at school and though I find it hard to recall his features I remember him as beautiful. He has become a dark, shadowy figure but if I think hard I catch glimpses of him. Then I see a boy with freckles across the bridge of his nose and piercing bright blue eyes. Sometimes our eyes connect and a terrible sense of confusion, lust, love, shame and admiration sucks at my stomach. It's as though I sometimes manage to force open a door into my boyhood and for fleeting moments can feel the surge of emotions I once experienced.

It had taken me several weeks to identify the source of my feelings towards Craig. Initially, I just desired his company and so we soon became friends and started visiting each other's houses. I was going through my FBI stage and planned to go to the USA to become an agent. Enthusiastically I counted down the days until my eighteenth birthday. When we met, he drank lemonade while I sipped black, sugarless coffee. Though I didn't enjoy it, it was something I had to become accustomed to. In films, FBI agents always drank their coffee black.

Craig's father was an officer in the RAF and they lived in a big house surrounded by a wood of sturdy chestnut trees. We shared several interests but the most passionate was making model aeroplanes. Walking and playing in the woods, out cycling, we were rarely out of each other's company. Over several weeks we avidly pieced together a Superfortress that his father bought us. Meticulously we filed the plastic parts so they'd fit together snugly. In the cockpit we paid every attention to detail even down to painting the buttons and zips on the pilot's flight overalls. In his company I felt happy and had a permanent smile on my face. I went swimming with him once. We were undressing together when I noticed him casting glances between my legs. He pulled down his pants and out poked a chubby erection. Little fuse-wire hairs sprung from the base of his cock whilst his foreskin had been neatly chopped off by a circumcision. Within moments I too had an erection. We defused the situation with laughter and waited in the cubicle until we'd both gone flaccid.

That week, in an agony column of a newspaper, I read about a teenage boy who was in love with his best male friend. In that instant I recognised that my feelings for Craig were feelings of love. Perhaps I too was a homosexual? I became confused, sullen and depressed. My father noticed the change in my disposition and coming up to my bedroom early one evening tried to initiate a father-to-son talk. Looking out of my window with my back to him, I had tears in my eyes and my throat felt like an apple had stuck in it. I stared out of the window at the fields that lay at the foot of our garden. The tears spilt down my face but I kept them hidden. I forced my breathing to appear regular and focused my mind on a row of trees far off in the distance. A momentary lack of concentration, a stifle, and all my angst would tumble out.

"You can tell me son, whatever it is I can help you. I know there's something bothering you and it's not fair that you should bottle it up. Is it school, something that's happened at school?"

"It's nothing Dad, really, I've just been feeling a bit under the weather lately. That's all, really." I wanted to tell him everything, to offload all my anguish and confusion, but instead I concentrated on the trees. I felt his hand on my shoulder, gently squeezing it. In my head I begged him to go away. His hand lingered, his finger tips massaged my neck.

"I'm just thinking," I managed to utter without sobbing. Then he quietly left my room. I often wonder what consequences would have followed had I confessed.

I don't recall Craig ever telling me he was leaving. He didn't appear in class and our form teacher suddenly stopped calling his name from the register. I knew he'd gone far away, as all RAF children eventually did. Nonetheless I visited his parents' house, its empty loneliness accentuated by the misty autumn evening, by the gloomy dank undergrowth of the wood. He'd gone. At the bottom of a great chestnut tree I sat and cried while lonely, golden leaves floated down from boughs above me. As an adult I've walked up the wooded road that passes his house. More than once I've been drawn into the woods that backed onto his garden. I can't remember which of the large houses he lived in but I take refuge in the fact it's one of them. Sometimes, if I concentrate I can hear a voice or see a face – though never clearly. In that fleeting crack of time I remember, in part, what it is like to be thirteen and in love with another boy. And with the erratic sensations of love are feelings of confusion, guilt and sordidness.

I have since learnt that the most traumatic aspect about being gay isn't coming out socially but coming out to yourself. Realising that you are 'one of them', a queer, abnormal is a lonely, difficult experience. Society taught us well, it taught us to hate ourselves; our parents taught us, our schools, the television, our peers. Why, we even taught ourselves.

I used a sewing needle to etch the crucifix onto my chest. It was about three inches long and positioned over my sternum. An etch it was, scratched onto my skin so that when the blood dried it was quite clear. Naturally my mates thought I was mad and could see no logic in such behaviour. Worse, I could give no rationale to explain my actions. My strange behaviour did little to endear me to other members of the band.

In the same attic corridor as the band practice room were the band offices, library, instrument store, individual practice rooms, bar and the squadron bar. There were rooms occupied as living quarters by three L/Cpls. At the time, it never dawned on me why these soldiers were housed so far from the rest of the squadron or why two of them had odd nicknames. They served in the regiment for many years and throughout the time I knew them their reputations were impeccable. Shaun, Daisy and Flower were respected regimental personalities.

Within the band I became the buffoon, the clown. I'd been befriended by several of the JNCOs. They found it entertaining to string me along with silly stories or get me to perform for them. I was their circus dog. They were AJ, a L/Cpl of twenty-eight who had a big handle-bar moustache; Spoons, a clarinet player, and L/Cpl Steve Scott, who played trombone. I didn't mind the humiliation or degradation, on the contrary I positively enjoyed it. One evening, AJ invited me to his house for a party to which some German women were invited. Though married, AJ's wife lived in the UK. He lived with the singlies but still had a married quarter. Before we even made it to AJ's house I'd been plied with copious amounts of Bacardi and was already finding it difficult to stand. My mates watched me march around the room and shouted orders to halt, about turn or mark time. Then they persuaded me to go to the bathroom and change my underpants back to front because German girls really hated Y-fronts. Later in the evening, after I'd staggered around the front room demonstrating a marching display, we headed back to Bhurtpore barracks. On the way they encouraged me to try and pull over lamp posts and traffic signals. The German women never arrived at AJ's party; they'd never been invited.

Towards the end of October we began getting ready for the regimental move to Cyprus. We spent weeks packing up boxes and being assigned to MFO duties in which we loaded boxes on and off lorries. Of course, it was the troopers and bandsmen who received the brunt of this fatigue work. I went to bed at night with forearms painfully throbbing. AJ was flying us to Cyprus, he told me one evening while we were walking to the NAAFI for a blackcurrant milk. Naturally, I believed his story. Whilst he was bullshitting his skill at landing a jet plane within the confines of a regimental square not much bigger than a football pitch, Steve Scott pissed down the back of my legs.

My barracks for the next six months was Polemedea Camp; this was under the jurisdiction of the United Nations, and we now came under their command. It was a sprawling camp of wooden barrack huts that each housed twenty men. The camp lay on a gentle sloping hill overlooking the coast several miles in the distance. On the edge of the shimmering sea lay the town of Limassol. The ground around our camp was a combination of light-coloured rock and compact gravel and sand. In the bright daylight you had to shield your eyes from the blinding, refracted light. The main huts in the camp were the regimental prison, the regimental square, RHQ, the cookhouse and Band complex. There were many other buildings, of course, but for me these were the most important.

The prison was a solitary black hut behind which lay an open-air gymnasium. It consisted mostly of barbells and weights made out of concrete. Bordering the gym was a neatly tended garden cultivated by the inmates. Outside the front of the prison lay several telegraph poles with which prisoners exercised. By the time we left Cyprus they'd been re-painted in the regimental colours of yellow and green. The poles always lay on their sides and were used by the RP to discipline offending troops. Every lunchtime the few soldiers in prison or on RPs struggled around the camp carrying a telegraph pole between them. Usually there were four or five men to each pole. The effort it took to run the perimeter of the camp was written all over their blue, sweaty faces. Their RP guard ordered a change of carrying position, though he always waited until one was ready to collapse. Sometimes it was above their heads, on a shoulder or on the hip. At regular intervals they stopped and put the pole down, and he ordered them to do a set number of sit-ups or press-ups. The telegraph pole punishment was banned in the late seventies.

Then there was the regimental square, that hallowed ground upon which one always walked briskly and with purpose. All regimental squares belong to the RSM who ensures that no one dawdles. RSMs in every regiment take an unhealthy ownership of squares of tarmac and patches of grass. It is through these spaces that they express and enforce their power.

The cookhouse in Polemedea always smelt of stale chip fat. It was a large wooden hut with a black corrugated iron roof. At lunchtime we helped ourselves to an endless supply of milk that came in small triangular packs and there was a copious supply of sliced watermelon. We learnt never to hang around in the cookhouse since it was infested with flies and cockroaches. Whenever we vacated a table it was invaded by flies, mostly clumsy, fat bluebottles. They swarmed onto the table turning it black. The pools of water-melon juice, bits of discarded food and bowls of sugar provided them with a feast. If you were forced to sit at a fly-infested table they had to be swished away before sitting. We rarely saw the cockroaches alive. Mostly they were squashed into the cookhouse floor. They were big brown roaches often reaching ten centimetres in length. Once I pulled one from a stew I'd been eating. Only a bony exoskeleton remained, all its meat steeped into the gravy. When I complained to a cookhouse Sgt, he laughed.

"This is the army, sonny. They're part of the regiment and very nutritious too."

The band complex lay in a secluded corner of the camp. There was only one building which housed a small rehearsal room, a few offices, store room and library. Behind the building lay a large patio where we rehearsed full band. It rarely rained and so we rehearsed outside. Psychedelic colours and patterns decorated the wall that faced the patio. It wasn't at all military, but then bandsmen can do this sort of thing. At the bottom of the patio lay a small pond shaded by a large date palm.

Farther up the hill, in the far right-hand corner of billet 110, was my bed space. I shared a room with the junior and senior NCOs. The BM and BSM, both WOs, were accommodated in their mess. My fellow bandsmen occupied the next hut along. Their hut stank since a cat had died and rotted under it. It stank further as it was home to a few hardened drinkers including Andy Lawrence, the band flautist, who besides being the most prolific boozer was a virulent farter.

Most of our engagements consisted of playing at UN officers' messes and at UN medal parades. Playing at other armies' parades was interesting. Many dispense with the mindless tradition that epitomises the British army yet is always used to assert British military supremacy. Of course most people who claim that tradition instils discipline in soldiers are either officers or SNCOs who wield the big stick. Failing that they're old die-hards who left the army when such behaviour was fashionable rather than traditional. Dutch soldiers paraded in their everyday uniform complete with dirty shoes. Swedish soldiers with long hair wore a hair net. The Canadians wore patent leather boots and plastic white belts, neither of which took much effort to clean and polish. No other army I have experienced could march with as much precision and such exaggerated boot stamping as did the British, nor did they wear such highly polished boots,

Our wooden billets didn't have running water and so showers were housed at the top of the camp whilst the toilets were at the lower end. The toilets were disgusting thunderboxes which were sucked empty every few weeks. Like the rest of the buildings they were wooden and consisted of a row of cubicles with stable-type doors. You rarely enjoyed a peaceful crap without some soldier walking past and looking in. I always used the cubicle at the far end of the row to avoid such disturbances. The wooden seats hadn't been sanded and a splinter in your arse was common. Rats lived in the bottom of the cesspool and sometimes, especially at night, you heard them rummaging over the top of the sewage. They made a crinkling sound as they snuffled about amongst the crispy, non-absorbent, army issue toilet paper. Visiting the thunderboxes was unpleasant, so much so that many of us stopped using them regularly. Instead, we held out for two or three days. Once I managed a week before having to go. In a thunderbox, no one did anything other than shit or piss. The gigantic flies, the same ones that snorted on the cookhouse tables, bounced off your face and the stink invaded your nostrils. You never visited there to vomit, you certainly never used it to wank, and you held your breath while pissing.

There were several ways to tell how full the cesspool was. One was by noting how long it took your piss to hit the sewage at the bottom of the pit. The other was by the intensity of the stench. I always shat at night since it was quieter then and with the cooler temperature there was a corresponding reduction in smell. The thunderboxes always stank; even in the cool evenings the breeze wafted the smell around the camp. In the midday heat, or when the pits were nearing full, you smelt the shit at a considerable distance. My gas mask was a constant companion on calls to the thunderboxes.

In Polemedea I began to get friendly with Charles. He lived in the band complex itself. My naivety prevented me from realising that he was gay and the process of discovering this was a lengthy one. He had this wacky pad at the back of the practice room. It was quite out of character for a soldier. His walls were covered in psychedelic posters and in the corner of his room an orange lava lamp hypnotically mutated. Joss sticks glowed on his bedside locker, filling the room with a heady scent. A brightly coloured civilian counterpane covered his army bed. He wore slippers when relaxing, something few soldiers did in barracks; they were considered 'unmanly'. He liked to have his hair close to the maximum permitted length and was always being told by Jake Potter, the BSM, to 'get a haircut'. He had an effervescent personality and stood out as an individual.

Life was exciting and any concerns about my sexuality were masked. Regular, solitary hand jobs in the shower served to quell any frustration. We spent both Christmas and New Year in Cyprus during which I celebrated my eighteenth birthday. Despite the way my room-mates derided me they also expressed a paternal concern. At times they protected me from the occasional mild bullying I experienced from other band members. They coaxed me with a great deal of patience in military and musical matters. How I incurred this paternalism I am not sure. Perhaps they detected something unusual in my behaviour that was a result of my sexuality. Their relationship with me was physical and often involved play fights in which I was pinned down, petted, stroked and even kissed. They especially liked licking my nipples and ears. It was all presented as a joke, a wind-up with the aim of drawing out my protestations. I always resisted but never enough to repel them. I'm tempted to claim that they found excitement in the physical closeness with a fresh, naive teenager. As far as I knew they were all straight and I drew no apparent sexual stimulation from their laddish ways. Perhaps it was a combination of my hidden sexuality and their own unspoken, unknown desires that elicited such behaviour.

3

Charles sat on the end of his bed cleaning his clarinet. He lived in a corner of the practice room surrounded by records, amplifiers and record decks. His lava lamp cast warm orange patterns onto the walls of his bed space. A fruity-smelling joss stick spiralled its smoky fragrance into the air. As usual, when Charles was relaxing, he wore slippers. His latest pair were of a mauve, shiny quilted material that only lacked a matching smoking jacket. We began showing our new comrade the band block and then Tony suggested we all have a blow.

"After all, Kieran, you'll need to get your lip in for the series of parades and concerts on our programme. We unpacked our comets, borrowing one from the store for Kieran.

"You'll get your own instrument in the morning, but it won't be as good as this one," claimed Tony, waving a dull, battered cornet around in the air. He pushed his glasses up onto his nose, licked his lips and worked his face into the mouthpiece. Taking a deep, gaspy breath he blew. What a noise! A rough, rasping sound vibrated around the room. A long note which for a moment mellowed and became a recognisable tone. He took another deep breath and looked down at the valves so that he went cross-eyed.

"Well, Tony, you are improving," I said. Then he blasted out a series of vulgar sounds more reminiscent of a foghorn. Putting my cornet to my mouth I began playing part of our *Regimental March*. I had memorised the first half of it. Meanwhile, Kieran began playing an overture which lay on one of the music stands. I waited until he'd started before playing along with him. That way he wouldn't notice my crude tone. Tony had stopped blowing and stood listening.

"Not bad, mate, a really nice tone," he said taking his personal instrument from out of its case

"Yes," I agreed. "Considering you won't have practised for months you sound pretty good.

"Hey, Kieran. Do you want to listen to the piece I've been practising for the last few days?" asked Tony.

"Sure, if you like." Tony went over to the third cornet stand, where he'd previously placed his copy of *The Carnival of Venice*, a difficult solo renowned in the cornet repertoire. He put his mouthpiece to his lips and twiddled his fingers over the valves. Then he began playing. It was masterful. Kieran stood up straight, his eyes wideswith awe. Tony agilely ran up and down passages with such precision that the chromatic runs melded into glissandos. He effort-lessly slid through the entire range of the instrument. By now Kieran was well aware that he'd been set up and wasn't offended by our joke. It wasn't until that evening, as I lay in bed, that I realised I was the one who'd really been made a fool of. I didn't have to fake being a poor player; I was. Kieran was much more proficient than I. He'd almost certainly be placed above me and was most likely to be put on first stand.

Kieran and I became mates, after all; we'd been trained by the same instructors, were the same age and both cornet players. In the afternoons we sunbathed, though Kieran, who liked an afternoon nap, always arrived late. He slept so much that we christened him 'Zom-bie'. I chose the name and it stuck. I've always been adept at giving people successful nicknames. When sunbathing, we rubbed lemon juice onto our torsos and legs. Apparently this helped to gain a good tan. We sunbathed on a blanket outside one of our billets where other band members stretched out beside us. As we became mates I began to develop a deep interest in him. I liked his personality, he was mild mannered and interesting, but I began to notice other things about him which raised my heartbeat and drew long sighs from deep inside me. The little rosy nipples on his chest, the whirled shape of his na-vel, the way his rib cage gently rose and fell, the way his ribs protruded with each inhalation. When his torso was glistening with sweat and lemon juice, he looked very sexy.

"What are you sighing at?" he asked.

"It's the heat, it's so bloody hot," I fabricated in response.

All the JNCOs and bandsmen had to practise the cavalry trumpet. Cavalry trumpets and trumpet duties were, and probably still are, a traditional part of cavalry regiments' daily routines. A cavalry trum-pet is simply a larger bugle and like the bugle is valveless. They were unlacquered and had to be regularly polished with Brasso. Attached to each trumpet were cords of intertwined green and yellow - the regimental colours. Every morning, just after first parade, which was at seven thirty, we assembled under the direction of the T/M, Ken Cort. T/M was a prestigious appointment with an important historic role in regimental life. In earlier times he was responsible for carrying out the whippings meted to offending soldiers. He could be any non-officer rank but was usually a Sgt. Regardless of rank he wore four inverted chevrons on his forearm which carried a set of crossed mini-ature trumpets above them.

It was his responsibility to ensure a high standard of trumpeting, to select the regimental trumpeters and trumpet team. Any trumpeter not selected as a regimental trumpeter automatically became a supernumerary. This entailed accompanying the duty trumpeter on his round of calls. On duty, trumpeters wore No2 dress trousers, shirt, stable belt and forage cap. Their gleaming trumpets had to accompany them all day. There were trumpet calls for Reveille, for Stables, for meals, for Office, for Guard Mount and for Last Post. If ever there was a fire or fire drill, everything halted whilst the trumpeters fetched their trumpets and ran out to all corners of the camp sounding Fire Call.

The T/M was also responsible for the performance and turnout of the regimental fanfare team. On official engagements the eight members of the team blew long silver trumpets from which hung embroidered regimental banners. Trumpet calls ordered military life. In the morning, the duty trumpeter and supernumerary marched to the guardroom. They marched with their trumpets slung over shoulders and the bell held against their thighs. They set off from the billets as the Greek regiment over the brow of the hill played their reveille on a record player. We knew it was a record player because in the few seconds before the call you heard a fuzzy, cracking sound. Once at the guardroom, as six o'clock arrived they sounded the Regimental Call followed by Reveille. At seven-thirty they marched back to the guardroom to sound the Regimental Call and Stables. Every morning, after Stables, the trumpeters assembled and were taken through exercises by the T/M. He listened to our individual calls, selecting them at random and criticising. I failed to become a duty trumpeter and was detailed to carry out supernumerary duties. For a cornet player this was humiliating, even the flautist and several clarinettists were duty trumpeters. Kieran and Robert Vickers, the euphonium player, were both put straight on the trumpet roster.

I practised hard to develop my musicianship and spent many of my free hours studying musical theory. I borrowed books on the elements of music, harmony, composition and military band and orchestral scoring. I even managed to find a book on conducting and spent hours in Charles's bunk playing classical records while conducting an imaginary orchestra. I quickly discovered that though most of the other bandsmen and NCOs were competent players, they were in general ignorant about musical history, form and harmony. Most of them were completely devoid of any interest in, or knowledge of, the immense musical repertoire. Indeed, most were devoid of any emotional feeling for music. At first some NCOs guided my study but soon I began to develop and before we left Cyprus I'd become the band boffin on all aspects of theory. Only the bandmaster had a knowledge that surpassed mine. This progress was nothing miraculous on my part, on the contrary, it was simply because the musical education and motivation possessed by most band members was so dire.

The future of my band life lay in an event that happened when I was fifteen. Through my best friend, Paul, I'd met a boy in our year but in a different class. It was a short acquaintance lasting only a month. He sold me a flute at a bargain price of six pounds. As I took it from him I knew it must have been stolen. At school I began taking lessons and though I only studied for a few months, I was able to play scales, chords and simple tunes. After that, the flute lay discarded in a drawer until I joined the army. The bandmaster asked if I'd be willing to move onto flute as Andy Lawrence was soon leaving the band. He argued his case stressing that we needed a flautist and that the job held good prospects. For the first time in four months of band life I felt useful and wanted. I agreed.

Having to spend rehearsals next to Andy wasn't a pleasant experience. He was a short chap of twenty-six with an enormous beer belly and a droopy moustache. On several occasions I was detailed to search the camp's numerous thunderboxes and find him. He had a habit of getting drunk in the evening and would then stumble to a toilet around midnight. He carried with him a selection of crisps, rolls and a tin of lager. In the stench of the thunderboxes, amongst clumsy flies and the snuffling rats he shat whilst eating his food. Eventually he fell asleep. Finding Andy was never easy. The camp housed eight thunderboxes and he never used the same one consecutively. When found, he was always in the same state, slumped against the side of the cubicle, unconscious and with trousers around his ankles. At his feet cockroaches and fat bluebottles gorged on spilt food. Any that weren't alert, I stamped on. Killing a few roaches was my reward for finding him. If they escaped there were always the ones that had squeezed into his can of lager and were trapped. My next task was to rouse him from his drunken stupor. He wasn't embarrassed at being found in such a degrading manner. Even with bits of shitty toilet paper welded to his buttocks, he smiled. He always thanked me when I helped him pull his trousers up, straighten his uniform and discreetly dropped his used toilet paper to the waiting rats. I generally knew when he was going to drink too much as he'd still have his uniform on late at night. He always shaved in the evening so that he wouldn't need to the following morning. That way, when found, he could go straight to work. Rescued from the thunderbox I led him to his room. The BSM always gave him a telling off but knew it was a waste of time.

Ten days before we left Cyprus the regiment held a 'Beating the Retreat'. This military spectacle is often performed when a regiment leaves a base. We rehearsed the parade for a whole week which culminated in a dress rehearsal. The entire regiment, minus those on guard duty, paraded attired in their No2 dress uniform: forage caps, beige and green uniforms, white belts and shining boots. The band paraded in blues: boots and spurs, green cavalry tights with a yellow stripe down each leg, blue jackets with chain-mail epaulettes, white sword belts and forage caps. The bass drummer, from whom came all our musical commands, wore a leopard skin over his blues. The bandmaster carried a sword and wore the traditional bandmaster's dress which included a knee-length black frock coat fronted with woven ornamentation. Before marching off the square the CO gave a regimental address. His oration, delivered with a poncy public-school accent, praised the regiment.

It was around the middle of the address that one of the bass players in the front rank took his dick out and pissed into the bell of his instrument. His name was Gary Flynn. We were stood at ease so the bass players had unslung their heavy instruments and held them against their legs. The rest of the band in the subsequent rows couldn't see him pissing, but though discreet, he wasn't discreet enough. Somehow, the CO spotted him and passed a message to our BM that Flynn would be charged and punished the following morning. When we were dismissed, Flynn was summoned and ordered to sterilise his bass. The following morning he was marched, minus beret and belt, to CO's office. As was usual with offenders and those on a charge, he marched at a ridiculously fast pace. Every fifty meters he was ordered to march on the spot while his charge caught up. Despite pleading a weak bladder he was charged with 'damage to army property' and punished with two weeks' RPs. This entailed confinement to barracks and parading in No2's at Reveille, Guard Mount and Last Post. In the hours between Guard Mount and Reveille he put on denims and suffered cookhouse duties: washing pans, scrubbing floors, or any job that was dirty and unpleasant. As well as this and a normal day's work, he received a daily dose of PT. The offenders were marched, or ordered to run in a squad to the Regimental Prison and there formed groups around the selection of telegraph poles. Lifting the poles onto their shoulders, they began the strenuous one-hour session of running around the camp to the screams of the RP.

The RP were the biggest wankers within the regiment. There were only four of them and they came under the command of the regimental Provost Sgt. The RP had to possess at least the rank of L/Cpl but unfortunately they were the dreg squaddies of the regiment. When a soldier was passed from department to department he often ended up as RP. The process began when a soldier was so inefficient within their squadron that he was moved into a store. Here he'd be expected to help the store NCO with the daily routine. If he botched this the next most likely shift was into one of the messes as a waiter or barman. It was from amongst the mess failures that soldiers moved into the guardroom as a member of the RP. Here, the reject was immediately promoted to a L/Cpl and given immense power.

During the period of Flynn's punishment Charles and I crouched down behind a window to watch his daily beastings by the RP. The prisoners always stopped outside the band practice room where there was a large flat patch of rock. Here they put their telegraph poles down and started doing forced exercises. We didn't like Flynn. He had red hair and a big mouth and knew everything about nothing. The RP in charge of the prisoners and RPs was a venomous shit. He barked out commands, his voice reaching that high-pitched squeal that all those with military authority seem to develop.

"Put down the pole!" he screamed. "Put it down now! On yer faces! Ready for sit-ups, assume the position... and go, one... two... three" (and up to twenty, sometimes even thirty). "On yer backs! C'mon! C'mon! Move it! Move it! You soldier! You! Yes you! What are you fucking looking at, soldier? Face the fucking sky. Ready for sit-ups! On my command... one... two... three..." (up to twenty). "Now stand up! C'mon you shits, move it. Marching on the spot! Mark... time! Left, right, left, right, lift those knees, higher. Halt! Lie down! ... Stand up! ... Lie down!" And so it went on for a good five minutes. Then they strained to lift the poles back onto their shoulders and staggered off down the road with the RP screaming at their heels. Charles and I sat and laughed, careful not to be seen otherwise we would have joined them. Then we waited half an hour until they returned to give us a second performance.

Back in Münster it was cold and damp, a severe winter hadn't quite conceded to spring. We unpacked our rooms, stuck our posters back on our walls and settled down to life in BAOR. Shortly after our arrival Andy left the band and so put me in a vulnerable position as solo flautist. Severed from the cultural excitement I'd experienced in Cyprus I began to reflect on the nature and implications of my sexuality. For months I managed to convince myself that all those cocks I'd played with as a boy, and my experience with the infantryman at Darlington station, had been part of a teenage phase. I still had visions of being married and a father by the time I was twenty-one. In a newsagent's in the town I saw a magazine rack that contained several rows of gay porn mags. Whenever I was in town alone I went into the shop and browsed. Of course I didn't dare pick up one of those mesmerising magazines, instead I blindly leafed through sports magazines while secretly, greedily, casting my eyes along the top shelf. I memorised the front covers of every magazine. After several weeks I decided that I'd have to buy one. I didn't have the gall to leaf through the magazines and select the one I found the most interesting. Instead, I marched resolutely into the shop, bought one that I'd targeted and briskly walked out. Back in the barracks I headed straight for the bathrooms, my magazine hidden away in a towel. Here I eagerly fingered through the pages of beautiful, and not so beautiful, teenagers. Boys lay on beaches, showered or lay in beds with their erections in their hands. Boys fondled themselves, they fondled other boys, they embraced each other, they kissed, sucked and fucked. I hid the book under the mattress of my bed.

My magazine was a momentary diversion from the ominous implications of my sexuality. Once I'd tired of its pages I began to yearn for the real thing. The porno photos forced me to accept that these boys were doing it with other boys and that sex wasn't just something that men and women did. It made me confront the notion that out there on the streets of every country in the world some boys actually preferred to have sex with other boys. How to find these lads was one problem. The other was that I was now beginning to act on my impulses and could see myself becoming a 'queer', a 'poof', a 'homo'. Worse, I was beginning to imagine Kieran on one of those glossy pages. I was succumbing to my inclinations and I knew that the mighty wrath of the military, of my friends and family, the hatred of society stood before me. I couldn't even have a good wank without the mores of society burdening me with guilt. On such occasions I was tempted to tear the photos into pieces and flush them down the toilet. It was me and a few still-life photographs embossed into my imagination, versus the world. Some nights, especially after I'd used my magazine for added stimulation, I sank into despair and loneliness. There was no one to turn to for help, no one onto whom I could offload my awful secret.

4

The following year saw our return to the UK. Our destination was Catterick for a tour of duty as the training regiment for the RAC. So it was back to Bolton Barracks, the home of my basic training. Every piece of equipment, except for the tanks and military vehicles, had to be moved.

Settling into a new barracks was a lengthy and tiresome affair. For weeks on end regimental life was in a state of disruption. Key personnel were missing and stores unable to function efficiently. Regimental symbols were absent or incomplete and the atmosphere of the barracks strange. The limits of discipline, set and enforced by the RSM, were shifted for the duration in which two regiments, two establishments, both inhabited the same barracks. Every room, every piece of equipment was cleansed rigorously as if to absolve it from the pollution of the departing regiment. Everything had to re-emerge and be reborn through this symbolic, institutional circumcision. An offering not of blood but of metal polish, floor wax and bleach. Eventually everything was made regimental and the regimental flag hoisted over our guardhouse and outside RHQ. Squadron lines were denoted by regimental-coloured plaques, every store run and co-ordinated by our regimental personnel. Finally, when our RSM's code of conduct asserted itself throughout the camp, our regimental calls sounded out across the regimental square. The camp now belonged to us.

In the evenings I jogged along the banks of the river. Out on the moors I felt free and relaxed. I always passed the spot where I first met Collings. On one occasion I even paused to see if I could find his footprints in the soft earth where he'd once stood. A northern winter, with its biting frost and blowing wind, had eradicated them. Besides, I wasn't sure if I was looking in the right spot. As much as I tried to ignore my desires the mere recollection of him in that toilet in Darlington railway station obliterated my futile defences and exposed the true nature of my inclinations. With my gay porn mags lying in a bin in Germany I was forced to look for stimulation in the life which revolved around me. I began to notice things that had previously escaped my attention when a recruit. I noticed how many attractive looking soldiers there were, and there were a lot.

My ability on the flute was progressing. I began to learn the piano and violin and the bandmaster, an aloof and private man, gave me lessons in music theory and harmony. In one of the spare barrack rooms I set myself up a small gymnasium, where behind locked doors I practised martial arts from books and magazines. I dreamt of becoming proficient in karate or kung fu and becoming a black belt, but it was a dream as unobtainable as becoming an adept musician. Shortly after our arrival the BM asked me to conduct the band at a Sgts' Mess dinner night. He was a tall, slim man with thick golden hair who walked around the barracks with an air of importance. He refused to salute junior officers but no one dared tell him off. His mannerisms did little to endear us to the regiment. At that time the band didn't have a good reputation. We were considered outsiders, poofs and treated with derision. His request was an acknowledgement for all the hard work and effort I'd put into my musical development.

Over the first few months in Bolton Barracks our band underwent some drastic changes as people departed for the civilian world. Several NCOs left, amongst them the BSM. His replacement, responsible for discipline and co-ordinating the running of the band, was Warren Patton. He was a well-built trombone player of outstanding ability, and a genuinely likeable person. There were several new promotions which included Tony Shaw's promotion to L/Cpl. While some had waited years for a promotion, Tony jumped them all after only nine months. I was too new, and too inexperienced, to be considered. To replace our losses two new bandsmen were posted in from JLR. They were Dean Firmin, a clarinettist and Ian Moore, a euphonium player. I now moved into a new single room within the barrack block, so I finally had all the privacy I needed. Dean and Ian moved in with Kieran.

My childhood friend, Paul Mann, joined the Regiment as a recruit. I'd known him since I was seven as he lived only doors away from my parents' house in Wendover. By late summer he arrived as a clarinet player. A blow-up doll provided a further addition. A group of singlies had bought her from a sex magazine and christened her Tpr Tanya. Her military identification was number 69 and she could be booked out in a small notebook kept for this purpose. She was kept very busy. I only met Tanya fully inflated twice, and never on a booking. Her limbs were stiff and shapeless, a coarse mat of black fur supplied her pubes, and bright yellow, synthetic hair sprouted from her puffed head and hung past her shoulders. Blue eyes had been painted on her plastic face and her lips, wide in a pout, were bright red. Her breasts were nipple-less mounds and a tight crease in her crotch provided a cold, lifeless vagina. Disinfectant scented her skin from the douche she was administered after being penetrated by a customer. The only rule in the booking book was that she should be cleaned with disinfectant after use. When not on call she was stored, deflated, in a carrier bag.

"How can anyone fuck that?" I asked as she lay on the bed on her inaugural inflation. "It looks fucking pathetic. If you can get a hard-on and fuck her you've got to be sick. It's a perversion." I pushed three fingers into her mouth and her entire head collapsed inwards around them. I had to pin her neck to the bed to retract them.

"Yes, she's terribly dry," laughed Paul.

"It'll be like wanking into a plastic condom," I said, shaking her head around as her mouth clasped my fingers. Her bright hair tossed around and all the time her big blue eyes starred. "Oooh, you're sexy, babe," I joked. Then Ian put his hands over her stomach and began rhythmically thrusting into her. With each thrust her arms and legs jolted and strained. On especially powerful thrusts her fingers splayed outwards and her head bulged.

"No more headache excuses," chuckled Paul. Ian gave an enormous thrust which blew her vagina inside out and a swollen sheath popped out.

"She can change sex," I shouted and we further humiliated her by bending her forward and forcing her mouth over her plastic dick. Then Paul put a forage cap over her head. Tanya lasted several weeks before a breast exploded and deflated her permanently.

Our duties whilst a training regiment for the RAC consisted of playing for the passing-out parades that occurred every second Friday. As winter approached the parades became a burden. The wind was bitter and cut through us. On several occasions the cornet players' mouthpieces froze to their lips. Charles and I stuck hot water bottles under our jackets which brought criticism from the SNCOs. As the wintry weather worsened the parades became painful. Before we'd even halted on the empty square to await the arrival of the recruits, the icy, persistent wind had found its way through our tunics and chilled our instruments. Then our ear lobes grew numb, our noses ran and our exposed finger tips hurt. The wind blew. It blew so hard that sometimes hats flew off and rolled across the square like tumbleweed. It blew so hard that our bodies swayed to and fro. Eventually the cold found its way through the leather of our boots and chilled our toes.

I began to develop a crush on Ian Moore, the euphonium player. His four-man room, which he shared with Kieran, Paul and Dean, was opposite my bunk. I'd gradually lost my infatuation for Kieran, especially since he'd started dating a local girl. He spent most of his evenings out with her and so I began to focus my attention on Ian. Both he, Paul and Dean were my age and shared my lowly position within the band hierarchy. Every Friday evening we held a meeting in their room which we called the front-stabbing session. In each session the minutes were written out into a red logbook:

> Dean complained that Nick leaves his dirty coffee mug lying around the room. Nick apologised and promised not to do this in future.
> Nick complained that Ian is sometimes moody and short-tempered. Ian asked for examples and it was agreed by Dean, Paul and Nick that he can sometimes be moody in the mornings – especially before having a cigarette. Ian explained that he needed some space in the morning but would try not to snap at us. All present agreed to be sensitive to Ian's early morning moods.
> Nick and Dean asked Ian not to smoke when having a wash. Nick thinks it is quite a disgusting habit and makes the washrooms unpleasant for non-smokers. Ian has agreed to cease this habit.
> Paul suggested that we put aside some money each week and use this to go out for a meal at the end of each month. Nick and Ian agreed and it was decided to put 2 pound a week into a kitty. Dean volunteered to look after our savings.

Though we were all new to military band life we were well aware of the intense bitching and back-stabbing that went on between all band members. The front-stabbing session allowed us to confront each other with problems rather than doing so behind one another's backs. It was a form of group protection.

My infatuation for Ian deepened until I soon found it painful to be in his company. He was over six feet tall and had thick, spiky brown hair. He'd an impressive physique and when stripped you could identify all the individual muscles of his torso. When he moved they rippled fluidly. Whenever his body brushed against mine tingles sparkled over my skin. I had to suppress a compelling sigh. Increasingly, I began to lock myself away in my room and even missed several front-stabbing sessions. Looking in the minutes book one afternoon I read the previous entries:

> Paul is becoming concerned with Nick's behaviour. He's become quiet and sometimes locks himself away for hours on end. Ian says he's almost stopped talking to him and always seems preoccupied. We decided Paul, as his closest friend, needs to talk to him.

One evening, in a bout of depression I cut my arms with a razor blade. It was a pathetic attempt to attract attention, a cry for help. I didn't even use a proper razor but a disposable type with a plastic guard above the blade. My forearms looked as if scratched by a thorn bush. Then, in the pit of despair I tried to hang myself. Suspending a rope from the ceiling, I stood on a chair and put my head through the noose. The rope was just tight enough to interrupt the flow of blood to my head and I began to go dizzy. Immediately, before I stumbled, I pulled the rope off my neck. I don't really think I wanted to kill myself and trying it deterred me from future attempts.

Charles, who lived in the bunk next to mine, was a source of support and frequently sat and talked to me. His effervescent personality drew my mind away from passionate fixations. It was impossible to be sombre in his company. His genteel mannerisms, his black curly hair and moustache, his bedroom slippers and tinted glasses infused his energetic personality. Five minutes in his company, listening to his gossip and bitching, soon drew me into a more optimistic world. On the other hand, Paul's insistent interrogation, though well intentioned, served to focus my attention on the nature of my plight. I kept my secret from them. When alone, I mulled through my predicament, weighing up the pros and cons of my options. Often, at nights, I lay and cried myself to sleep.

I started taking harmony lessons from an old German doctor of music. He lived in Middlesborough which was thirty miles from Catterick. Charles drove me there and then sat in a pub for an hour while I had my lesson. Charles and Robert bought wigs that they wore outside the barracks. Both were long enough to cover their ears and hang onto their collars. Charles's was a fluster of tight black curls. With his moustache he looked like a character from a spaghetti Western. Robert's was fair and collar-length. Whenever possible, Charles wore his blue-tinted glasses; they mellowed his bubbly appearance. Several SNCOs had ordered him not to wear them in uniform. Even in civvies the RP sent him back to the accommodation if he tried to wear them out of barracks.

Charles was a DJ and had all the equipment – various decks, amplifiers, a smoke machine, lights that threw patterns on walls or ceilings and hundreds of records. He transported his show around in a small grey Minivan. Flowers decorated the vehicle's side panels. He bought himself a little stitching gadget and made himself hessian shoulder bags in which to carry his records. When on a gig, he'd unashamedly strut down to the car park wearing his wig and shoulder bags. His eccentric, un-military behaviour was excused by his trendy,

DJ identity. All Charles's idiosyncrasies, the conflicts of two opposing identities, were attempts to resist the system. His hair, moustache, slippers, glasses, joss sticks and flowery-patterned sax sling were all weapons with which to fight back. He was the naughty boy of the band and his behaviour endeared him to us. Charles pestered me to tell him why I was acting so strange, every time he took me to Middlesborough he gave me the third degree. After several weeks of resistance he claimed he knew what was wrong and that he'd known for ages.

It was in the early hours of Friday morning that we were woken by the duty guard. We heard them crashing about in their boots on our corridor. They woke up the Trumpet Major, Ken Cort, who was in charge of our accommodation. I lay awake in my bunk anticipating a crash-out. These were exercises in which we had to activate the military machinery for a potential crisis. There were muffled voices out in the corridor. I waited for the banging and shouting to start and began fretting about where all my crash-out equipment was, my combats, webbing and back pack. Then I heard the guard's footsteps disappearing down the corridor. Quiet returned, an eerie quiet when the ears strain to differentiate between the sounds of the building and those that are alien. The sort of straining that makes the ears rush as if listening to sea in a shell.

I heard breathing, muttering, outside my door. Any moment and the banging and shouting would start. I waited, my ears rushing. Then with a gentle click my door opened and a beam of light cut across my bedroom. I could see the T/M's dark, ominous outline.

"Nick? Nick? Are you awake?"

"Yes," I mumbled.

"I'm afraid I've got some really bad news. The guard have just been over."

"Yes, I know, I heard them. What is it?"

"There been a car accident!"

"Oh, fuck!" I exclaimed, pulling myself upright. "Kieran and Robert are dead. Martin and Stanley are in hospital." We were silent. "I've put the percolator on in my room, I doubt any of us will sleep."

I sat in the darkness of my room, numbed by the news. Then I joined the procession of bandsmen going quietly from room to room, comforting each other, pouring out cups of coffee, quietly talking or lost in thought. No one cried in public apart from Charles but I wept in my room. Out of selfishness I cried for Kieran; what a waste of life, a waste of beauty. Outside, dawn began to break. It was a drizzly, dull morning that unveiled itself before us and exposed our reddened eyes. Down the hill, at the camp's entrance, Reveille was taking place.

A Reveille from which two comrades were absent.

That morning we paraded for a passing-out. There was a sub-dued atmosphere amongst us. No one complained that we played wrong notes, that our boots were dull, that our quick marches lacked vigour. And in front of us, in the corners at the head of the square, flags flew at half mast.

They had been travelling back from a party in Ripon and in driving across the moor had skidded on a cattle grid. Robert had been killed outright, his head severed from his body. Kieran was thrown from the car and impaled on a fence post. Stanley Walters, one of the two survivors, told us that as he lay beside the car he heard Kieran crying out. Late that afternoon we packed their belongings into cardboard boxes. Kieran's music system, which he'd proudly bought tax free in Germany, was cased up. Their clothes were folded and put into little brown boxes. I stripped Kieran's bed clothes. His pillow slip still lingered with his scent and one patch of his white sheet was sputtered with semen. A photo of him in Cyprus hung above his bed; I'd taken it as we sunbathed outside our huts. I placed it carefully on the top of an open box which I then sealed shut. By Last Post their bed spaces were empty, their beds stripped and awaiting their replacements when life returned to normal.

Days later we buried them. Robert went home to his parents while we buried Kieran in the garrison cemetery. We paraded at the church in full blues. It was another wet day and we wore our dark blue capes. When his mother and girlfriend walked down the aisle they began sobbing. Several of us joined them. We carried him out into the cemetery, out into the misty drizzle. A Union Jack covered his coffin and his forage cap and white sword sling lay on the closed lid. Stifling sobs, the coffin bearers, fellow bandsmen, lowered him into his grave as Tony sounded Cavalry Last Post. Then we observed the traditional two minutes' silence; heads bowed towards the ground. I didn't think about Kieran. I drove his memories and the pain away by singing Reveille in my head. It focused my mind and stopped me crying. Then, out of the crushing silence, the bold optimism of Reveille. He was buried in a pleasant site between two large trees and his grave later marked by a headstone bearing the regimental crest and motto.

I missed Kieran for a long time and often, in quiet moments, I think of him. I wonder what life would have held for him? What he would be like now? I regret never having come out to him. He never knew who I really was, he never knew what Nick Elwood was all about. Would he have accused? Cursed me? Supported me? Even embraced me? He was never given the opportunity to do anything. I had loved him from afar, lived with him and was a mate yet he'd never known me. I decided that I would have to come out. I was tired living a lie, denying my inclinations and hurting.

I decided to tell Paul first as I'd known him since I was seven. Besides, we had wanked and sucked each other off during puberty. At the time, however, I didn't perceive this as sex; it was what schoolboys did. So one evening I told him I wanted to talk and he drove us into Richmond. We went for a drink during which I either evaded the issue or clammed up. The pubs closed and we started walking the streets of the town. Paul kept prompting me, promising to support me, insisting that it couldn't be anything that bad. Eventually we stopped by a footpath.

"Come on, Nick. You can trust me. Whatever it is that's been bothering you all these months, it can't be something that we can't deal with? Can it?"

"I just don't know if I can tell you. I keep trying but it just won't come out. Once I've told you, well, that's it."

"Are you ill?"

"No, I'm not."

"Well, is it something to do with money?"

"No, its not money, and I've not broken the law or made anybody pregnant."

"Well for fuck's sake tell me what it is. Christ! I've known you since we were kids. I thought I knew you, could sense what was wrong. You must surely be able to tell me?"

I paused, summing up all my energy. Finally, I blurted it out. It was like being verbally sick.

"I'm a fucking queer!"

"A what?"

"A fucking queer," I repeated, gnarling the word 'queer'. He collapsed against the wall and slid down onto his haunches.

"I don't fucking believe it."

"But that's not all," I sobbed. "I'm in love with Ian."

"Well I never. How long have you known?"

"Long enough... I suppose I've gradually come to know since I was twelve or thirteen."

"What, even when we were doing it?"

"No! No! I didn't know then. I knew that I enjoyed it more than I felt I should have done. But I didn't fancy you or anything, it was nothing like that."

"Well, thanks," he joked. "What, I'm not your type?"

"No! It just wasn't like that. It wasn't sex. We all did it. Fuck, we wanked off every kid in the street, it seemed normal, secret but normal."

"Look! It doesn't bother me, Nick," he said, pulling himself up. "And I won't tell anyone."

We walked back to the car park as he asked me the same sort of questions I have since been asked by most straight people to whom I've come out. When did you first find out? Were you overly mothered in childhood? What made you gay? What sort of men do you fancy? Do you think it's a phase? Have you had sex with a woman? And of course, I defended my sexuality as if some perversion that needed an explanation.

My mates sensed that Paul knew something. They sensed that I'd opened up and relaxed. Now they too wanted to know. If Paul knew, they argued, then so should they. They pestered me constantly, affectionately pledging me their allegiance and loyalty. Eventually I gave in and told them one by one. One evening Dean drove me to a nearby chip shop. Along a quiet country lane I confessed.

"I'm queer," I said. Coming out a second time was much easier. The car shuddered to a halt.

"Never!" he exclaimed with a laugh. "You're fucking bent!" He continued laughing. It intensified. "Fucking queer!" He laughed until tears ran down his face. He wiped the corner of his eyes.

"You're not supposed to be laughing," I complained. "It's difficult for me." He continued laughing.

"So that's it! That's what's been up with you all these months. I wasn't expecting that one... deary me," he said wiping at his tear-stained cheeks with the back of his hands. "So is that it?"

"Is that what?"

"You're gay? That's all that's up with you? Shit! I was expecting something major, something like cancer or something."

"Well, there is something else, I suppose I'd better tell you."

"What! You mean there really is more." He started laughing again. "Don't tell me, let me guess... you're gay and you've got cancer." He laughed. "Cancer of the arse," he interjected hysterically. His laughing continued until he looked up and noticed my sullen face.

"I really can't believe that you find this all so funny. I've just told you my deepest secret, my greatest shame and all you can do is sit and laugh."

"I'm sorry, I'm sorry. Look... all serious now," he said pulling his best unemotive expression. He coughed, sat up straight and placed his palms on his thighs. I paused a moment.

"I think I'm in love with Ian."

He burst into a fit of uncontrolled laughter and began slapping

his knees with his palms. "Fuck, fuck, I can't believe this is for real."
He began wiping his eyes again. "Tell me you're joking?"

Eventually he calmed down, looked at me and became very serious. "Well," he said, "what am I supposed to do? Fucking kick you
out of the car. Throw my arms up in the air and start condemning
you? Or maybe I could report you to the RSM?" He stared at me
intently. "It's no problem, it's cool. Okay?"

"Fine."

"But I wouldn't tell Ian how you feel," he continued, almost as
an afterthought. "I mean, you know what he's like. He'd probably
run a mile."

Shortly afterwards we continued on to the chip shop and on the
way he asked me the same sort of questions that Paul had asked.

I chose to tell Ian on an afternoon when we were both out on a
run along the river. We'd run as far as we could along the bank and
then turned onto the bleak and churned-up tank manoeuvre area.
Eventually, we stopped to catch our breath and sat on a small concrete bridge. Our conversation soon got around to my secret problem.
The moment was right, and this time coming out was even easier. Ian
was shocked but as with Dean and Paul, he claimed it was 'no big
deal'. Of course, I didn't tell him that I was in love with him. I'd have
to let him deal with my homosexuality before I told him that he was
the object of my desires – if I decided to tell him at all, that is.

Finally, I told Charles early one evening when he drove me to
Middlesborough. I hadn't planned to tell him but he initiated the
conversation.

"So Nicky, are you going to let me in on your little secret? I
mean, I know anyway but I just want you to tell me. Just in case I'm
wrong, but I don't think I am."

"I don't know if I'm quite ready to, Charles. And anyway, I
really don't think you know what it's about."

"Don't you bank on it. I think it's pretty obvious. I'm not stupid you know. And anyway, you've all ready told half the corridor,
why can't you tell me? Besides, I might be able to help you, give you
advice."

"I doubt it, but I suppose it's only fair, anyway I've only told a
couple of people. Has someone, one of them, told you something?"

"Hell no! No one's said a word... honestly."

"Well, what do you think's wrong?"

"Hey, I'm not starting that, either you tell me or that's it. I'm
not going to drag it out of you by guessing. If you're not ready to tell,
well, that's fine. But when you are ready I'd like to know... as a friend."

"Okay, I get the message," I said. "I'm queer. That's the problem in a nutshell."

"I was right then."

"Well how on earth did you know, I've never said anything or done anything to give it away, have I?"

"Look, Nick, do you really think that you've just invented the word, that you're the only one, the only one anywhere in the world?"

"What do you mean?"

"Well, that there are other people just like you, you're not alone."

"Oh! Fucking great! Well, where are they? Down the regimental stores? In the cookhouse? The point is that I don't know any. I've never met a queer, I've never even see a queer."

"The word's gay, not queer,"

"I'm not using that word. What does gay mean? Limp wrists and a fairy's voice. I'd rather you'd use the word queer, please. It's the most comfortable of the two. Not that I feel in the least bit comfortable with queer in the first place."

"Whatever! The fact is that there are plenty of other queer people around, not just you."

"Well, I don't know any."

"Yes you do. It's just that they've never come out to you, so you wouldn't know anyway."

"I would know if someone was queer, I'd be able to tell."

"Would you? I mean no one in the band has ever suggested that you might be gay... queer. You've kept it hidden. So have others."

"How do you know all this?"

"Look, where do you think I've been going every time I hang around Middlesborough when you've got a music lesson?"

"I don't know. Why, I thought maybe you went around the shops or went for a drink. I've not really given it any thought."

"What! You really thought that I drove to Middlesborough just to look at the shops for an hour? Middlesborough? It's a bloody dump."

"Well where have you been going?"

"To a gay pub!"

"You're joking?"

"Straight up. I've been going to gay pubs for years, obviously because I'm gay, I'm queer, too."

"God! I don't believe it. I would never have thought that you were gay." I was overjoyed.

"See, you're not alone, there are others just like you and you've met them and not recognised it. Not all queer men are camp."

"What does camp mean?"

"It means effeminate, you know, like limp-wristed."

From that moment onwards I began my new life as a gay person, even though I found it hard to refer to myself as gay. On the way to Middlesborough we asked each other all the typical questions: when did you first find out you were gay? have you had sex with a woman? and many others. After my music lesson Charles introduced me to my first gay pub, it was aptly named The Queen's Head. I was surprised to meet Charles's boyfriend, Malcolm. Less than a week ago I'd been the only queer person I knew and it was my secret. Now all my mates knew and I was sat in a pub surrounded by men like myself. My best friend sat arm in arm with his boyfriend. The pub was packed with men of all ages, they weren't just any men, they were queer and there was something similar about them. It was their mannerisms, their dress, the way they looked at you. Their casual clothes were smart, their hair combed and their faces mostly shaven. A variety of aftershave scented the air. Some younger men wore earrings, many wore tight white T-shirts, some were sun-tanned and some had defined, muscular bodies. If I had walked into this pub a week ago I'd have immediately sensed that this bar was different. Straight men just don't take such meticulous care of their appearance when socialising. Already I was beginning to identify with this queer culture and I felt a slight twinge of pride at being a member of such a group.

From that moment my depression evaporated. I could hardly claim to have come out in a big way but it was enough to ease my sense of alienation. Besides, this was the army. A week later we went back to The Queen's Head and during the evening a young man began eyeing me up. He was good-looking, tall and skinny and not at all camp. He kept looking over at our table and when Malcolm returned from a visit to the toilet he asked me if I wanted sex with him. All I had to do was leave the pub and the lad would follow. His name was Steve.

"He's a pretty little chicken," said Malcolm.

"What's a chicken?" I asked.

"A sexy young lad under twenty-one."

"And preferably with a big knob," added Charles.

If I'd been on my own I might have rejected his offer. However, I felt somewhat pressured into proving my sexuality. I had to do it in order to become a member of the fraternity to which I had finally admitted I belonged.

I left the pub and sure enough Steve followed me out to Malcolm's parked car. Although I'd had sex with boys in the past this was to be the first sexual experience in which I was fully aware. For years to come this would be the event from which I'd affirm my sexuality. This wasn't some hand down a pubescent boy's pants in the fields back home. It was going to be a homosexual encounter; my first conscious, homosexual act. It would confirm or deny my proclaimed sexual identity.

We climbed into the back seat of the car and talked nervously for a while. He was a nineteen-year-old trainee hairdresser. Our hands caressed each other's knees and thighs as we spoke. I told him I was in the army, a musician. He told me he was from Ripon. Then his hands found their way to my crotch and we began kissing. Our conversation was over. Shirt buttons opened and the windows of the car began to steam. I didn't know what I was supposed to do, after all, no one had ever taught me. I had more idea of what to do with a girl than with a boy. So I lay back, and trying to be as casual and cool as possible, said: "Do what you want, man." So he did, and what he did I then did to him. It was like look and learn. When I walked back into the pub I had a bright love bite on my neck and a sticky wet patch on the front of my shirt. I wore them with pride. On my face was a big grin.

"Did you enjoy it?" asked Malcolm.

"It was fucking brilliant," I replied. I felt different. I felt the warm glow that comes after having had a good shag. I felt strong and contented. An enormous weight had been lifted from my shoulders. Being homo would never be the same again.

A few weeks later I went out for a drink with Ian and Dean. With a new confidence bolstered by alcohol I told Ian that I'd a crush on him. Having a crush didn't sound as bad as telling him I was in love with him. It all happened so quickly. In the second I told him, he cursed under his breath, banged his glass down, snatched up his coat and almost ran from the pub. With drooping jaws Dean and I watched his hurried exit. His beer was still sloshing around in its glass. Dean looked at me; a subdued smile hung on the corners of his mouth.

"Don't you just know how to ruin a party, Nicky?"

"Fuck! Now I've gone and done it!"

We returned to barracks in John's car. I had visions of the Military Police waiting for me at the camp entrance but they weren't. Ian locked himself in his room and wouldn't even let Dean in.

"Come on, Ian. Where am I supposed to spend the night?"

"I don't know," he shouted from behind the locked door. "I'm sure Queer Boy Elwood can give you a bed for the night."

"God, Ian! You're really over-reacting. What the hell's your problem? What do you think he's gonna do?"

"Well I sure as fuck don't intend to give him the opportunity for me to find out. "

"But you can't just keep your door locked. What happens when

Paul gets back? Are you gonna keep him locked out too?" He didn't reply. "Come on, Ian. I wanna watch telly. 'Space 1999''s about to start. Please let me in? I've watched every episode so far." Still he refused to answer.

Dean sighed heavily. "This could cause real problems," he whispered.

"Tell me about it. It's going to be all around the barracks."

"If I miss this episode I'll lose the gist of the next one."

"You wanker!" I sneered.

"He's still there, isn't he?" shouted Ian from the safety of his room. "I can hear him. Hey, Queer Boy?"

"What?" I replied.

"Just you go lock yourself in your room. And I wanna hear your door lock. Then I'll know I'm safe."

"Come on, Ian," I pleaded. "I'm not going to do anything. I just wa..."

"I don't wanna talk. Just lock yourself away!"

"You'd better do as he says otherwise he's going to have the whole corridor out here wondering what's going on," Dean suggested. I opened my bunk, entered, and locked my door loudly.

"He's gone now," said Dean. "You can let me into my room and you'd better have the telly on!"

"Are you sure?"

"Of course I'm bloody sure, now let me in!" I heard their door open and moments later, with a clunk, it locked.

Next day, I was expecting the singlies' floor to be in a commotion when news of my 'crush' became common knowledge. I was prepared for the worst; a summons to see the BM or RSM. In the washrooms everyone went about their business as usual. The first place to hear the latest gossip was while having a shave or cleaning your teeth. All morning I waited nervously for an NCO to order me to the BM's office but thankfully such an event never occurred. Ian ignored me for almost two weeks during which our weekly front-stabbing sessions were quietly forgotten. Every night that week I heard their door lock shut but from the following Tuesday this ceased. Whenever Ian walked past, he looked straight ahead. I didn't exist. He washed and dressed before any other bandsmen were out of bed. Dean and Paul kept me abreast of their room's developments and insisted that they were 'working on him'. Returning from a shower several weeks later I found a note on my table:

I've been a right arsehole. Sorry. I've never met a homosexual before and certainly not one that fancies me. You really

freaked me out! Ian. PS. I've left a small present on your window ledge.

I drew back my curtains and on the ledge lay a teaspoon. It was a Trust House Forte spoon we'd pinched from a motorway stop. I picked it up. It was filled with a yellowy-white liquid that I instantly recognised. What he expected me to do with it I don't know. I poked it. It was still warm. Between my fingers it felt slimy. It smelt of fresh dough. I'd never yet swallowed an oyster but when I eventually did, the sensation was similar. Ian became one of my best mates and though I never managed to swallow his oysters live, he supported me for the next twelve years.

5

The summer season, a busy one, approached and we were given a two-week block leave. I went home to Wendover with Paul. We spent the days driving around in his car and meeting old school friends. One particular friend was Will. He lived on the main road where his parents owned a transport cafe. I'd always had an attraction to him. Why, I don't know, he wasn't particularly attractive. He had dark brown hair, was slim and had a greasy complexion. He had an appalling sense of humour. Whenever we told a joke, he stared dumbly as we delivered the punch line. Then we had explain it to him. Except for the rare occasion, he'd given up telling jokes. He either muddled the plot or simply forgot the punch line. His redeeming factor was a wealth of dirty stories. As a homosexual fourteen-year-old, this is what had drawn me to him. He amused us with his most personal intimacies. Without any prompting, he admitted that his younger brother wanked him off and that when he was thirteen he'd had sex with his grandfather, who was in his sixties. According to Will, people with no teeth gave excellent blow jobs.

"You've gotta be joking!" I exclaimed.

"You're bloody sick!" said Paul.

"No, really, he did. It was great."

"But no one has sex with their granddad. It's a disgusting thought," I argued.

"Well how did it happen?" asked Paul.

"I was having a bath and feeling randy, as you do. Anyway, he wanted in for a shave so I opened the door and then got back in the bath. Then I got an erection and he saw it. He asked if I could use it yet. Eventually, after a bit of talking, he showed me how to wank it."

"And then he sucked you off?" asked Paul.

"Yep. I was too far gone on his hand to bother about him sucking it. Besides, it felt great. He sucked just like a baby calf."

"What?" I asked.

"Just like a baby calf, you know – no teeth."

Naturally we were shocked and found his exploits difficult to accept but there was something convincing about them.

"Does your bum hole feel sexy if you poke it?" he asked one day, during religious education. Paul and I recoiled in revulsion.

"Shut up, Will, you're sick!" I complained. He told us about the variations he practised whilst masturbating. His favourites were sticking the end of his cock into a greased-up milk bottle and wanking with a palm full of salt. He claimed the sting of the salt was an added pleasure. "Pain and pleasure, what's the difference? They can be mixed together."

"What do you mean?" I asked.

"It's hard to explain. But wanking with just a tad of pain makes a feeling you can't describe; it's wonderful. I call it the twilight zone." Neither Paul nor I empathised with his theory. His most bizarre story, and one whose genuineness I tend to doubt, centred on his attempts to fuck his cat. Out of all his stories, this one I found hard to accept. However, in the boys' changing rooms that afternoon, I noticed scratches on his thighs. At fourteen I hadn't seen gay pornography. The only magazines I had seen were the straight versions boys brought to school. Each of Will's stories were engraved into my memory and a vital source of fantasy imagery. His explicitness we listened to with ardour.

I had another close friend at home. His name was Damien Gorst. He played the trumpet in our school band and was several years younger than me. Out of my whole school, he was the boy who'd appealed to me the most. His fresh, clean appearance was an immediate attraction. His blond hair was short and neatly parted and he always looked as if he'd just had a haircut. His bright blue eyes flashed with a sparkle. He'd often been the centre of my boyish sexual fantasies which included shooting him full of arrows or stabbing him. He never died an easy death, simply because my fantasies never lasted long enough for him to die. My pleasure lay in manipulating and morphing his experience in the twilight zone and thus I needed him alive. Sometimes I did him with arrows that thumped heavily into his buttocks, between his ribs or into the soft flesh of his belly; at others with the thrust of a spear that sliced into his taut muscles. I finally understood Will's theory. Damien's expression was the convergence of pain and pleasure. His mouth formed an O. It was a mouth of pleasure, like the sigh of an orgasm. As if in another dimension, his eyes were expressionless. The blue eyes of someone about to ejaculate or faint.

We met through the school band, and were friends for about four years. Our joint interest in music was a bond between us. At weekends, or in the evenings, we listened to records, practised our trumpets or walked in the fields and forest that surrounded Wendover. Sex had become a topic during our country walks. Initially it began with references to pin-ups he'd seen in a paper or magazine. During our initial conversations we impressed each other with manly, suggestive comments such as how we liked 'big tits' or 'blonde birds'. Later, when our friendship was secured, we confided in each other the ambiguity of our sexuality. Eventually I confessed that I'd had sex with men but tempered this revelation by claiming I was bisexual. At the time it was a trendy statement to make since so many pop stars proclaimed it. He told me he'd wanked off a couple of freinds on camps with the Air Training Corps.

In the last few days of my leave we met and after listening to Mahler's First Symphony, went for a walk in the hills. Inevitably our conversation meandered around to sex. We strolled up a secluded country lane that led to the edge of the Chiltern Hills. Dusk was already falling.

"You know, Nick," he said. "I really find it hard to believe that you're bisexual. I mean, you're in the army, it's supposed to be illegal."

"I am! Really," I insisted. There's not a lot I can do to prove it, is there, other than telling you that I am."

"No, there's not," he replied thoughtfully. I looked at him but he diverted his eyes to the ground.

"I find it hard to believe that you are too."

"And there's little I can do to prove it either?" He looked up; momentarily our eyes met. "Well, not unless we do it together, I've got a busting hard-on, I really need a wank."

"I've got a fucking stiffy too, I've had it for the last hour, my balls feel like shot putts." We stood in silence. All around the only sounds were the cracking twigs under our feet and the song of a blackbird chirping high in a tree. He moved towards me, his hand reaching for my shoulder. I stepped closer, aware of my erratic panting and rushing head. My hand gripped his biceps and I felt the rhythm of his arm massaging his erection.

"I've wanted to have sex with you for ages," he said in a soft exhalation. "Since I was fourteen." He moved closer so that our jackets brushed together. His hands dropped to my crotch where he fumbled breathlessly to undo my jeans. I ran my fingers through his hair, over his beautiful, shadowy face.

"I've fucking dreamt of this," I gasped.

"Me too," he replied, pressing his head against my chest. Then he dropped to his knees and the world around me become all woozy and wobbly. I had to stop him from finishing me off and suggested we found somewhere more comfortable. We decided to walk back towards the village to a place he knew.

He led me to a deserted railway shed not far from his parents' house. By now it was getting dark. The shed was derelict and once inside we had to stumble in the darkness, our feet knocking against the rubbish-strewn floor, to find a suitable spot to continue. At the back of the shed we found a sort of stage, it was dusty and our prying fingers felt shards of glass. In blindness we cleared a place of rubbish and then our hands fumbled to find each other. I was horny, but Damien was uncontrollable, out of breath and all prying fingers that undid buttons and slid down flies whilst aggressively wanking himself off at the same time. I got my hands under his T-shirt. His body was hot and clammy. He had a scrawny physique where each rib stuck out like the black keys on a piano. I wish it had been light enough to see his features, to see the twisting and twitching expressions on his face as my hands sought out his most intimate places. In the darkness of the filthy shed we released passions repressed in both of us. It wasn't just a sexual passion but a passion for the very nature of the act itself. His hands ran down my sides and found places on my body that were uncharted erogenous zones. I could smell the scent of sexual excitement seeping from our bodies.

We left the dirty rail shed expended, exhilarated and with dusty clothes. Damien's blond hair had been dirtied by my passionate hands and smears of dirt grubbied his face. Our hands were filthy from the shed's ancient dirt. For most of the walk towards the village we were silent. It was only briefly interrupted when he asked if I still preferred 'big tits'. I thought for a moment.

"Not half as much as I like little tits, tiny little titties." We chuckled. "But I still prefer blonds."

Back home, the post-ejaculation guilt began smothering me. I hadn't experienced such feelings for a long time. Was it because of his age or because the innocent nature of our friendship now felt transgressed? Nothing could be the same between us again. I wanted to ask him if we could meet again but couldn't say the words. In the village we said our farewells casually. I knew he wanted to ask to see me again. I saw it in the way his blue eyes lingered and sought out contact, in the way his body language was reduced to that of a floppy puppet. But he, too, couldn't say it.

That evening I met up with Paul and Will in a pub. When it closed, we decided to watch the late-night horror film in Paul's bedroom. His parents always went to bed early and so we made ourselves at home. Will went upstairs to the toilet whilst Paul and I made a pot of tea. Suddenly Paul become very quiet. "What's wrong?" I asked.

"I'm okay. I was just thinking."

"About what?"

"I've been wanting to ask you if you fancy Will at all? Would you have sex with him?"

"Do you know, I've been giving that some thought myself," I

whispered, anxious in case Will should hear me. "There's something I find attractive about him. I find him a bit sexy, perhaps it stems from all those dirty stories he used to tell us. But then I don't really think he's all that physically attractive. If I saw him on the street I probably wouldn't notice him."

"So would you have sex with him?"

"Yes, I suppose I would. In any case, why do you ask?"

Paul turned his back towards me and began pouring the tea. "Well, your luck might be in, he's got a nice cock," he answered.

"What are you on about? What do you mean, he's got a nice cock?"

"Just that, and he's circumcised."

"Well, that makes two of you. Anyway, how do you know?"

He finished pouring the tea and turned to face me. "We've been having sex for the last eighteen months. That's one reason why we went on holiday together," he said, grinning. I stood, frozen on the spot, riveted by his revelation.

"I don't fucking believe it! But you're always eyeing up women. Are you queer... gay?"

"No, I don't think so. A bit bi perhaps. He's just someone to have sex with. I don't fancy him." Upstairs we heard the toilet flushing.

"Why didn't you tell me before now? Fuck, it would have been the most consoling thing you could have told me when I came out to you. Why didn't you?"

He thought for a moment. "I don't know why," he insisted. Will was on his way down the stairs. "Don't tell him you know," he whispered.

In the bedroom we turned on the television and settled down on Paul's bed. My mind was racing with questions I wanted to ask but that would now have to wait. The film was a gothic horror. Will lay outstretched and I cast my gaze over the length of his body. I would have sex with him, I thought. Besides, I was feeling horny. Paul's hand slid silently onto Will's thigh. He didn't move and continued watching the television. At first, his hand moved ever so slightly and gradually shifted onto his inner thigh. At that point Dracula began terrifying a young woman, he parted his lips and exposed his infamous fangs. The woman, as in all such films, began screaming hysterically. Her hands over her jowls, she was paralysed into immobility. Paul's hand pressed along Will's inner thigh towards his crotch. His eyes remained on the screen but in the television's silvery light, I watched his chest rise as he silently sighed. The woman screamed.

"Do not be afraid, little bird," said Dracula, his lips quivering over his sharp teeth. For a moment the woman stopped, she was trembling uncontrollably.

"Please! Please don't hurt me," she gasped. Dracula stepped closer. Will sighed again and pressed his hips into Paul's probing hand.

"Come, little one, it will only take a moment," said Dracula putting his hands on her bare shoulders.

"Oh no! Please, please don't hurt me," cried the woman burying her face in her palms. Between the screen and me, Paul's fingers busily explored Will's erection. Dracula tried to subdue the woman into submission and began to caress her shoulders.

"Just one small kiss and you can join me in eternity. You should not be frightened. I offer you life everlasting, pleasures and dreams beyond your earthly imagination." Will looked away from the screen and at Paul. He moved his hand from behind his head and began stroking Paul's shoulder. Then he looked back at the television. Paul's caresses were no longer subtle. With Will's tacit consent his hand intensified its movement by pressing fingers along the outline of his erection. Will's knees began twitching. On the screen the woman raised her head, tears streaked her cheeks.

"Come, calm yourself," said Dracula, his hands feeling her neck, searching out the pulse of her carotid artery in anticipation of his strike. His bloodshot eyes fixed upon her; they were intense and hungry. My breathing became irregular and I felt my face flushing. I already had an erection. Paul's hand found its way into Will's flies and enthusiastically burrowed around under his clothing. Dracula moved close to the woman, almost as if to console her. His head moved towards her pale neck. Will's cock sprang out from his pants, in the silvery light it bounced gently to a halt. He turned his head away from the screen and looked up at the ceiling. His eyes closed. His hand coaxed Paul's head closer to his erection. The discordant music reached a climax and the violin's screeching harmonics tore at my ears. The woman released a long sigh. Dracula had struck. Paul's head sunk over Will's dick and he too let out a stuttered gasp. In a moment of impulse my hand reached over to Paul's groin. He didn't resist my advances and immediately began rhythmically moving his hips into my hand. I missed the rest of the film.

It was exciting but it wasn't like the sex I'd had with Damien. Neither of us had just wanted sex; we'd wanted each other. Between Paul, Will and me something was lacking, something missing. Our communion lacked tenderness and commitment. Perhaps because there was no strong attraction between us. We'd avoided kissing and no words of affection passed our lips. But nonetheless it was a fun experience.

Over the next few days the three of us had sex most evenings. Our intimacies took place in Paul's car. One evening we drove into the Chiltern Hills and through dark lanes found the local lovers' land. Here we parked on a grass lay-by which looked down on the brightly lit town. Several other cars were parked alongside, their windows misted. In the last few years since I'd last played with Paul's dick, it had grown tremendously. It wasn't just long but incredibly thick. The thought of it up my bum made me wince. When he came it had a horrible bitter taste. It was such a bad taste I wound down the window and spat it onto the grass. It was an insulting thing to do but Paul wasn't perturbed. His attitude suggested it was merely sex between us. Once I arrived at this understanding I began to recognise that they weren't gay, their hearts weren't really into it. Sex with them was no different from the pubescent fumblings Paul and I had enjoyed in our early teens.

Amidst the bleak moors of Catterick, in the solitude of my room, I began to realise that there was more to sex than the purely physical act. That with the right person, it could be so much more than just a helping hand to ejaculation. I was quite prepared to have sex with Paul but felt I could take it or leave it. Paul and Will's homosexual experiences weren't an important part of their identity. It was just a temporary condition borne out of boredom, horniness and lack of women. Eventually they'd drift off with girlfriends and the events of the past few days would be forgotten, ignored and denied.

During the autumn months the band's 'gay' clique regularly visited gay bars. Dean began a brief relationship with a man he'd met, though I never met him. Over a period of weeks they shared a vibrant exchange of letters. Then Paul and Dean met two sisters and began their own relationships. The sisters were very unattractive. Not just unattractive; they verged on hideous. One was goofy whilst the other had a rodent zit problem. They were both extremely dense and spent most of their time giggling and laughing like horses on helium. One evening, just before I was going to bed, Paul returned from Richmond. He sat on the end of my bed and chatted away about his evening.

"Oh, by the way," he said, "smell my new aftershave." He stretched his hand towards me and I sniffed his fingers.

"Ugh, yuk, what the fuck is that?"

Paul started laughing. "It's my new girlfriend!"

I can't remember her name but on the way home to Wendover in Paul's car that Christmas, she asked if I wanted to feel her tits. She was that kind of girl.

"Get them out then," I said. "I've never felt a pair before, perhaps I'm missing something." She lifted her T-shirt and her ample breasts fell out and swung around with the lilting of the car. They resembled two enormous melons on a bungee. My fondle was more of an examination; it was clinical. I palpated them with my fingers and weighed them in my palms.

"Very nice," I said, unconvinced.

In the spring, potential recruits visited our band for interviews. They were mostly teenagers. Sometimes they arrived alone and on other occasions there were a group of them. During the morning they were given a tour of the barracks and invited to join in one of our rehearsals. In the afternoon they were introduced to the bandmaster who gave them a short interview and audition. Throughout the day the senior ranks busily tried selling them army life, emphasising the glamour, sport, travel and camaraderie. With their audition complete they were shown to the band accommodation where a bed space had been arranged in one of our four-man rooms. The senior ranks then left the singlie bandsmen to entertain them for the evening. Once in our company we gave them the alternative version of army life. We regaled them with stories of basic training; of the intricacies of boot bulling, bed packs, inspections and the endless block-job routines. We felt no guilt or betrayal in providing this information and believed that with a balanced view of army life they'd be better able to make a decision regarding enlistment.

Whenever we entertained a potential recruit our four-man room was visited by most singlies. Some visited out of politeness, others for a conversation and a few to check out their looks. Then we subjected them to our clandestine leching. Word spread early in the day if a sexy boy was staying with us. Often we'd enact pranks on them. Sometimes it was arranged for me to arrive as the lad was beginning to feel relaxed. I then entered the room and introduced myself in a camp accent. I might say something like: "Hello, I'm Nick. God! You're a real sweetie, aren't you, darling." I flounced around the room like an over-the-top queen and on occasion sat next to Paul or Dean and stroked their knee or perhaps kissed their cheek. Of course, it was all an act but one too real for potential recruits. The bandmaster realised something was afoot as not one of the interviewees enlisted. He delivered a stern lecture to us on regimental pride and allegiance. Despite this we resumed our old ways within a few weeks.

One of the last potential recruits to visit our band was an attractive cornet player. He was seventeen and came from Brough, near Warcop. I nicknamed him the Brough Boy. He drew a roomful of admirers and as we were still wary about frightening him off army life, we refrained from putting on a show. Instead, we introduced the subject of homosexuality and with the relaxed manner in which he received this, I confessed to him that I really was queer. By now the nature of my sexuality was common knowledge to most of the band other than the SNCOs. It was with ease that I suggested that we go to my room for a coffee. Shortly after, I persuaded him to take his pants down so I could administer him a good sucking. The Brough Boy really was a boy. His cheeks were void of even the faintest stubble and his body skinny and narrow. He'd a fat, veiny cock on which I chumped vigorously. After a few minutes his face began to flush a blotchy red. He came very quickly and with a grunt sprayed a jet of jism up into the air and onto the little orange army-issue carpet beside my bed. The stain remained visible until I handed it back to the quartermaster on my next posting. The Brough Boy, so we heard from the BSM, enlisted a few days later.

Towards the end of spring, when Catterick and the surrounding moors were turning a multicoloured patchwork of green, Will came to visit for a weekend. At the same time Charles's boyfriend, Malcolm, stayed. Will arrived on the Friday evening and after a shower and change of clothing we went to a gay pub in Darlington. There we met Daisy and Flower who had lived at the end of the band practice corridor in Münster. Daisy was camp, both in and out of barracks. He spoke with a high-pitched squeal, was limp-wristed and turned every minor crisis into a drama. He was slight of build and apart from a patch of hair on the back of his head, he was quite bald. He always wore big, round glasses with clumpy black rims. Flower was much heavier-set, with a thick moustache. He didn't look or act camp until he spoke, when his favourite expression was "Oh! darlings." At that point his arm popped upward and his wrist collapsed.

Daisy worked as an orderly in the Medical Centre and Flower was a clerk. Both were full Cpls and in their early thirties. That evening Daisy had drunk too much and was tipsy. After we'd sat a while talking, he suddenly became agitated and halted our conversation.

"Hey listen, I've just remembered a story I've got to tell you. You've just got to hear this!" He wriggled around on his seat in excitement. We stopped our conversation and gave him our attention. All around the hubble and bubble of the pub continued. A practised drama queen, he paused for effect.

"How many gays are there in the band?" he asked.

"Gays or bisexuals?" asked Charles, who was wearing his spaghetti Western wig and blue-tinted glasses.

"How many blokes do you have who would have sex with men...

or have had sex with men?" We looked at each other inquisitively, mumbling and counting in our heads.

"Four of us," said Paul. Charles and I nodded in agreement.

"Well," continued Daisy, "a few weeks ago, I called up to your rooms to visit someone whose name I won't mention. It was almost midnight and the place was quiet. Anyway, I knocked on the door and..."

"Whose door?" interrupted Charles. Daisy pouted his lips and gave him a disapproving frown.

"Do you mind, dear, I'm telling a story. Please don't interrupt." His hands clasped together on one folded knee.

"As I was saying. I knocked on this door and as I was in a rush went straight in. Normally I'd wait a few seconds before entering, but like I said, I was in a hurry. Well, as I went into the room, I must have interrupted something because I caught one of these two individuals jumping into his bed. He was naked. The other one, who was in bed, was all flustered and pulling his covers over his body. They were at it!" Flower started chuckling. A line of beer froth coated the bottom of his moustache.

"Oh! darlings. Fucking bandsmen, they're all at it."

"Who the fuck was it?"

"Wouldn't you queens just love to know?"

"What did they do?" asked Paul.

"Nothing, they just lay in their beds as if nothing had happened. But I knew."

"Did they say anything when you went in?" I asked.

"Well, one of them pretended to be all dopey, like I'd just woken him up. I asked if so and so was around and they both said he was still out. Then I left the room."

"Go on, tell us who it was?" insisted Charles. Daisy was enjoying his power trip and wiggled on his little bottom.

"But I haven't finished yet, I've still got more to tell you."

"Come on! You've got to tell us!" I said.

"Yeah," added Paul. "There's no way we're going to tell anybody. Really!"

Daisy paused – we waited in eagerness.

"All right then. It was Mervin and Horton."

"Mervin and Horton?" I gulped.

"Now let me get on with it!" said Daisy. "Last week, when I was on evening duty, one of these two fucking benders comes down to the MRS."

"Which one?" asked Charles.

"Horton, it was Horton. I was on a late duty. He was sort of limping and looked in some discomfort. Well, to cut a long story short, he had a salt cellar stuck up his arse."

"Fucking no way," exclaimed Paul.

"It took ages for me to get him to tell me what was wrong. I had to call out the doctor. I wasn't going to fish around up his dirt track."

"Oh darlings," chuckled Flower. "Fucking bandsmen."

"Didn't you ask how it got there?" I asked.

"There was no need. I knew."

"But what on earth did the doctor say?" asked Charles.

"Oh, he's used to it. It happens from time to time. My mate at the garrison MRS says the wives are even worse. Says they're always coming in with things stuck up their micks."

"He probably told him to use a real cock," laughed Will.

"Was there still salt in it?" I inquired.

"Yeah," said Paul. "If he ever ran short of salt for his crisps he could just shake his arse over the packet." We laughed.

"Fucking bandsmen," mumbled Flowers into his beer glass. No one paid him any attention.

Over the years, the story of Horton and the salt cellar became part of a restricted band folklore. Little intimate oral histories that were the occasional topic of factions within the band but were never fully public knowledge: stories about what wives or husbands got up to behind each others' backs or about the sexual encounters between bandsmen. Some were personal, others were stories based on carica-tures: the big noses, the acne-ridden, the greasy-skinned, the big or little cocks and so forth.

Bands are bitchy places. Even the malicious queens I've met in Civvy Street don't exceed the biting bitchiness of bandsmen and their wives. It stems from the claustrophobic lives that bandsmen lead, liv-ing in close proximity, rehearsing together, socialising together and having a bar within their living quarters. There were factions within factions. A myriad of friendship networks. There were factions be-tween and across the ranks, between the pads and the singlies and between the wives and the men. Factions could decide promotions or stifle an individual's progress. They could bring couples together or rend them apart. Great care had to be taken in how factions were manipulated and there was an art in doing this. If used properly, fac-tions furthered your self-interest. The informal rules that operated were learnt in the doing. Over the last few months a new faction had arisen, it was the queer faction and their peripheral mates.

Hence the salt-cellar story became a taboo topic only ever re-ferred to by certain groups and never in the presence of Horton. Amongst my mates Horton became known as Shake'n'Salt.

The following morning we were up early to travel to Halifax for a concert. The presence of two civvies on the bus caused an uneasiness amongst the senior ranks and those who weren't up to date with the latest developments. They kept giving us little, shifty glances and were perturbed that we'd upset the bus seating arrangements.

Most army bands had an unwritten code concerning where individuals sat on a bus. The bandmaster always sat at the front with the BSM in the opposite aisle. The remaining senior ranks, that is the S/Sgt and the Sgts, sat in the rows behind the WOs. The most junior members of the band were relegated to the back seats. Promotion within the band necessitated moving farther towards the front of ths bus.

The senior ranks and the uninitiated sensed something afoot but didn't dare levy accusations without absolute proof. That morning the gay faction were in high spirits and we countered hostile glances with an arrogant smugness. I knew that some SNCOs were aware of our intrigues. I had a bright purple love bite on my neck that I made no attempt to hide. That no one asked about it confirmed they suspected. Had any believed for one moment that I'd slept with a female they'd have slapped me on the back and asked if she'd been a good ride. Tony spotted it as I was packing my music stand in the luggage compartment. His eyes bulged in his chubby little face. Each time I turned my head to confront his stare he quickly looked away. The T/M, Ken Cort, was momentarily transfixed. Their silence, their frozen, shocked looks exposed their suspicions. There was little they could do other than gossip. To be homo was such a weighty crime within military law that to point fingers without good cause was foolhardy.

6

My mates in the band had all arrived while we were in Catterick and had never been to Germany. In the first few weeks of sight-seeing around our new garrison town, Osnabrück, they anxiously begged my company as I spoke some German. Charles, pining for Malcolm, rarely ventured out. One of our first outings was to the local sex shop. Porn shops on the mainland fascinated me. Row after row of shelves, each sectioned into different types of magazines. Gay mags stood in one corner and were divided into those to suit clone lovers, military admirers, S and M fans, teen enthusiasts and lesbians. Amongst the heterosexual shelves were magazines depicting big-breasted women, schoolgirls, water-sport activities, dwarf sex and even animal sex magazines. The first thing I realised in my visits to these shops is that there is an incredible diversity in the nature of human sexual expression. Porn shops are among the first port of call for soldiers arriving from the UK.

In the months passed since coming out I'd gradually come to terms with the fact that I was gay. To acknowledge my new identity, and to try and find potential partners, I put an advertisement in the lonely hearts column of *Gay News*. It was a short advert: '19 year old male, 6"6', well built, seeks friends.' I received over a hundred replies, and in the following weeks another twenty-six. I callously threw in the bin any letters that were accompanied by photos I found unappealing. I also kept aside any I found outrageous. One letter I kept provided an explicit account of what the author would like to do to me. This included a vivid description of rimming my arse. I showed the letters and photos to my mates and we laughed at them. Afterwards I felt a sense of guilt. People had written to my advertisement in good faith. They'd volunteered their time to reply and I subsequently made their intimacies a public joke.

Within a few weeks of arriving in Rawlpindi Barracks, my life took a new turn. I joined a karate club in the town and immediately developed a new circle of friends. It's strange how random choices can shape our lives and afford us new experiences. I asked a taxi driver to take me to a karate club and he drove to a school he'd merely heard of. There were many clubs in the town as the martial-arts fad of the '70s was still at its peak. There were various Japanese styles, several Chinese kung-fu schools and two Korean schools which taught Hapkido and Taekwon-do. The taxi drove me to the Taekwon-do school. On the wall outside the club hung a plaque bearing the insignia of the International Taekwon-do Federation and the name of the school, Song Do Kwan. Inside the training hall white-suited students were busy sparring. On their hands and feet they wore brightly coloured mitts. Some, mostly those wearing white and yellow belts, were clumsy. However, those wearing blue and brown belts moved with grace and precision.

The Song Do Kwan was run by a Greek Cypriot named Georg. He spoke perfect English since he'd served in the British Army. He was a short, stocky man in his mid-thirties with a German wife and three teenage sons. Georg led me to the changing rooms where I put on my judo suit. Moments later I was in the training hall undergoing my first ever martial arts instruction. Though I made technical errors I adapted quickly. Even though I was a mere white belt, Georg befriended me and took me under his wing. It was a big club and occupied two floors. Downstairs was a reception room with seats so visitors could watch the training through large perspex windows. The training hall was walled with mirrors and in the corners, near the reception, hung sparring mitts. Upstairs was a room equipped with judo mats and an assortment of weights. It was a lively club that ran three classes a night, five nights a week: one class for beginners and two for advanced students.

Georg was a third-degree black belt. His certificate, from the International Taekwon-do Federation, hung on the centre of a wall in the reception. Several other black belts helped instruct the classes. Within two weeks I started staying on after the beginners' session to train with the advanced students. I began training outside our band block which was in a secluded corner of the barracks and surrounded by silver birch trees. Between trees I tied a rope on which to stretch my legs and around one I fixed a foam pad which I could strike with hand or foot. My progress was rapid and six weeks later I took part in my first fighting competition. As a white belt I was officially unable to enter since the lowest fighting grade was that of green belt. I fought wearing a borrowed green belt and won third place. Afterwards we celebrated in a local restaurant.

Since we'd arrived in Osnabrück, Charles had become sullen and spent most of his time writing letters to Malcolm. He had wild mood swings and suddenly began acting overtly military when in uniform. Now a L/Cpl, he'd been placed as second-in-command of our accommodation. Tony Shaw, as Cpl, was overall in charge. A block-job rota, which changed every Monday morning, hung on our foyer noticeboard. One Saturday evening, we read a message:

From henceforth there will be a block-job session every Sunday afternoon at 1500. An inspection will follow at 1600. All living in bandsmen will be in barracks by 1455 – without fail.

> Cpl T Shaw. i/c Block Jobs
> L/Cpl C King. 2i/c Block Jobs

We were infuriated as the order meant our weekend terminated on a Sunday afternoon. Those bandsmen who went away for the weekend now had to return to barracks early. I complained to Charles but he insisted the session wouldn't be altered and his word was final. On the first Sunday afternoon we refused to begin our jobs. Charles and Tony strutted around the accommodation ordering bandsmen to begin work. The bandsmen's faction was united and no broom or toilet brush was lifted. Charles tried persuading me to call the strike off, appealing to our friendship; I refused. The following morning, after Tony and Charles had spoken to our new BM, we paraded in front of the BSM, Warren Patton. He asked for a spokesman to put his hand up and five of us thrust our hands into the air. We aired our grievances.

"It's just not fair, Sir. It ruins our weekend because we have to return to barracks on a Sunday afternoon," argued Dean.

"I think it's bloody outrageous," I shouted angrily. "I mean, if you're a married Bdsm, no one comes around inspecting your house at the weekend. Why should we be treated differently to the pads? It's always the same. If you're a singlie you get hounded left, right and centre. But pads get nice clean homes and are left in peace."

"We keep the place clean," said Dean. "We've put posters up on the hall walls, it's not as if we don't look after the place. We could surely be given some credit for that?"

For a moment, the BSM's silence and expressionless face suggested we might have won him to our side.

"We're not saying we don't want to do block jobs. Just that 1500 on a Sunday afternoon is a bit unfair," pleaded Dean. It was obvious from the outset that the issue would become our insubordination rather than the unfairness of block-job timings. Suddenly the BSM began shouting.

"We're not saying we don't want to do block jobs!" he repeated. "This is the fucking army! You do as your told. This is mutiny! Do you know what the charge is for such an offence?" He paused. "It's a court-martial offence. Under active service punishable by firing squad! Now the next soldier to step out of line will find himself in the guard-room and in a cell. Is that clear?"

"Yes, Sir," we mumbled.

"Right! Dismiss yourselves and get to work." Subdued, we returned to our individual practice. Minutes later, Tony and Charles were called into the Bandmaster's office. Our new BM had arrived days earlier. It should have been obvious to us that this insurgence was a test of his authority and that stamping on us was his only recourse. However, sometime that day the block-job order was removed from our noticeboard. Although Tony and Charles never admitted it, we knew the BM had given them a telling off. Charles never forgave my part in what became known in band folklore as 'The Revolution'.

There are several events that bandsmen hate, usually those that detract from normal routine and consist of activities for which we had not primarily enlisted. Manoeuvres were detested, as were guard duties, crash outs and medical training. All these events required dragging our creased combat uniforms from the bottom of our lockers where they'd been thrown the last time they were worn. Few bandsmen can wear combats with the same credibility as squaddies. Those who could were looked down on by fellow musicians and often, with a sneer, called 'squaddies' or 'grunts'. Our berets, squashed for most of year at the bottom of drawers, sat awkwardly on our heads. Our combats generally looked new since we only ever wore them a few times a year. The puttees, worn around our ankles, looked un-stylish and the hang of our combats never looked quite right. We felt as awkward in combats as did the squaddies on the rare occasion when they wore blues or ceremonials.

The most hated event of all was the bi-annual BFT. By departments and squadrons, the whole regiment paraded in boots, denim trousers and T-shirts. Our heavy boots made the task all the more strenuous. The BFT was hated as it was a tiring slog. Failing to pass incurred early morning physical training sessions until you passed. As a result, there were various ploys soldiers employed to make sure they didn't fail. Running on the inside of the road and cutting corners knocked a small distance off the overall route. PTI staff generally policed any corners but if they failed to do so we took full advantage of their absence. Snorting asthmatic inhalers, eating glucose tablets and even taking amphetamine-based slimming pills made it possible for weaker soldiers to pass. There was great camaraderie on a BFT. Soldiers who found it difficult were encouraged by their mates or paternal SNCOs or officers, and even weak senior ranks were coaxed by their subordinates. The exertion of the BFT, under whose rules we were all equal, defused the rank structure. Everyone helped and encouraged anyone who seemed to be struggling.

On a sunny afternoon when I was practising my flute in the foyer, two strange men appeared at our block. They both had short, military haircuts and wore dark-coloured civilian suits that gave them an ominous appearance. They disappeared into the bandmaster's office. Within minutes, gossip was around the band that something strange was going on. One of the married pad Cpls arrived at our rooms and told Charles he was wanted. For over an hour Charles remained in the BM's office whilst the BM sat in the bar talking to the BSM. Bandsmen and JNCOs busily speculated on what might be happening but no one gave a feasible account. Then we heard footsteps and voices from the foyer and saw Charles, one of our Sgts and the two suited strangers entering Charles's bunk. His door closed and here they remained for over half an hour. When the strangers left, they turned down the path towards the guardroom. Shortly after, Charles was ordered back to the BM's office.

When he returned, he refused to give in to our probing questions and firmly told us that we'd find out in good time. However, that evening, Charles called me into his bunk and told me that he'd visited the MO and admitted being gay. The MO wanted to examine his arse, claiming that a stretched anal sphincter would provide all the proof he needed. Charles refused to submit to such an invasive examination and so the MO contacted the Military Police to instigate an investigation. Hopefully, on finding evidence of his homosexuality he'd be given a medical discharge and returned to the UK. This was the only way to leave the army, other than being a communist, that guaranteed a free discharge without having to give a year's notice or be put in jail.

That evening I decided to remove any gay pornography from my room. I stuffed anything incriminating into a briefcase and stored it away in our box cupboard. The next day began the first of my two experiences with the SIB. I saw them arrive. Walking down the path outside our block in their dark suits, they sent shivers down my spine. I was called for and went to the BM's office where they told me I was under investigation for being a possible homosexual. My room was to be searched. Escorting me to my bunk they told me to choose a senior rank who could be present as a witness to the search.

"I don't care, as long as it's not Sgt Webb," I said. If knowledge of my sexuality was going to be made public, Frank Webb was the one most likely to be homophobic. I'd no choice anyway since they deliberately called Webb in as a witness. He stood against the wall whilst the two officers pulled my room apart. It was a tight squeeze, Webb's beer belly taking up much of the space in my tiny room. They scrummaged through my locker, throwing clothing and shoes onto the floor and nosing through pockets. Each shoe was inspected even to the point of examining the heels. In a trendy pair of platforms, bought in Münster, a stone had become lodged inside the heel. It rattled when shook.

"It's only a stone," I said. The officer, on his knees at the foot of my locker, held it to his ear and shook it again. Webb looked on, his little eyes glinting. Taking a penknife from his pocket, the officer cut a hole into the heel and prised out the stone.

"Only a stone," he spat sarcastically. Throwing the shoe down onto the pile of clothes at his knees, he continued searching the corners of my locker. They searched my coat and jacket pockets, eventually finding my *Spartacus Guide*. Finding a jar of Vaseline on the top shelf of my locker gave them evidence enough to begin implicating me.

"So what's this, then?" asked the officer with the penknife.

"A jar of Vaseline, Sir."

He held the jar to my face. "Your bum jelly. Eh, laddie?" he snarled.

"Bum jelly?"

"Yes, bum jelly. That you might use to lube up your chums." Behind, the second officer busily searched my personal drawer. Webb stared at the Vaseline; his jaw slumped in shock.

"I use it for cracked lips and lubricating parts of my flute."

"Okay, sonny! But we've not finished yet. This jar is probably only the beginning."

Then they went through my letters, reading each one in turn until they came to one of the *Gay News* replies. I'd forgotten it was amongst my letters. I remembered its sordid contents and began to panic. As an officer unfolded it, I suddenly felt a need to shit. I suppressed an urge to drop one into my trousers and went to snatch it from his hand.

"That's private!" I shouted. He moved the letter out of reach. Their faces smirked, they knew they were onto something. I wanted to cry. There was no way I could explain away the possession of such a letter without incriminating myself. I was doomed. Holding it between thumb and forefinger, as if it was contaminated, one of the investigators read it. Skim reading and mumbling, he scanned for dirty bits.

"I would just love to lick around your fat knob end," he quoted.

"You filthy queer," snarled his companion. Webb's jaw sagged gormlessly.

"Then I would stick my tongue right up your arse and give you a good rimming." They stared with pinched and sneering eyes that burnt into the centre of my body.

"So what's rimming, boy? Eh? Have you ever had a good rimming?"

I was silent. He waited. "You dirty fucking pansy. Got to rout perverts like you out, keep them away from our lads."

"Yes, Sir!" I replied. The one with the letter laid it down on top of a *Gay News* that they'd also discovered. I'd left it unnoticed in a pile of music. Besides putting aside anything that could be used as evidence of my homosexuality, they took my Buddhist text, Queen Kunta and my joss sticks. With my confiscated possessions they escorted me to the BM's office for an interrogation. One SIB sat in the leather chair behind the desk while the other leant against the radiator. The one at the desk began sifting through my possessions. He picked the Buddhist book up and leafed through the pages and colour prints.

"I suppose you're a weirdo Buddhist, are you?" said the one leaning on the radiator.

"No, actually I'm not."

"Why have you got it, then?"

"Someone conned me into buying it in London. I've never even read it."

"Easily conned... are you?" he asked. The one at the desk began browsing through my letter.

"I don't think so," I replied. The room was silent for what seemed a long time. The one at the desk passed the letter over his shoulder to his partner, who began reading its contents.

"Looks like you've been a bad boy, doesn't it?" I didn't reply. "Looks like you've been having a very busy social life. Have you been to many of the clubs in this book?" said the one at the desk, holding up the *Spartacus Guide* for me to see.

"Only one," I mumbled.

"Who d'you go with?"

"Charles King."

"When was this, then?" he asked. The man on the radiator silently watched me, observing every minute twitch and fiddle I made.

"A few weeks ago. But it wasn't a gay bar, it was normal."

"Are you a queer, then?" asked the man sat on the radiator.

"I don't know."

"What d'you mean, 'I don't know'? Why's this among the things in your bunk?" He shouted, moving to the side of the desk and picking up the *Gay News*. He waved it around wildly in front of my face.

"Is this the kind of perverted shit you find in normal soldiers' rooms, eh?" I felt myself beginning to panic and knew I'd have to mount a defence.

"I read *Woman's Own*, but I'm not a fucking woman."

"No, not quite, but you're halfway there," said the investigator standing up from the radiator. The seated one continued.

"So," he said almost soothingly. "Have you ever had sex with a man?" His voice was calm and reassuring.

"No, I haven't. Well, I suppose it depends on what you mean by se." The standing investigator sat back on the radiator.

"Let me put it another way, then. Have you ever taken part in homosexual activities such as arse fucking?"

I diverted my gaze towards the floor. They must have spotted my guilty body language, I thought.

"Occasionally, when nothing else has been on offer. But I've never had anal sex!"

"Have you ever kissed a man?" he spat. I twiddled my fingers together, staring at them intensely. The interrogation was turning into a confession and I felt it impossible to lie. Their power, their authority seemed to effortlessly suck information from me.

"Well?"

"Yes, I have."

"Was it a deep kiss or just one on the lips?"

"It was a deep one, but I wasn't really into it. He started it and I just let him. He was driving the car so it really wasn't a very good kiss."

"Fucking disgusting! Would you have preferred it if it had been a good kiss?"

"No! I told you, I wasn't really into it."

"And what other sorts of things did you get up to? Did you just kiss or did you do anything else?"

I paused, staring at my twiddling fingers. "I suppose we played around a bit," I whispered. The man on the radiator began fidgeting. He sensed I was hooked and was preparing to land me.

"You fucking played around a bit," he quoted. "What the fuck does that mean? Sounds like you sat and played fucking Monopoly or something. You know what we fucking mean. Answer the question! Did you wank him off or suck his fucking cock?"

I began to feel angry and humiliated; my hands were hot and clammy. My mind was frantically trying to find a way of defusing the implications of my confession.

"Yes! Yes, we did. But that was all, and it happened only the once."

"How old were you?" the one seated asked.

"Nineteen, I suppose." I thought for a moment. "Yes, I was nineteen and he was about twenty-one."

"I see. And have you ever had homosexual sex on any other occasions?"

"No! It was just the once, the only time."

"Have you ever had any girlfriends?"

"A few. I had a girlfriend when I was at school. Her name was Donna."

"And did you ever have sex with her?" I deliberately held his gaze, aware that this was the most difficult lie to sound convincing.

"Yes, we did."

"So why the sex with men, then? Why the gay newspaper, the gay guide?"

"I don't know; I just felt like it at the time."

"But that doesn't explain these away," he said passing his hands over my possessions strewn on the table.

"I don't know," I reiterated looking back at my sweaty hands.

"Are you fucking gay?" the man on the radiator asked. I looked back at his partner behind the desk; I felt more comfortable talking to him.

"I don't know. Sometimes I fancy girls, other times men. Perhaps I'm bisexual. I think everyone has the potential to be both ways."

"Well I've got no queer genes in my fucking blood, sonny!" snarled the man on the radiator.

"Perhaps it's got nothing to do with fucking genes."

"Homosexuality, bisexuality, whatever you like to call it, it's all the same. It all involves practising perverted acts, unnatural acts. It's fucking sick!" A long silence hung over the room.

"And what about this letter?" asked the seated man.

"Yes, it is rather incriminating," I said. "Well, several weeks ago I put an advertisement in *Gay News*. I wanted to meet people and I kept this letter because it was so disgusting it was funny. I never replied to the bloke who wrote it. I know you probably don't believe me, but it's the honest truth. I suppose my career's finished now?"

"We'll have to see," the man seated said.

"How did you find out about me?"

"In Cpl King's letters from his boyfriend. You were mentioned several times."

The investigators finally let me go after ordering me to their headquarters the next morning. They arranged a car to pick me up from outside the band block. That evening I went out with Paul for a meal. It was one of my training evenings but I was in no mental state to practise Taekwon-do. Instead, we went to a Turkish restaurant not far from my training hall. We sat considering what I could do in Civvie Street. Towards the end of the meal Paul said that he was willing to confess in order to be discharged. Dean was likewise considering a confession. For Paul it was a convenient exit from army life but I didn't want to be forced to leave, I enjoyed the military lifestyle. His revelation didn't console me. Paul wasn't settled in army life. He wasn't committed to the self-discipline necessary to produce a good instrumentalist. He was an awful clarinet player who sat on the bottom stand and had become a musical liability. I knew Paul well enough to know that he'd easily confess and happily return to civilian life. In contrast, I visualised a career in the army; I wanted to become a bandmaster and to one day have my own band. That evening, when I went to bed, I couldn't sleep.

The following morning people acted as if nothing had happened. Apart from having discussed my interrogation with friendly factions, no one asked me what had happened. Just before the mid-morning NAAFI break, I left the band block to be driven to the SIB headquarters. We drove through the town. All around life went on as it did every day of the week. I was oblivious to it all. I was inside my head, contemplating the outcome of my pending interrogation. At the SIB headquarters I was interviewed by one of the investigators I'd met the day before. He was the more pleasant of the two who'd been sat at the BM's desk. He interviewed me for over an hour and we began to relax. We ended up having a frank discussion about the nature of sexuality. I was aware that perhaps this was a ploy to lure me into revealing any new information. Nonetheless, though I altered the truth I denied little about my identity and inclinations. I told him that I fancied men and fantasised about them. The investigator even agreed that all people have the potential to be bisexual. In the conversation I mentioned that several other band members were thinking about confessing. The investigator was momentarily shocked but quickly pointed out that they weren't conducting a witchhunt. At the end of our discussion he left me alone in his office. Against his office walls were large steel filing cabinets. I wondered how many soldiers' lives were in those drawers. Little snippets of information that had either condemned individuals or lay waiting to be used when more damning evidence could be found to corroborate them. Somewhere, in the depths of those steel drawers, in some cardboard file, was my name. Would the SIB's findings condemn me, close my file, or put its evidence away to use at a future date? They couldn't possibly let me go, I thought. I've committed homosexual acts whilst a serving soldier and I'd contravened Queen's Regulations. I was guilty.

When he returned, he sat himself down at his chair. He was silent and began looking through my book on Buddhism. On the wall a clock noisily ticked. After a few moments he spoke.

"Could I borrow this?" he asked holding the book up.

"Of course."

"I'll return it to you at a later date."

"Later?"

"Yes, you're free to go." I wanted to shake his hand and hug him.

"You know you're a good-looking bloke. Somewhere out in the big world there's the girl for you."

"Yes," I agreed.

"You've been very honest with me and perhaps the confusion you've experienced is all part of growing up, coming to terms with yourself. But we can't have you doing it with other men and especially with other troops. You've got to realise that. You've got to be normal."

"Yes," I said again in earnest.

"Messing around, playing around with men might only be a diversion from the real thing but you've got to stop thinking about it. Get down town, you speak some German don't you?"

"Some."

"Then get down town and meet some German girls. Now I'm going to give you my phone number," he said passing me a printed card.

"If you ever discover any soldiers, bandsmen, taking drugs I want you to give me a call. It will all be confidential. Have you got that?"

"Yes, definitely," I replied putting the card into my pocket.

I left the SIB office and was driven back to Rawlpindi Barracks; out through the Military Police Headquarters and through the town which now thronged with midday activity. Finally, I passed the married quarters and entered my barracks. The regimental portcullis and the motto *Forever Onwards* welcomed me. The sun shone, flowers scented the air and I felt exhilarated. My future was safe.

Years later, at the end of one of my life's little eras, I threw the card into a bin. It had remained stuck on the inside of my locker door until discarding it. I can still recall the card's appearance. It had been printed on a material that had a bamboo texture. Embossed on the front, in blue and red, was the cap badge of the RMP and underneath this the SIB detachment number and address. After my interrogation I became straight, I wiped the image of men from my fantasy. I threw away any gay pornography and bought myself some straight porn books. I began to objectify women and to nurture every glimmer of heterosexuality in my psyche. My wanking sessions became a therapy during which I struggled to cure myself by using images of women. It was futile. I had to pump vigorously to gain an erection and maintaining it ached my arm and chafed my dick. Soon, tits began to turn into pectorals and hairy crevices sprouted penises.

Later, I recovered from my malady and reaccepted my sexuality. However, the incident left me with a morbid fear of the SIB. Just the mention of them raised my heartbeat and sent shivers down my spine. Whenever suited strangers appeared at our block, I panicked. The BM's office was never the same again and for several years, whenever I entered it I experienced a fleeting sensation of fear.

Within a month Charles was preparing to leave the band. Why he was leaving was information only a small group were party to. To the remainder of the band he was leaving for personal reasons. On the night of his farewell party, held in our band bar, I took my examination for my first Taekwon-do belt. I did so well that I advanced straight to yellow belt. The magnitude of Charles's departure hadn't dawned on me but at his party, listening to his farewell speech, I realised that tomorrow he'd be leaving. I suddenly became aware of the place that he'd carved out in my personality, of the support and advice he provided when I came out. Further, he was the only truly gay person with whom I'd had a close friendship. He introduced me to a gay world and coaxed a pride in my sexuality. That evening, after we'd drunk much beer, we went to his bunk. We talked and reminisced about Cyprus then we cried together. Eventually we found ourselves having sex. I don't think either of us really wanted this, but the closeness of our bodies made us feel secure. The next day, Charles left our regiment and his bunk was taken by the next senior Bdsm. Apart from an annual phone call we've seen little of each other since. Years now separate us and lie strewn between those sunny days in Cyprus and the present.

7

In the middle of our band block, between the living accommodation and the practice room and offices, stood our band bar, the 'Brahms and Liszt'. It was a big bar, almost a third of the total Band block. The bar itself was built by members of the band under the direction of the BSM, who was an excellent carpenter. With our band funds we bought bar furniture and a microwave, and a local brewery installed fruit machines, a pool table, a space invader game and all the necessary pumps, glasses and optics. All of us took turns to run the bar for a week at a time. Some of the singlies, myself included, pinched bits of chicken or ham from the cookhouse and used these to make sandwiches and rolls, thus ensuring a healthy profit. It was possible to make money while duty barman though some boozers always ended up drinking away their profits. Despite being a BM, Murray Leigh threw himself into building the bar and worked harder than most of us. It was completed within two weeks. The final touch, a red and white Coca-Cola sign bearing the bar's name, was hung above the entrance. It was the most envied bar in Rawlpindi Barracks and its most avid supporter throughout the next nine years was Murray Leigh.

Within Rawlpindi were four squadron bars and the bars of the NAAFI, Cpls', Sgts' and Officers' Messes, REME and the band. Ten bars serviced an area of no more than half a square mile and with less than seven hundred occupants. Up the hill, a mere five-minute walk, was another regiment. Here, on our doorstep, were more bars, including their regimental band bar. We shared a close relationship with both our neighbouring band and other bands within Osnabrück garrison. Army social life revolved around boozing; it was institutionalised. Singlies had a disposable income and cigarettes and alcohol were very cheap. Every regiment had its hardened alcoholics who were occasionally sent to the nearest military hospital for drying out in the aptly named P Wing. Whilst one puff on a joint was enough to send you to the military prison in Colchester, having a drink problem was acceptable and to many soldiers, admirable. Tolerance for alcohol and the copious amount one could consume were criteria used to judge masculinity. Apart from the NAAFI, the regimental bars rarely closed when supposed to. Instead, the doors were locked and drinking continued in private. The duty officer or members of the guard often drank behind the locked doors they'd checked were officially closed. Most bars closed when the barman felt tired. However, in the SNCOs' and Officers' Messes, the bar closed when the senior soldier present deemed it convenient.

Life in Rawlpindi was comfortable, cosy and hidden. We decorated our rooms with posters, photos and paintings and bought coffee percolators, toasters and music systems. If we bought electrical goods in the NAAFI they were tax free. In the alcove entrance and the corridors we fitted old Axminster carpets and hung posters. Though old bumpers stood in our cleaning room, there was also a vacuum cleaner. Thankfully, never again did I have to use a bumper. A coffee table and armchairs welcomed visitors to our alcove and on an old mahogany table we fixed a large goldfish tank. Our band accommodation was the plushest in barracks. Visitors and friends were welcomed with the placid mouthing of goldfish, the aroma of coffee and buttered toast.

Shortly after Charles's departure the annual regimental concert was scheduled. Rumour and conjecture were gossiped all over the barracks about our new BM. Soldiers wanted to know what he was like and the officers wanted to know how good he was. A bandmaster in an army regiment occupied a prestigious position. Their character largely determined the regiment's attitude towards us. In the WOs' and Sgts' Mess they held a position equal to that of the RSM. Technically they were the only person in the regiment who could officially have their surname prefixed by the title 'Mr'. This tradition dates back to Victorian times when army bandmasters were usually German civilians. However, most officers used Mr, it was a snobby habit which lower ranks were unable to follow since they were always denoted by rank. For Mr Leigh, the annual concert was his first appearance in front of the regiment.

All week we rehearsed the programme. We were to open with the march from 'Suite Algérien' by Saint-Säens. The first three opening chords, if played at a slower tempo, are exactly the same as those to 'God Save the Queen'. Murray cued a timpani roll prior to the chords so that the audience would think we were about to play the National Anthem. After the introduction, with the audience standing, we'd resume the music's rapid tempo and continue the piece as written. Murray thought this would be amusing but the bandsmen thought it a pretty dull joke.

The concert served not only to welcome and accept Murray into the regiment but to endear him to us as our bandmaster. It was a great success. The Sgts and officers were detailed to attend, if possible with their wives, and many of the soldiers were present. At the beginning of the concert the BM appeared out of the wings to a round of applause. For many people in the regiment this was their first glimpse of him. He was a short rotund character with a moustache and balding head. He strolled out to the front of the band where his conducting dais stood, turned to face the audience and bowed deeply. Then, he straightened up and turned towards us.

In the moments before a piece of music begins, a band is always focused, everyone clearing their thoughts and getting into the frame of mind that the music requires. In those seconds Murray had a twinkle in his eye and a cheeky smile on his face. He held our attention. With a snap of his wrist his baton slowly rose and we raised our instruments to their playing positions. The hall was silent. With an almost imperceptible nod of his head the timpani loudly struck a roll that quickly diminished until it was barely audible. Heads in the audience began to turn, anxiously looking for someone from whom to take a cue. The CO and his wife stood up followed by the rest of the audience. When silence returned to the hall and the audience were stiffly at attention, the baton fell and the first three chords sounded. Murray suspended the third chord before resuming the music's original tempo. For a moment there was an astonished look on the faces of the audience which quickly gave way to laughter as they realised they'd been fooled. In those brief seconds, Murray won both us and the audience over.

I was to play under Murray Leigh for the next ten years. He was eventually promoted out of our band as an officer. He was an excellent bandmaster who was respected throughout the regiment and in the wider world of army music. Wherever we played, be it to pensioners, children, soldiers, or the general public, he was able to sense where to draw the line with his humour. He could recite joke after joke and in doing so take the audience to the very threshold of permitted decency. When the audience were soldiers he gave free rein to his well-developed, crude sense of humour.

After Murray's regimental debut, he instantly became a success and joined the elite ranks of those regimental characters who personified the regiment. Individuals around whom the regiment revolved, who were themselves an ineffable essence of the 15th Dragoons. Often they were key regimental characters. They were quick-witted, often crude, extremely efficient, strict yet fair. Regimental personalities had charisma; it was their middle name. Coming to know a personality took many years. If one stayed in the regiment long enough their exploits were learnt, passed by word of mouth as part of the regiment's oral folklore. With promotion to their mess their finer traits, good and bad, could be observed. Even though you might not be able to identify why such individuals were outstanding, their charisma seduced you. Soldiers took years to become part of the regiment but most passed through our ranks without ever becoming regimental history.

The Gentleman Club was situated in a small square in the quaint back streets not far from the centre of town. It was a residential square of tall, old buildings with high, pointed roofs and blue shutters on the sides of windows. Opposite the club was a small square of trees, large chestnuts that loomed up in the darkness of night or cast a dense shadow in daylight. We rang the door bell; after a few moments it opened. Behind the little iron grill a nose and moustache appeared.

"Kann ich Ihnen helfen?"

"We're English," Paul said.

"Sind Sie militär?" the nose asked.

"Yes," I replied.

"This is a private club," the voice said with a heavy German accent.

"Yes, we know," said Paul.

"A gay club."

"Yes, we understand."

"You are military and you want to come to a gay club?"

"Ja, bitte," I added. The door opened, revealing a handlebar- moustached, walrus-figured man in his fifties.

Inside, the row of stools along the front of the bar was occupied by men. As we entered their heads turned and we heard the word 'Soldaten' whispered. We sat down at a table opposite the bar whilst one of us ordered drinks. The club's lighting was subdued and mostly supplied by the little camp lamps that were at the centre of each table. A small dance floor stood in the middle of the club. The portly gentleman was the owner, his name was Theo.

Paul and I began to visit the club regularly, and within a few weeks Theo would welcome us with a kiss. It was never a kiss on the cheek but one directly on your mouth. His spiky moustache scratched your lips and sometimes, like an animated slug, you felt his tongue-tip probing for an opening. He kissed all his customers.

At the end of the summer season some new bandsmen arrived, one was Colin Yardley. He'd been posted directly from Bolton Barracks in Catterick. He was a clarinet player. As I got to know him, I discovered he was incredibly thick. Not just gullible, that would have been acceptable for an eighteen-year-old, but truly lacking in common sense. One day someone asked him who had composed Beethoven's 5th Symphony? Colin didn't know. That's how stupid he was. He was also one of the worst clarinet players I've heard – even worse than Paul. On one rehearsal he managed to play the wrong piece of music. The BM, for a laugh, didn't say anything and let him struggle on, completely lost in his own world. He could play whole passages of wrong notes and not realise anything was amiss. Colin's dumbness didn't deter me from being attracted to him, if anything it spurred me. He was so dumb it made the chances of seducing him easier.

Colin had come to the attention of another gay soldier in the regiment. On a night out to the Gentleman we met Flower and Daisy. Daisy, who loved to gossip, told us that Shaun Grace, a Cpl in one of the regimental stores, fancied Colin. At first, Paul and I were cautious and refused to believe Daisy's rumour. A week later, however, Shaun, an occasional visitor to our bar, began visiting every night. Within days he'd managed to strike up such a good friendship that he was able to call into Colin's bunk. After several weeks they were frequently in each other's company.

Bored one evening, a group of us, including Colin, decided to visit the NAAFI for a drink. We ended up playing fizz buzz. Colin made most of the wrong calls, shouting out 'twelve' or 'thirteen' when he should have shouted 'buzz'. The forfeit was to drink a glass in one go. After a few mistakes and a few large pernods, Colin began to make even more errors and very soon was drunk. Around the numbers twelve, thirteen or fifteen, he suffered a mental seizure. The quick succession of numbers that were multiples of or contained the number three confused his drunken brain. I don't think our game ever progressed beyond the number fifteen.

"Fuck, you're so incredibly stupid," laughed Dean. "You've got the memory span of a goldfish!"

When we left the bar Colin couldn't walk straight and kept stumbling, so putting an arm around him I guided him along the path. Our mates walked on ahead and left us behind. Colin put his arm around my waist and gripped tightly to hold himself steady. I'd drunk a few shorts myself and wasn't particularly sober but how we started kissing I don't recall. I vaguely remember that we used a large birch tree to steady ourselves and there began groping each other. When we reached our block we went straight into my bunk. Colin collapsed on my bed whilst I quietly locked the door. We resumed kissing and groping but then he began drifting off to sleep and eventually couldn't be roused. A few of my mates started banging on my door, shouting, laughing and chanting, "We know what you're doing." After a while they gave up annoying me and went back to their rooms. As for Colin, I couldn't wake him and giving up, I slept on the floor.

On our free weekends we often visited the nearest Schützenfest. These are a kind of carnival that most towns and villages celebrate each summer. On one particular Saturday evening, Colin, Dean and I drove out to a festival on the outskirts of Osnabrück. Dean had to stay sober as he was driving, but Colin and I drank more than enough. In the car on the way to Rawlpindi Colin and I sat in the back and started playing with each other. Dean kept moaning about messing his seats up – we just told him, "Belt up and watch the road and stop being jealous." "If you want to join in," I said, "just stop the car and jump in the back." He didn't. By the time we reached Rawlpindi Barracks we were uncontrollably all over each other. We left Dean to lock his car whilst we headed straight for my pad.

Colin was my first introduction to anal sex. It was an unpleasant experience. He was as clumsy in bed as in social interaction. There was little finesse in his technique and I felt more like Tpr Tanya, the blow-up doll, than I did a person. Grunting and groaning in a frenzy of sexual excitement he rolled me onto my front. It was a horrible encounter that lacked any care or consideration. He stabbed blindly with his dick until eventually, with a long sigh, he managed to stick it in. For the next few minutes his technique consisted of a series of grunting thrusts which were so forceful they knocked the breath out of me. When he came, and I couldn't tell at which point he did , he withdrew and my stretched bum painfully collapsed like an imploding black hole.

"Cor, that was great! Just what I needed," he sighed. Lifting the edge of my cotton sheet he wiped his gooey cock clean.

"You seem pretty experienced," I said.

"Well, I've never fucked a bloke before. But the girls I've done enjoyed it. How about you?"

"Oh, you were great," I lied. Next morning I couldn't stop farting. My gut felt as if inflated by a high-pressure airline and I had an aching arse. For the next few evenings, shortly after the NAAFI closed, Colin knocked on my door. Pre-empting his visit, I'd locked it. His dumbness and lack of musicianship I could accept, but his selfish, clumsy attempt at sex I couldn't. All infatuation for him vanished and was replaced with a sense of disgust.

I nicknamed Colin 'The Animal'. He didn't have any wrists. His forearms just melded into his hands rather like a lizard's. As usual, it was a name that stuck, though only a few people understood its significance. The Animal only stayed in our band a few years and in that time had a brief affair with Shaun Grace. We never spoke about our liaison and apart from a few occasions when he was drunk and feeling randy, the affair was forgotten.

At the same time that Colin arrived in our band another recruit joined us from JLR. His name was Ashley Brown. He too was a clarinet player, but this time one with potential. Ash became one of my closest mates and for a while one of the best straight allies a gay man could have. He was so supportive, so empathetic that he resembled a male version of a fag hag. Unfortunately, as happens with most close friendships, we also had some bitter disputes. Ash was quickly accepted into our faction – the faction of gays, bisexuals and their supporters. Our revelations and exploits failed to shock him. He knew who all the gays and bisexuals were at JLR, and was familiar with their exploits and affairs. He was a knowledgeable source of gossip concerning gays in other bands. We could immediately tell that he'd been party to a similar faction while at Junior Leaders. Amongst Ash's JLR mates was a fellow clarinet player named Carl Powell. He was gay, 'totally gay' according to Ash, who excitedly told us of Carl's sexual adventures with the soldiers and NCOs of Junior Leaders. Carl, he said, was an excellent musician, funny and very intelligent. He even had five O-levels which as far as soldiers went made him a super-brain. He'd passed out from JLR at the same time as Ash but had gone straight to KH on a one-year pupil's course. Carl sounded interesting, like someone worth getting to know, perhaps even a potential partner. At the end of his KH course he was due to be posted into our band. I awaited his arrival in anxious anticipation.

In the autumn of that year, Paul decided that he wanted to leave the band and move into the regiment. He'd been under pressure to improve his standard of playing but despite this did little extra practice. He left our accommodation in early December. Had he not decided to leave he would probably have been transferred into the regiment by the BM, a polite way of kicking him out of the band. In the time he'd been with us he displayed little interest in music and made insignificant progress. He took up a post in the officer's mess as a waiter. Musically Paul was a waster, a passenger we couldn't afford to carry. His transfer from the band into the regiment as a waiter was the typical relocation that such people followed.

Officers' messes are generally situated in a secluded corner of a barracks. Soldiers rarely, if ever, see inside them. Bandsmen, on the other hand, are never out of them. In fact, it is safe to say that most bandsmen can expect to visit more officers' messes than officers themselves. No expense was spared in decorating and maintaining them. Thick, fitted carpets covered the floors and when floors weren't carpeted they were covered with rich parquet. Paintings adorned the walls, usually of regimental significance. Armchairs and sofas, generally leather, were grand affairs into which you comfortably sank. Most messes had a bar, an anteroom, and a dining room. Officers were waited upon at meals and ate their food with silver cutlery from bone-china plates on regimental place-mats. Their food was as grand as the surroundings: they always had butter, while we only ever had margarine; their chops were meat instead of chunks of fat; their vegetables crisp, never boiled tasteless, and their bread white never yellowy. When we played at an officers' mess the cooks were expected to provide us a meal after our performance. Usually we were served the same vegetables as the officers' but with fish fingers or bratwürst replacing the fancy poultry or meat. We rarely had starters or a sweet.

Paul only stayed in the officers' mess for a few months and in the spring of the following year left the army. In civilian life he became a lorry driver, then a telephone engineer. Later he formed his own telephone engineering company. Two years after leaving he married and now has four sons. Occasionally we meet up for a drink and reminisce about army life, such as old comrades do. Though he always inquires as to my sexual well-being, our intimate past, however we individually wish to define it, has become unspoken history; perhaps as much through my silence as his.

8

Carl Powell arrived in 1978. I was busy in my bunk dry-knacking when there was a knock at my door. During working hours it was practice to knock and then enter. In the evenings you always paused a while and gone 2300 you generally waited until asked to enter. The door opened. Sunlight streamed into my room, skimming off the table top and stereo system. For a moment my eyes squinted to recognise the two figures silhouetted in the doorway.

"All right, Nick?"

"Hi, Ash," I replied, getting up from my chair. The person behind him, whom I didn't recognise, stepped into the room.

"I take it you're Carl?" I said.

"And you're Nick?" he replied, shaking my hand. "I've heard about you."

"Fame at last," commented Ash.

"Oh, dear me, nothing bad, I hope?"

"No! Not at all. Being the tallest piccolo player in the British Army is hardly something you can hide."

"The biggest guy with the smallest instrument," added Ash.

"Yes Ash. But at least I know where to put it."

"Like fuck," he laughed.

"Ignore him, Carl, he's got a very poor sense of humour. As I'm sure you already know."

"Yes, but then he can have his moments," added Carl, without changing his serious expression. He gave Ash a sideways glance. It was the sort of condescending glance that a parent gives a child. He licked his thin lips in a very quick and almost imperceptible manner. It was one of Carl's little idiosyncrasies, a habit he repeated when in a thoughtful or sombre mood.

I'd hoped that Carl might fulfil my dreams, some stunningly beautiful gay Adonis with wit and intellect to match. On the contrary, he was mediocre. There are some people who even in youth bear the features of middle age. Carl's dark hair was fine and thin. The bright sunlight from the alcove doorway behind him reflected off his scalp. He already had a receding hairline, or was it just a high forehead? I could see the future in his youthful face, the sagging eyes and the places where lines would eventually be scoured into his features. But there was something captivating about him, even charismatic, though I was unable to identify the origins of these qualities.

Ash, as a close mate of Carl's and a committed gossip, took no time in giving him all the news on our band and its members. Carl was provided character portraits on everyone. All those little snippets of intrigue which were privy to my faction were paraded freely in front of Carl. At least I wouldn't have to broach such issues myself. Ash was an animated gossip who could tell the same story in a variety of different ways, this was part of the fascination of his personality. Though I heard his stories many times he always made them sound new and interesting.

To my surprise, I discovered that my gay identity was common knowledge both at KH and JLR. The web of factions spread far beyond the perimeter of our barracks. According to Carl, our band was referred to as the fag band. From JLR young soldiers and bandsmen, quite a few of whom were gay or bisexual, were posted to regiments were there were suitable vacancies. They went to bands all over the country, many to Germany and some to places such as Hong Kong or Belize. At KH, where bandsmen attended a one-year pupil's course, individual regimental cap badges were subsumed under the RMSM crest – the musicians' lyre. Old friendships were consolidated and new ones formed. At the end of the course musicians returned to their units and the extensive, subliminal network of the pink parade was invigorated. To wipe out homosexuality in the armed forces, establishments such as KH would have to be dismantled. Along with other similar institutions it served as the hub from which we discovered others like ourselves, sought out straight allies, formed relationships and learnt all the intriguing gossip and rumours. In turn those gays and associates would create their own history which in time became part of gay regimental folklore.

Carl and I were spared the need to come out through the usual ritual of dropping hints, confessing and then exchanging histories. We had both been fully briefed on each other's personalities. We were able to engage straight away in exchanging information. Carl, newly arrived from both Junior Leaders and KH, was a great source of intelligence. He'd had sex with several student bandmasters whilst at the school. Student bandmasters were junior or senior NCOs who'd been selected to undertake the intensive three-year course leading to promotion to WO, first class, and the subsequent posting to a band as a bandmaster. He had also had a variety of encounters with other bandsmen. I memorised their names: Ellie and Lance of the Fusiliers, Marc and Zelda, both of the Devon and Dorset Regiment, Lloyd Morton, a euphonium player in the Household Cavalry, Jamie Forbes, a trombone player with the Paras, and Edward Banks, a saxophonist.

Another Bdsm, Patrick Mitchell, joined us from JLR. Though

he was over eighteen, his voice still hadn't broken. He was an unattractive boy with pinched, weasel-like features. He wore small round glasses that were always steaming up. We nicknamed him Bumfluff as his cheeks were soft and downy. He was an ambitious musician who played the clarinet. However, his eccentric character occasionally upset his roommates. Within weeks of arriving he bought himself a cuckoo clock. Every hour, on the hour, a little plastic, arthritic cuckoo popped out of the clock face and announced the time. It was a big clock from which hung two weighted chains. The cuckoo's hut was revolting. It was made of plastic that had been moulded to resemble wood but failed to do so. Little window boxes adorned the alpine facade. From each box sprouted stiff flowers painted in gaudy, bright colours. The cuckoo was cheap, and tiny plastic umbilicals marked where it had been separated from its mould. Its eyes were red and splodged on so that it looked more like a goldfish. Yellow gloss paint sealed the bird's beak permanently shut and stiffened surrounding feathers. Its mechanism was clumsy. A cheap plastic clatter catapulted the cuckoo back and forth. The bird flew forward so fast that its beak smashed onto its supporting platform floor. As muffled cuckoo imitations sounded from within the plastic hut, the bird bounced crazily on its spring before being wrenched backwards. Its constant ticking and cuckooing annoyed his three roommates. In an attempt to minimise the irritating imitations, they glued coins onto the back of one weight. Despite this the bird still appeared at regular intervals. One morning, Bumfluff awoke to find the cuckoo silent. In the afternoon he packed it into its box and took it back to the NAAFI.

"My clock's not working. I've only had it two weeks." He placed the package on the counter.

"Do you have a receipt, sir?"

Bumfluff searched through his wallet to find the sales slip. He handed it to the assistant.

"Right, let's have a look at it first." He began to unpack the box. and laid the clock on the counter.

"Oh, sir, I don't think they come supplied with coins attached to the weights," he said holding out the weight. Bumfluff squinted through his thick, round glasses.

"I don't know how they got there," he exclaimed.

"I take it you share a room in barracks?"

"Yes, with several others."

"It's a common prank in barrack rooms. We're always getting clocks returned that have had the weights adjusted. Mind you, that wouldn't stop the mechanism working so I best look inside." He rattled through a drawer, produced a small screwdriver and began to remove the back cover.

"Fucking wankers," Bumfluff muttered under his breath. The clock cover came off and the assistant's eyebrows suddenly knotted.

"Well that's original, sir. Are you a vegetarian?"

"No, why?"

"Well, you've got a meat pie squashed in the mechanism. Steak and kidney, I believe."

"What?"

"A meat pie; it's been stuffed into the springs. Basically it's ruined." He turned the clock around for Bumfluff to inspect. Pliant pastry clogged coils and strands of soft meat and purple kidney jammed springs. The assistant prodded the meaty mechanism with his screwdriver. With a clatter the cuckoo shot out of its door. A clump of kidney flew off its head and landed on the counter.

"Any chance of a replacement?" asked Bumfluff.

"I'm afraid not, Sir," replied the assistant. The corners of his lips quivered as he suppressed a grin.

"Fucking wait, I'll kill 'em," squeaked Bumfluff. His face was bright red and his glasses were beginning to steam over.

Within weeks of his arrival I'd sucked him off. I kept the encounter a secret from my mates as he was far too unattractive to admit having sex with. Bumfluff was feeling lonesome and horny and suggested that if I was gay I should prove it. It was a brief encounter because his roommates were talking in the room next door.

"Suck me off," he asked.

"Yeah, okay then." I got up and sat on his bed. He put down his book. I began unzipping his flies and then tugged down the waistband of his blue underpants. His dick was already hard. For a boy with an unbroken voice it was surprisingly long and thick. Swollen veins bulged along its shaft and a pink tip poked out from his foreskin. It was an attractive dick. I gripped it and began tugging it up and down. His foreskin slipped back revealing a broad, strawberry-shaped head. Leaning forward I sank my mouth over it and felt his body relax. It was a clinical blow job from which I gained little arousal. His dick might as well have been sprouting out of the wall or the mattress as my hands and eyes went no further. Eventually, when I sensed the right moment, I aimed his dick towards his shoulder and let him squirt up his T-shirt. His hands gripped the sides of the bed. When he'd finished wriggling and his fat dick had begun to soften, I wiped my hand on his yellow counterpane. He stared at the ceiling with glasses that were skewed unevenly.

"Thanks," he sighed. I left the room and immediately washed my hands.

In December we began rehearsals for the annual military concert known as Hallemünsterland. It was an impressive multi-function hall which when arranged for a concert seated a vast audience. This was one of the largest regular engagements on our calendar and saw several hundred musicians assemble under one baton. The event gave us the opportunity to perform challenging pieces of music, often from the classical repertoire. They were always pieces that showed off the military band, noisy, driving overtures or symphonies, or little novelty pieces which displayed the dexterity of our soloists. The year Carl arrived, we opened with Rossini's 'William Tell' overture and so I spent weeks rehearsing the difficult pastoral flute solo. Massed concerts, such as Hallemünsterland, always had at least one superior band present. These bands were classed 'staff bands' as opposed to 'line bands', and consisted of regiments such as the Guards, or the Household Cavalry. Instead of a WO1 bandmaster, they were directed by an officer. On massed bands, such as Hallemünsterland, the senior director always took charge of the programme, rehearsals, concerts and always conducted the flashy pieces of music.

For a week we rehearsed in a large gymnasium in one of Münster's barracks. It was a chance to get to know people and catch up on gossip. It was also an opportunity to meet some of the individuals of whom Carl had spoken. New to Osnabrück garrison was one of the Parachute bands. They were billeted some distance from Rawlpindi, too far to socialise with. After the rehearsals both our band and the Para band shared the bus on the hour's journey back to Osnabrück. Despite bands sharing a bus, the same hierarchy of seating arrangements was maintained. The bandmasters and SNCOs sat at the front and the bandsmen in the rear seats. It was odd seeing our yellow and green side hats intermingled with the prestigious maroon berets of the Paras.

On massed bands, I made a mental note of the sexy looking soldiers and where they were positioned within the band formation. It was one way of passing time during rehearsals. If I craned my head around far enough, I was able to look up through the tiers of stands to one particularly attractive-looking trombone player. On one occasion, when the flutes were resting during the music, I glimpsed up through the legs of the stands. He had a lean body which was tightly hugged by his green army pullover. His maroon belt extenuated his narrow waist, and his maroon Paratrooper's beret lay beside one foot that gently tapped to the rhythm of the music. Lost in an erotic daydream, I mentally undressed him. I gazed for too long. He took his trombone from his lips. A bright red mark, caused by the pressure of the mouthpiece, swiftly faded white and then blended into tone with the olive complexion of his skin. He placed the trombone on its stand and looked down to catch my eye. I was brave, foolish perhaps. Our eyes met. He tilted his head slightly. His black hair shone as if greased and flopped down above one eye. His eyes were dark and sparkling. Then, almost imperceptibly, he raised his eyebrows. It was a neutral expression that neither admonished or encouraged me. Embarrassed, I turned back to face my stand.

Carl and Jamie spent most breaks in each other's company. One evening, on the journey back to Osnabrück, they were sitting together towards the back of the bus. I sat opposite. All around bandsmen joked and laughed as they tried to outdo each other with their jovial piss-taking. For a while I sat silently looking outside my window at the cold landscape. Winter had stung the land with its frosty bite. Many of the houses and farms had traditional colourful Christmas lights adorning small trees in their gardens. My spirits lifted. The biting cold, the hoarfrost, the sparkling fairy lights in the gardens, made it so much more Christmassy than in Britain. When I looked back across at Carl and Jamie, their faces were stuck together. They were as oblivious to the company around them as the others were to them. Carl, in his excitement, lay partly on top of Jamie who was pushed up against the window, his hand busy burrowing away inside Jamie's flies. Carl's side cap fell to the dusty floor unnoticed. You lucky bastard, I thought jealously. It was an outrageously erotic sight; two young soldiers, in barrack-dress uniforms, snogging and groping away with their superior officers sat only yards in front. I had desires on Jamie but knew nothing would ever develop. Eventually, when the noisy joviality of those around us died down, they disengaged themselves.

That evening, back at Rawlpindi, Carl suggested we went to the Gentleman where we could meet up with Jamie.

"I don't know if I really feel like it."

"Oh! Come on. We'll have a good time. Besides, we haven't been out for a few weeks. It'll do us good."

"Yeah, maybe, but I don't know if I'm in the right mood to be a spare prick at a wedding – if you get what I mean?"

"No! I don't get what you mean. What are you talking about?"

"You and Jamie," I paused trying to find the right words. "You seemed to be doing very nicely on the bus. I just assumed you were making a hit on him." Carl started laughing.

"I was just horny and it seemed an outrageous thing to do."

"So you're not after him?"

"No! I felt like sex at the time but not necessarily with him. It was just convenient. I don't fancy him."

"Why not?"

"I don't know, he's good looking, but I don't fancy him."

"Have you ever done it with him?"

"On a few occasions, nothing serious."

"I think he's gorgeous. I'd fucking give him one."

"I know," stated Carl.

"How do you know that?" I asked defensively.

"He told me. Jamie told me."

"Oh yeah, I really believe you."

"No, he did, really. He said he caught you looking at him a few times during rehearsals. Says you've got a really obvious glint in your eye when you do it. He knows you're gay, you know?"

"I'm not particularly bothered if he does. Its obvious from his randy behaviour on the bus that he's hardly Mr Straight himself."

"We've all heard rumours about you down the school. You're famous. Who knows, perhaps Jamie's into fucking celebrities."

"I doubt it."

"Well, you'll never know if you don't come out, will you?"

I paused for thought. "When's the bus?" I asked.

That evening there was a touch of optimism in my mood. I showered in the ablutions as Carl occupied the adjacent cubicle.

"Is he gay?" I shouted over the sound of splashing water.

"Stick a finger up his arse. Then you'll find out."

"What do you mean?"

"Straight boys never look after their bumholes cause they only ever use them for shitting. Once you start to use it for other purposes you keep it clean. Straights always have shitty arseholes." His voice was strained, as if he were occupied in some task.

"I always keep mine clean," he grunted. "Get my finger right up it and hook out any crap. Then I soap a finger, slip it up and swish it out a few times. When dry I dab it with witchhazel."

"Interesting," I shouted back.

"There, all done and nice and clean," he said sounding pleased. Suddenly his head appeared over the top of the cubicle partition. He waggled an index finger at me.

"Fuck off, you dirty bastard!" I shouted.

"Do you want to sniff my insides?"

"Go away!" I replied throwing a handful of water over the partition.

In my room I dressed and put on my canvas baseball boots which were a gay trademark of which the squaddies were unaware. I gave my face a blast under my portable tanning lamp and rubbed Nivea into the exposed parts of my body. In the army at that time, using hair conditioner, face and skin creams, hairdryers and the like were seen as poncy pursuits. Today they're part of every thirteen-year-old boy's daily life. Carl had a well-stocked boudoir of body-beautiful products which I sometimes used. Every night when he went to bed he smeared the oily Nivea into his face and he always kept several expensive bottles of aftershave. Before leaving for the bus into town, I made up my bed. In anticipation I sprinkled some talcum powder between the crisp, white sheets. I sighed deeply. "Who are you kidding?" I asked myself aloud.

The Gentleman was busy but we managed to find ourselves a stool in front of the bar. The Village People's 'In the Navy' and 'YMCA' played incessantly on the jukebox. Jamie hadn't arrived so Carl and I started drinking banana liqueur, our favourite. Every time someone pressed the bell outside the club door, a set of orange lights above the bar flashed. Then Theo or his boyfriend Walter answered it. Sometimes, when Carl and I were in particularly high spirits, he pressed the doorbell in time to the beat coming from the jukebox. Carl said it was necessary to announce our arrival. Every time the lights flashed our heads turned, waiting to see if it was Jamie.

Some squaddies entered the bar, identified by their short hair, lack of earrings or tight jeans. They huddled amidst the crowd at the bar. We watched them, waiting for the moment one of them realised they were in a gay bar. They ordered their drinks and began to relax. Eventually one of them noticed the bar was full of men and turned to tell a companion. Their heads converged as if in discussion and they began peering around the room with panicked faces. Then they quickly finished their drinks and left.

The light flashed again, it was Jamie. He smiled widely when he found us; the white of his dark eyes flashed in the subdued lighting. He removed his jacket. Through his white T-shirt I could trace his firm pectorals and the impression of nipples. He wore a pair of black Farah trousers that were just tight enough to extenuate the curve of his buttocks. He had one of those butts which protrudes in a beautifully curved bubble.

"Well, sorry I'm late, missed the bus." He leant towards Carl and kissed him on the cheek. His olive-coloured skin was clear and smooth, and boyish sideburns grew down from above his ear. Down the centre of his back I could count each undulation caused by his spine. Then he turned and kissed me. Hair brushed against the side of my head sending a tremor down my neck. It was a gentle kiss, his breath hot on my cheek.

"Rather brave of you to wear an earring," said Carl.

"Yes," he replied putting his hand to his ear. "They're banned. I have to put it in my pocket and stick it in once I'm outside the barracks."

"They're not banned in our barracks yet. Not unless you're in uniform, of course. But then you're a rufty tufty Paratrooper. Aren't you?" Carl laughed.

"Of course, darling. All male. One hundred and ten percent." His campness was momentary and obviously acted.

"So what are you having?" asked Carl.

"I'll have whatever you're drinking."

"Even banana liqueur?" joked Carl.

Jamie looked at him. "God! You cavalry are so pathetic." With a huff Carl motioned to Theo that we wanted serving.

"I'll have a banana liqueur," said Jamie reluctantly.

We progressed from banana liqueur to Pils by which time Carl was already starting to get tipsy. He began making eyes at blokes around the club in whom he was interested. Eventually he went and sat at someone's table and we hardly saw him for the rest of the evening.

I was nervous talking to Jamie and aware of my desires yet convinced he wasn't interested in me. But once the alcohol started coursing through my brain, giving me tiny hot flushes, I began to relax. Over the blaring music we strained to talk, gleaning most of our dialogue through lip reading. We sat close; almost head to head. His fresh scent invaded my nostrils. When he looked up, his eyebrows slanted upwards at an angle. Then a pang struck at my stomach, and his beauty overwhelmed me with a sense of hopelessness. I became lost in my thoughts and either missed cues or nodded when I should have shaken my head.

"Fucking hell!" I said. "If it's not 'YMCA' again. It's starting to really bore me."

"We should have a dance," replied Jamie.

"Dance! I'm useless at dancing. I'm a musician and I've no sense of rhythm." Jamie stood up; I remained firmly on my seat. "I haven't had enough to drink."

"Come on! We'll have fun; I can't dance either." His hand tugged at my arm, imploring me to join him.

"Just the one," I said reluctantly.

I hate dancing; being tall I can see over everyone's heads. Perhaps if I'd been a bit shorter I'd have been able to stare at peoples' chests rather than down at their faces. I've always wanted to be able to lose myself in the dance but have never been able to let myself go. Once, when I was fourteen, I went to a teenage disco. I can remember standing on the very edge of the dance floor, really wanting to dance, to enjoy it. My favourite pop tune at the time was 'All Right Now', by

Free. I was on the very brink of starting to dance but something held me back. Every time I've danced since, I've wanted to let myself go but have had that restraining feeling which I first encountered as a fourteen-year-old. It's as though I still have to cross that threshold.

After 'YMCA', Jamie wouldn't let me sit back down and so I jerked around the dance floor convinced that most of the club were staring at me, mocking me. I tried to alter my rhythms, finding out little combinations that worked, or at least seemed dance-like. Occasionally I tried copying other dancers' movements but most of the time bodged it up with my awkwardness. Eventually a slow ABBA number played. I went to sit down but Jamie moved towards me and pulled me into his arms.

"Come on, slow ones involve less movement. Just shuffle and gyrate your hips." He put his arms around my waist and nestled his head against my chest. I felt as graceless with him in my arms as dancing on my own. My mind was occupied with how to hold my hands on his back. Conscious that every little movement might be construed as sexual, as a come on. The last thing I wanted was a cold rejection. His proximity induced a growing erection which I tried to keep from his notice. The warmth of his cheek on my chest increased until it felt like a comforting, warm hot-water bottle. Fingers began to pit and pat across the top of my buttocks. I responded by squeezing my arms tighter. The game had began and my body switched to auto pilot: I tensed my grip, he pressed his chin against my sternum, my fingers probed his spine, his crotch banged against the inside of my thigh, I pressed my cheek against his hair, he pressed his erection against my leg. Soon we were bonded together in an embrace. All around us was a merry-go-round. A peripheral sea of swirling colours, unnoticed faces and sound. Suddenly I was dancing, I was relaxed and my surroundings insignificant. I was in the dance, in the merry-go-round. Our lips met and my eyes closed.

Later, we took a taxi back to Rawlpindi Barracks. Behind my locked door we began undressing and soon shirts lay at our feet. Nibbling my chest his hands caressed my back. His breath was hot and laboured. I knew then he was gay, his eagerness for a male body expressed it. My face burrowed through his dark hair busily licking and smelling. His lips found my nipple and I felt his teeth clamp around it. His bite was gentle but fixed me momentarily in pain.

"Fuck," I gasped. My hands slotted under his armpits and ran down his flanks. His muscles quivered gently. I arched my back pushing my dick against his stomach. Again his teeth pinched my nipple and I tensed.

"Yeow, that's fucking great."

"Yes," he moaned as my knee pressed under his crotch.

"Do you have a clean bumhole, then?" I asked. He looked up, startled. "Carl says gay boys always keep their bumholes clean."

"I'm not really into arses, Nick."

"No, neither am I. We must have dirty arses then," I laughed. I broke our embrace, sat on the edge of my bed and tugged my jeans off. Jamie's fingers flicked open his bulging buttons and his trousers fell to the ground.

"Hey, boxers," I exclaimed. "Very aristocratic." His erection stretched the blue cotton into a tent. He moved to pull them off. "No, leave them on. They're sexy." I reached out and pulled him towards me.

"In my band they call boxers 'old man's pants'," he said laughing and swung his hips so his dick swayed in front of my face.

"Only officers wear them in my regiment," I replied. I ran my hands up the inside of his legs until I gently cradled his balls. I passed them between my fingers. Reaching down, he stroked my hair. I slid my palm up his shaft and massaged the end through soft material. The muscles in his thighs twitched and he rose up onto his toes. Falling on top of me we rolled onto the bed. Working his hand into my pants he began exploring. His weight pressed onto me, his tongue smothered my face in licks and he sucked on the side of my neck. Anxious fingers pressed into the very base of my dick and I felt it surge with pressure. With our faces twisting together, we kicked off our underwear. Then he knelt abreast my chest so his balls dangled above my face. His dick jutted upwards, its skin so taut it was ribbed. It curved slightly to one side like a banana. He pressed it against my face and eased his hips forward so that it pushed over my chin, mouth and nose. Like a snake it rolled over my face until the foreskin unpeeled and a pink head appeared. The head was edged with a swollen purple ridge. The wiry hair on his balls tickled my chin. His hips continued moving and pushed his dick all over my face. His hand was jerking on my dick and it was beginning to hurt. I pushed it aside and took over.

"Sorry Jamie, but I'll never come with you doing it like that." He moved forward and placed a palm on the wall.

"Suck my cherries?" he asked. I opened my mouth and they flopped onto my tongue. With a slight suck each popped into my mouth. He wrapped his palm around his dick and began wanking. His dick head speedily slid in and out of its sheath. My tongue swirled over his hairy balls and pressed into testicular recesses. I breathed heavily through my nose. When he came I felt his sac tighten and his balls clenched. For a second he paused, his red head glistening. Then the base of his dick throbbed and a long jet of spunk flew up and splatted on my Bruce Lee poster. It dribbled down his face and slipped onto the wall. I closed my eyes and shot up his back. My jerking hips tossed him up and down.

"That was fucking great, Nick." He pulled himself beside me and kissed me on the cheek. I felt his sticky, deflated dick on my thigh.

"Are you going to stay?" I asked.

"If that's okay."

"Of course it is." I smiled. I leant over and flicked on my cassette player. We drifted off into the woozy state that only sex can swaddle you in, to the final, gentle strains of Bruckner's Ninth Symphony.

Early next morning Jamie left to drive back to his barracks and ready himself for rehearsals. I didn't hide the bite mark on my neck when I shaved in the washrooms. Having such a mark got you talked about by the SNCOs. The unfortunate thing was that the presence of love bites on both our necks meant we had to avoid each other all day. Whilst I wasn't bothered by others' suspicions, Jamie's band weren't so liberated. His regiment was the ultimate in macho pride.

Jamie and I had planned to meet outside my barracks in the late afternoon. Before he left that morning he'd insisted we wear our barrack dress when meeting. I hung around outside the camp entrance for ages, he was late. He should have arrived just before Guard Mount but didn't. From outside the main gate, I watched the camp's barrier drop in order to halt all traffic while the parade took place. One of the trumpeters, whom I couldn't see, sounded the Regimental Call, followed by Guard Mount. It wasn't a particularly good call and several notes were split. No more than a few minutes later, I heard the guard being ordered to dismiss and the barrier lifted. I'd began to think that he'd stood me up. What a fucking comedown, I pondered. Resentful thoughts began to impinge themselves on my mind. At the barrier, the RP sentry left his post. Even at this distance I could read the big brass letters RP on his arm. A sentry dressed in combats took his place. All over Germany, in hundreds of other barracks, an identical ritual was taking place. From the guardroom entrance prisoners and RPs appeared dressed in their fatigue overalls. They were all armed with brooms and began sweeping the kerbs opposite the guardroom. A guard NCO supervised them. I was beginning to consider returning to my bunk. It was an unpleasant thought since it involved re-evaluating the previous night's adventure. I sighed, tutted and was beginning to feel rejected, when Jamie's car suddenly pulled up in front of me. I broke into a wide grin and forgave him in elation. We drove into town and drank coffee in a small, rather up-market cafe which overlooked a shopping mall. All around sat little old ladies, all impeccably dressed and with painted faces. We sipped coffee and ate gateau but under the table we stroked each other's legs and pressed our knees together. The naughtiness made it nicer.

I'd already won several karate tournaments and had progressed to wearing a blue belt. I was one of Georg's prize fighters. In one tournament, held in the town of Gelsenkirchen, I was up against a fighter from a neighbouring club. My opponent's instructor was Lütz, the young black belt who'd often instructed me during my first year at the Song Do Kwan. I knew it was going to be a difficult fight. Lütz had visited the club on several Friday evenings, under the premise of a social call, but Georg reckoned that he visited to watch me training. My first opponent I demolished with a series of side kicks, blasting him out of the fight area on the final kick. My German team mates were constantly encouraging me not to be so friendly; they said I smiled too much. I was christened the bull of Osnabrück. When the time came for me to fight Lütz's student, neither of us drew any points. Every technique I employed, he countered. We were forced to play two tiring extra rounds during which I managed to beat him on points. The next day I suffered. My shins were tender, my forearms bruised from blocking kicks and punches, and my toes bent beyond their usual extension in both directions.

My size has always lulled opponents into a false sense of security. Being tall and heavily built they usually expect me to be slow moving, which I am. But through lengthy sparring sessions I had developed a very good reaction speed. Some evenings were entirely devoted to sparring during which we constantly changed partners. Once launched an opponent is committed to following their attack through and if countered at the right moment he is left completely vulnerable. Most fighters prefer to attack but I am a defensive fighter, preferring to wait until my opponent launches their offensive. I read books on the subject of timing and was an avid admirer of the techniques of Bruce Lee who stressed the importance of timing and cadence. I trained most lunchtimes in the gymnasium, putting myself through rigorous aerobic circuits and improvising all sorts of training accessories. I toughened my fists and finger tips in a sand bucket, used pulley devices to stretch my legs and various hand and foot weights to improve my power and speed. I perceived myself as a martial artist.

Most nights Jamie slept in my bunk, there was no need to keep our relationship a secret from the other singlies. After strenuous training sessions at the Song Do Kwan I rushed back to Rawlpindi to meet him. Whenever I slacked in the training the thought of his soothing hands focused my mind and hardened my resolve. In barracks we showered together, his soapy palms massaging away my muscular tensions.

We joined a German fire brigade band in the town. It was a revelation to experience a band where the emphasis was on enjoyment rather than musical perfection. The band had players of all ages, men and women. They rehearsed twice a week with schnapps and Pils under their seats. They swigged whenever they wanted even if it meant missing a cue. Few of the older players spoke English but they tried.

"Hey, Nick, Jamie, you drinking schnapps now, ja." And a bottle was passed across the band to one of us.

"Drink! Then you hear no wrong notes," they ordered with rosy faces. Mostly they played marches, proud Prussian stomping music like 'St Petersburg' or 'Preussens Gloria'. There were some horrendous players and the schnapps didn't prevent my ears from aching. They played with two marks of expression, 'loud' and 'as loud as possible'. Their faces puffed out, their eyes bulged; their enthusiasm was admirable. If they took a break from march music and drinking it was to sing a rousing song, the Huntsman's Chorus from Weber's 'Freischütz'. Then they swung their bottles, slopping Pils onto the stands, the music and themselves, conducting as ineptly as they played. Who cared?

Gert was a gnome of a man. He played the E-flat clarinet badly. Wrong notes, squawks and being out of tune were all merrily ignored. We visited his house on several occasions and though he and his wife spoke little English we managed to converse through hand signs and our basic German.

"Nick, how do you say in English, would you like a cigarette?" his wife asked when we were all pissed. I lifted a packet of cigarettes from the table and flicked the top open. Then I offered one to her husband.

"Du muss sagen, would you like a blow job?"

"No zank you," replied Gert proudly. Jamie put his head down and stifled a chuckle. I didn't dare look at him in case I started laughing too.

"Jamie, what's wrong?" asked Mutti, Gert's wife.

"Nothing, I think I've drunk too much." Mutti took out her cigarettes and turned to Gert.

"Vould you liking plow jab?"

Jamie started laughing, his head hung between his hands.

"No zank you," replied Gert smiling broadly.

"Are you going to be sick, Jamie? asked Mutti in German.

"No, really. I've just drunk too much."

"Mutti, you have to be clearer. Say, would you like a blow job?

"Vould you like a blaw job."

"Blow job, not blaw," I advised slowly.

"Blow job," practised Mutti.

"Vould you like a blow job?" said Gert.

"Vould you like a blow job?" repeated Mutti.

"Yes please," replied Gert and Mutti passed him the packet.

In February I was promoted to L/Cpl. It came without warning. I was called into the BM's office early one morning and given the news. It was a shock since promotions were speculated weeks in advance and normally the prospective NCO tipped of the event. There then followed weeks of anxiously waiting for the promotion to be announced through Regimental Orders. These contained details of promotions and postings in which everything that appeared was the outcome of the military administrative bureaucracy. On the date that my promotion became effective a welcome party was held in the Cpls' mess. As was custom, I bought the mess and RSM a round of drinks. Promotions were always boozy affairs and a good excuse, though never needed, to keep a bar open until the early hours of a morning. By the time the promotion was official my uniforms carried my new insignia.

Most of the time the band were left alone by the regiment. We only had to do guard duties when the squaddies were out of barracks. We pulled our combats, berets and squaddie boots out from under the piles of dirty washing and went out to guard an eerie, lifeless camp. Guardrooms always give a superficial illusion of cleanliness. The floors, walls and windows are mirror bright and pristine, but the mattresses are absolutely rank. Smears from boots blacken one end and grimy hair wax pollutes the other. They are impregnated with the smell of oil from squaddies' uniforms and stained by tea, coffee and food. Such beds wouldn't have been so unpleasant if you could sleep but this wasn't possible. The bright light from the guardroom reception was a constant annoyance as was the guard commander's shufflings and the frequent rotation of patrols and sentries. It was pointless going to bed early as no one else did, and besides, four hours sleep was the longest you could take. The whole room stank of floor polish and after a while you developed a headache.

One of the most important objects in the guardroom was the Regimental Guardroom Log Book. This was an official document that all guardrooms were required to keep. In this log were recorded all events that happened during the evenings and early mornings, i.e. those hours when the guardroom was manned by personnel other than the RP. Reading the log always temporarily relieved the boredom of the duty. It was full of grammatical errors, illegible handwriting and spelling mistakes, and written in a stiff, military manner:

Sir, at 2330 a fight broke out outside the Cpls' mess. The to men involved both whom were highly intocksicated were L/Cpl Goreham of A Squadron and L/Cpl Jones of B Squadron. The to soldiers were escorted to the guardroom and questioned. L/Cpl Goreham claims that he caught L/Cpl Jones quote messing around with my wife end quote. They then started fighting and had to be stopped.

Sir, at 2347 hr's, Mrs Goreham arrived at the guardroom she was very drunk and told us that she quote wanted her fucking husband end quote. I then told her that it was best to keep her husband in the guardroom overnight and that he would be released in the morning. Mrs Goreham then said quote I want to see the fucking Commanding Officer you can't keep my fucking man in jail end quote. I told her that the CO couldn't be disturbed for such a minor incident. She then kicked over one of the brass shells outside the Guardroom entrance and called me quote a cunt. She was very abusive.

Sir, at 2400 another wife arrived at the guardroom (Mrs Webster, w/o Cpl Webster, A squadron.) She calmed Mrs Goreham down and escorted her home.

Sir, at 0130 hr's in the morning the guard patrol reported back to the Guardroom that they had apprehended a soldier walking around the back of the barracks in his underpants. When the guard questioned him he said he was looking for a rabbit which he had seen. After further questioning the soldier who is reported as 29675841, Tpr Keith. J, of C squadron, said he had seen a six foot tall rabbit jumping around outside his window. When he went to look for it it was gone. The guard told Tpr Keith to go back to bed. The guard are sure that he wasn't drunk. I have ordered the guard to check on him at regular intervals and to also check the outer perimeters of the barracks for anything strange. Sir, I have nothing further to report.

When we finished a guard duty, at 0830, it was up to the cookhouse for a big, greasy fried breakfast. At the end of a guard we always took a shower, it was needed to wash away the stench of a duty. In most cases we had the rest of the day off. Band guards were easy going.

After Easter leave I lost interest in Jamie. I stopped seeing him straight away. I was registered to attend a one-year pupil's KH course and it was the choice between him and my career. Once I had decided, I put him out of my mind. I didn't return his phone calls and ignored the letters he sent me. He could have called in to see me but didn't. My selfish attitude hurt him and pushed him away. Georg told me that a Para called Jamie had begun training in the club during my leave. I treated it as a joke and made flippant remarks about him to my mates. Eventually he was posted back to the UK. Jamie's gay inclinations were eventually found out by his regiment, probably following some indiscretion on his part. They unceremoniously discharged him but not until his inquiry would drag me into yet another investigation by the SIB.

9

Kneller Hall, known to bandsmen as the Crotchet Factory, was a place where the most unbelievable things happened. It was the army's most prestigious music school and run in a strictly military manner. Most pupils hated KH and many tried, usually in vain, for an RTU. The obsession with bullshit was taken to the extreme. Block jobs, inspections, Padre's hour, drill practice and morning parades ruled our lives. Reveille was sounded at 0600. By the time we'd finished bulling, bumpering, polishing, picking up leaves and the morning parade, it was 0830. By then, few of us had any interest or energy for music. KH had the facilities to be a first-class school of music but was instead an institution run on pettiness, punishment and inconvenience.

The hierarchy of the school was split a number of ways. At the very top of the rank structure came the CO, a colonel who was the Director of Army Music, then came the school Commandant, another colonel responsible for everything that wasn't musical. Under the two colonels came the adjutant, who was an officer. The SNCOs included the School Bandmaster and the RSM – again a musician and a squaddie. The student bandmasters were all acting SNCOs but in reality could have been of any rank from L/Cpl to WO2. Instead of chevrons or warrant badges they wore a lyre on their sleeve or wrist under which was the word 'student'. At the very bottom of the hierarchy were the pupils who were mostly bandsmen but sometimes JNCOs.

Ash and I arrived at KH several hours earlier than detailed. But the gate guard was under instructions to forbid new arrivals from leaving the barracks. Unable to explore, we unpacked our belongings. Of the school's four companies, we'd been attached to A company which was housed on the ground floor of one of the two accommodation blocks. Ash was billeted in an eight-man room whilst I had the privilege of a small single bunk. Within two hours of my arrival I received news from a student messenger that I'd been promoted to full Cpl by my band. It was another surprise promotion. I unpacked my uniforms and took them to the school tailor as new arrivals began to occupy the barracks, all wide-eyed, bewildered and mostly teenagers. I was one of only three full Cpls on the course and was put in charge of the squad that occupied the two eight-man bunks at the bottom of my corridor.

Each company was divided into two squads. I had to wake my

squad in the mornings, inspect their rooms and block jobs, and march them around the school when going from place to place. Every Thursday at 1730, which was outside usual school hours and thus in what we considered our own time, I had to call my squad's roll and march them to the main building. This was Padre's hour; Catholics went to one room, Methodists, United Reformers, and Baptists to another, and Church of England elsewhere. Nowhere else in the army were adult, trained soldiers expected to receive religious instruction. I tried to get myself excused. A few days after my arrival I went to see the RSM who had an office in the administrative wing of the main building. His nickname, passed from course to course, was Bumtwig. Pressed against the wall in a narrow corridor deep in the main building, I waited until he was ready to see me. Eventually he called for me.

"Right! Who's next?" his voice bellowed out.

"Cpl Elwood, Sir!" I walked into his office and stood in front of his mahogany desk.

"How bloody dare you walk into my office in that manner!" he screamed.

"Sorry, Sir!" I said, pulling myself to attention.

"You can jolly well get back outside my door and come back in properly!"

I turned around and briskly marched out of his office. Then I turned around, paused, and marched back in. When I halted in front of his table I thumped my feet heavily onto his floor, so that the pens on his desk shook.

"Cpl Elwood. 'A' company, Sir!" I announced loudly.

"You should be setting an example, Cpl. After all, you are a squad commander. We do things here the Guards way, none of your Cavalry slouching around this school."

"Yes, Sir!"

"Now, what do you want?"

"Sir! I wish to be excused Padre's hour."

"Oh, you do. Well, I'll have to make a note of it." He opened a notebook and began writing.

His office was immaculate. His pens and pencils were on parade in a little holder on his desk, flanked by his tidy 'in' and 'out' trays. His mahogany desk shone deeply. On the front edge of the desk a brass name plate read 'RSM Browntree'. To the side of this sat his forage cap that bore the cap badge and colours of his Guards regiment. In the tradition of the Guards his forage cap's peak had been slashed so that it slanted downwards to touch the bridge of his nose. He mumbled slowly to himself as he wrote. He clearly found the act of writing simple statements an intellectual feat. "Cpl Elwood requ..e..st..s excusal from the weekly Padre's hour." The pitch of his voice rose up and down in a singing fashion. Then he looked up.

"And what's your reason for wanting to be excused?"

"I'm a Buddhist, Sir, and you have no facilities for Buddhist education."

"Well, we might have to jolly well provide those facilities, Cpl. You're the sixth Buddhist I've had in here today."

"Really," I said in surprise. He continue writing in his notebook, tunefully mumbling as he scribbled.

"Claims to be... of the Bud... dhist... religion." He looked up. His face was bulldog-like and he had a neck as thick as his head. Whenever he spoke he bore an expression of great concentration; it was evident that a struggle to communicate raged inside his head.

"Well, what religion is on your official documents?"

"Methodist, Sir. But I've not practised that religion for several years."

"Well, until you change it officially you'll have to attend the Methodist meeting."

"How do I go about changing it, Sir?"

"You'll have to bring me proof... a letter from your guru, rabbi... whatever you call them."

"Fine, Sir. I'll do that," I lied.

The main practice room, the only one large enough for the entire full band of a hundred and sixty musicians, was located in an enormous air-dome tent which stood at the back of the school. It was kept inflated by vents which blasted hot air into the interior, day and night, winter and summer. Within the first week we met Lieutenant Colonel Graham Foot, the Director of Army Music. He was a short fat man with little square glasses that perched permanently on the end of his nose. I only ever saw him in uniform when conducting concerts. At all other times, even during rehearsals, he wore civvies. We spent most of the afternoon running through 'Mars' from Holst's 'Planets' suite. Foot conducted the opening several times, stopping at various places to instruct the students that stood behind him. Then they took it in turn to start the piece. 'Mars' is difficult to conduct since it is written with five beats to the bar. Not one student could keep the beat going. Foot constantly stopped the band by waving his hands madly in the air. Then he nastily scolded the student conductor. They were so afraid of being shouted at that they really couldn't concentrate on keeping the awkward beat going. After four or five students had attempted the piece and progressed no farther than the first few bars, Edwards waved his arms about.

"Can any pupils conduct? Perhaps we can find one with more

feeling than these musical numskulls here."

"Cpl Elwood, Sir, he can conduct," someone shouted.

"Shit!" I muttered.

"Cpl Elwood," said Foot, peering down at us over the top of his glasses. "Cpl Elwood, where are you?" I put my hand up.

"Well come up here then, lad."

I put my flute down and walked up to the conducting dais. "Can I have the stick, please," I asked him.

"The stick, you mean batón," he replied sarcastically, handing it to me.

Conducting was my strongest musical talent. I lifted the baton and a hundred and sixty musicians raised their instruments and poised their timpani sticks. Silence gripped the stuffy air dome. My wrist flicked and the first beat fell to an ominous, impending rhythm. I hardly had to follow the score, I knew it so well. When the final chord died away, the musicians applauded and a few made whooping noises. As I turned from the dais to sit back down, I noticed embarrassed students rubbing their necks and whispering to each other.

With autumn the large trees that grew in the grounds began to shed their leaves over the paths and roads. Along with the daily morning routine of picking up bits of litter and fag ends, a routine called 'areas', we now had 'leaf fatigues'. Every morning, just before breakfast, I had to accompany my squad to its designated area and ensure that no leaves or litter cluttered the ground. Until the last leaf had been blown from the trees, Bumtwig was obsessed with 'leaf fatigues'. He even detailed those soldiers deemed 'sick but walking' to form a daily posse to stumble and stagger over the camp raking up piles of leaves. When no leaves offended the road and pathways, they were expected to attack the ones on the vast grassed areas. Ash, who'd broken his leg and was on crutches, spent a week hobbling around the barracks on the endless hunt for leaves. When these were located, which was never a problem, he precariously propped himself on one crutch and stretched down to apprehend the offenders.

In harmony and instrumentation, I'd been placed in the top class and had the privilege of being taught by the School's Professors. The remaining seven classes were taught by suitable students. Twice a week, I received individual flute lessons from the Professor of Flute who performed with the London Philharmonic. He was an ageing Irishman in his sixties, with a balding head and cheeks that were a map of tiny capillaries. He kept a large hip flask in the inside pocket of his jacket. He would instruct me to play an exercise, always a long one.

"Now you play this," he instructed, placing music on my stand, "while I sit and listen." I scanned through the music, noting keys, key changes, tempo markings and the general structure of the piece, then took a breath and began playing. The lesson always followed the same format. At first he stopped me to correct my phrasing, tone or interpretation. Thereafter I played on uninterrupted. I was always positioned with my back to him but could smell the whiskey on his breath. In the reflection of the window in front of me I watched him secretly sipping. When his flask was empty he left to refill it.

"I'm just going to the professors' room for a few minutes; just you keep playing." He returned, selected a long exercise, instructed my initial attempt and then fell asleep.

The flute section of the full band was seven strong and was without doubt the best of all the instrumental sections. Although I was in the top class for harmony and instrumentation, I sat sixth person down; the five above me, four of whom played in prestigious staff bands, were excellent instrumentalists. I shared my stand with a WRAC flautist and Paddy, an infantryman. Paddy and I were both reasonable players of the same standard. However, our ability was dwarfed by the dazzling technique of those above us. All were in the top classes. Two have since become bandmasters, and one a director of music.

I quickly began to make friends. My position as squad commander, a liberal one, encouraged friendships. My squad, and other mates, often used my room as an escape from practice and fatigues. Most afternoons entailed individual practice and our company commanders ordered checks to make sure that is what we were doing. Skiving was punished with extra duties. In my small bunk I could hide up to eight men. With a military issue counterpane draped over the side of the bed until it touched the floor, I could comfortably provide a hiding place for two at a squeeze. If we heard footsteps, I sat at my desk working and when a student appeared looking for people to do fatigues or some messenger job, it looked as if no one was in my room. JNCOs were never asked to perform dirty work. A secret knock was used so mates could gain entrance when I had locked my door from the inside. It was the opening dot dot dot dash from Beethoven's Fifth Symphony.

I sought out friends who were passionate about music – especially classical music. When my boxes having arrived I had a large collection of records and tapes, many scores and a good quality stereo. In the school multi-gym room I became friends with an artillery clarinettist named Tom Seymour. He was a keep-fit fanatic and interested in classical music. In my bunk, I offered him sherry, olives and cheese from my military-issue suitcase box, white, which were fitted to the tops of our lockers. The sherry and snacks were a comfortable foible which impressed my guests. Tom and I began to train together and then ventured into town to watch films or visit pubs.

Tom was attractive. I wouldn't have offered him my sherry otherwise. Over the weeks we developed a closeness and were quite physical with each other – this can't be avoided when training together. In the gym we pushed ourselves hard, always doing more sit-ups or reps than the day before. Exhausted, we retired to my room where the buzz from training infused us. One evening we ended up wrestling on my bed. He was a strong lad with a compact muscular physique and we were evenly matched despite my weight advantage. Tom managed to force me into a head lock and began pulling my hair.

"Fuck, that's really painful," I yelled.

"Give in?"

"No fucking way." He pulled harder. I thrashed with my arms but couldn't reach him. Tears were welling in my eyes.

"Do you give in?"

"No!" The pain was excruciating and I knew I either had to admit defeat or grab his balls, which were within reach. The pain from the roots of my hair was intense but I wasn't going to give in. I thrust my hand between his legs and grabbed him. For a moment both of us stopped struggling. In my frozen hand I grasped a solid erection.

"Oh!" I muttered.

"What are you going to do now, then?" he asked, casually.

"Take it out?... If it fancies some exercise, that is."

"Yep, it sure does feel very tense." My hand began to rub him through his tracksuit trousers.

"I think a little massage would do him good, might get him to relax," I suggested.

"Good idea. He's not had any exercise from a trainer for ages," he sighed. My fingers slipped into the top of his waistband and let his erection spring out.

There is nothing more exciting than setting a cock free of its clothing, especially a new cock, an uncharted cock. All cocks are different, but then some are more different than others: the length, girth, proportion, whether it is cut or not, its colour, the pattern of veins along the shaft, the way it hangs. Each and every cock is an individual. Cocks are beautiful, if they're not it's because their owners are ugly – in personality or looks. Artist have taken great pains to replicate male genitalia as they have done to animate female breasts. Michelangelo's David has balls that look like he's just stepped from a hot bath. They float in their thin bag crying out to be fondled and have their mettle tested. The only cocks I can't stand are of little baroque cherubs. They're repugnant – tiny, chubby dicks, void of character and movement; no fun to paint or fondle. But real, stiff cocks come out of their pants sometimes like a weighty pendulum, swaying in the air, at other times with a thwack against the belly, and on occasion poking straight up at their owner's chin. Working that swollen pink head until it is bulging a deep, angry purple is a heavenly pursuit.

Tom's cock sprung out from his waistband and swung in the air, then he lay back, sighed, and closed his eyes. My door was unlocked. When the foreplay reached fervour pitch, I locked the door, confident that he wasn't going to change his mind. The sweat of training had given his skin a salty taste, his armpits scented his presence with a faint musty odour and his balls had the sweet aroma of digestive biscuits. We huffed and puffed, swathed in oblivion.

"I'm going to come in a minute," gasped Tom.

"Yeah, me too."

"Think I should shoot it up your wall... as a sort of trophy."

"I want to drink it." There was a pause in our breathless conversation.

"You can drink it next time, but you can come off in my face." Suddenly Tom gasped and a spray of semen flipped onto my wall. It immediately began to slide downwards, a clump of blancmange leaving a silky, slimy trail. A second spray landed next to it. Then I bore towards him and let a gush of jism splat onto his chin. Tom stayed the night and in the early morning, minutes before the duty trumpeter sounded Reveille, he slipped silently back to his room on the next floor. In the daylight yellowed trails decorated the wall by my bed. I didn't bother cleaning them off, they were a trophy. I would even add to them.

Tom had known I was gay. News of my sexuality travelled from company to company. I hadn't attempted to hide it. One of the L/Cpls in my squad had clambered under my bed to hide from a student and there found some magazines.

"What's this?" he asked, starting to unfold them. "Your stash of porn?"

"No! Actually they're copies of *Gay News*."

"Oh! I see," he replied, slightly embarrassed.

One Friday night in early November, Tom and I took the train to Nottingham where we were going to spend the weekend at his parents. We bought two bottles of red wine, a bottle opener and two wine glasses. On leaving London, we opened a bottle and began drinking. It was early evening and the train was full of City types whose eyes were constantly upon us as they listened to our boisterous conversation. Tom began to get horny and suggested we go and do it in the toilet. I agreed and when the cubicle light showed 'vacant' we stumbled down the aisle of the carriage and locked ourselves in the loo. I had my dick out before he bolted the door.

"Give us a blow job," I implored, waggling it around in the air. Willingly he got down onto his knees. I squeezed my legs between the toilet bowl and the narrow walls. As I shuffled into a comfortable position against the wall, he eagerly tried sticking it in his mouth. It stabbed into his eye, poked into his jaw and squashed against his nose. We laughed.

"C'mon! Or I'll jolly well have to do it myself," I joked. Jolly was the RSM's favourite word. "Jolly well fucking suck it, pupil!" I ordered.

"What key do you want me to jolly well suck you in, Cpl?"

"I think I can have a jolly good time in A flat," I replied.

Once anchored to my dick he began fumbling in his flies and pulled himself out. His knob dribbled in anticipation, seeping from his tiny pink lips. He sucked in A flat for a while until I asked him to change key. The change was noticeable as his tongue suddenly intensified its slurping and his sucking became harder. Involuntary twinges of pleasure tweaked at my knees and buckled them. The train began jolting as it reduced speed. Our shoulders bounced from wall to wall with the lull of the carriage. Scratching teeth accidentally gouged my dick head and slipped me into a twilight zone between pain and pleasure. Soft moans of contentment squeezed past my throat. The lull intensified into a series of lurches as a stop approached. Throwing out a hand I braced myself. Tom's mouth sucked away whilst his fingers frantically twiddled my balls. I felt the tightening bite of an approaching ejaculation.

"I'm gonna come," I hissed.

"Mmm," Tom hummed into my cock. In my abdomen a generator activated and electrical pulses surged. They intensified until with a twitch, I pumped into his sucking mouth. In ecstasy my head flopped forward. Tom was a brilliant clarinettist, a soloist. I'd never seen him so absorbed in playing as at blowing my cock. His cheeks sucked in and out as he hungrily drew on my offering. His eyes gently closed as if sucking on the most pleasurable of lollies. Between his legs his hand feverishly tugged his rigid dick. I could tell by his twitching face he was about to come. Suddenly the toilet door opened, thumping into Tom's shoulder. It was a City type wearing a striped shirt and three-piece suit. My dick was still twitching out its juices and Tom still sucking.

"Hello," I gasped.

"Mmm," sang Tom in panic, his eyes bulging. The City gent's jaw fell in disbelief.

"My God!" the intruder muttered. Then, looking past him I noticed the shocked faces of passengers stood in the carriage exit. They were all similar boring, suited, City types. Tom still had my dick stuffed in his mouth. As suddenly as the door had opened, it closed. Leaning forward, I locked the latch only to discover it was broken.

We hid in the toilet, laughing, until the train pulled away and we'd lost our erections. Then we slipped out and went back to our seats.

In Nottingham we began walking to his parents' house, stopping at a public telephone booth for more fumbling since he had yet to come. It was a damp, misty evening and the phone box windows misted up quickly to obscure our activity. Before we could really get going we heard impatient footsteps outside and giggling we left the box. We took a short cut through a graveyard. Away from the street lighting, the cemetery was dark. Great trees stood black against the starry sky. Tom propped himself up against a headstone and dropped his trousers. It was an old grave with a small stone sarcophagus in front of the headstone.

"Perfect, you've even got a seat. You won't have to get your knees wet," said Tom.

"It's a perfect blow-job throne. Do you use it regularly?" I laughed.

"Fuck! We'll go to hell for this. It's sacrilege."

"Maybe, but we'll have fun on the way," I replied, licking the end of his dick. "Anyway, heaven must be so boring."

"Why?" I sat back on my knees and busily jerked his growing erection in my hand.

"Well, imagine it. Heaven, a place where you live forever and every wish is fulfilled. That's really hell. After a few weeks of heaven you'd be bored stupid. I'd rather go to hell. At least there you'd experience moments of bliss. Heaven is the short break you experience in hell between exchanging a red-hot poker up the bum for the biting nip of the nipple clamps. In the moments of release from pain, you'd experience heaven. Anyway, pain can sometimes be pleasurable." I yanked his foreskin back hard and his body jerked. "See, bet that felt a bit sexy." However, Tom's dick didn't want to play. Too many interruptions had dampened his enthusiasm. Coming quickly was essential before we were interrupted again. He had already insisted that we wouldn't be able to fuck around at his parents, so I got to work slurping away. Tom responded as his hips took up my rhythm.

"See that house over there?" he asked. I stopped and looked without disengaging myself.

"Mmm," I nodded. At the far end of the cemetery, beyond the old wall, stood a row of houses. I took my mouth off him and let my hand take over.

"Which one?" I asked.

"One... two... three... third from the right."

"Yes, I see it."

"See the woman in the kitchen?" My eyes squinted.

"Yes! I've got her."

"Well she's my mum." With mum at work in the sink, I busily worked on her son until he eventually exploded in my mouth.

I liked Tom but our relationship wasn't romantic. We were convenient fuck buddies. Astute musicians, and even some students, were aware of the nature of our friendship. One Sunday afternoon, we were on guard duty together. The commander was a third-year student, Jonathan Ford. In the guardroom was a small portable television on which we were watching the 1948 film *Scott of the Antarctic* – the sort of black and white movie that typifies British Sunday afternoons. Ford sat by the television whilst Tom and I sat side by side next to him. Occasionally, we pushed our knees together or gave each other affectionate glances. We thought we were being discreet.

"Do you two see much of each other, then?" asked Ford. I looked at him with a puzzled expression.

"How do you mean?"

"Do you two hang around together?"

"Me and Tom?" I asked.

"Yes, of course, you and Tom."

I looked at Tom and shrugged my shoulders. "I suppose we do. We train together and go into London and all that. Why do you ask?"

"I just wondered. The pair of you look close friends... I always see you together around the school... Look, why don't the pair of you pop over to the NAAFI, you can get me some fags while you're there." He dug into his pockets and handed me a five-pound note. "There's no hurry. Just be back within the hour."

"That's very good of you, student," said Tom, getting up from his seat.

"What sort of fags do you want?" I asked.

"Silk Cut. And get me a can of Coke as well."

Tom pulled on his beret and walked out of the guardroom entrance. I went to follow him but Ford called me back.

"Cpl Elwood."

"Student."

"It is obvious, you know? Not to everyone, but to some of us."

"What is?"

"Rumours get to students and some of us can recognise the signs."

"I don't know what you're talking about."

"Make sure you're discreet. Won't you?"

"Me, of course, student." I checked my beret was straight and walked out of the entrance.

"I really have no idea what you're talking about," I said grinning.

One of the guard that Sunday was a Bdsm from another cavalry regiment, Gig Ingham. I first met him one evening after I'd been training in Twickenham. Together we walked from the station in Whitton down the hill towards the school. I took an immediate dislike to him. He had a brash manner and a heavy Brummie accent. We started talking about classical composers and at first I thought he was waffling.

On the Monday morning, just after the guard had gone off duty, the fire bell sounded. As was the custom, trumpeters ran out of their barracks sounding Fire Alarm. Fire calls were so frequent in army barracks that we never took them seriously. From the guardroom, where I was involved in the routine key count, I could hear voices shouting, "Fire! Fire!" Students began pouring from the main building, where their accommodation was situated. They carried fire hydrants, blankets and buckets of sand. From the side of the guardroom the duty fire guard hauled a red fire-hose cart. On the main square we began to parade for roll call. Soon the whole school was assembled and behind the columns of soldiers lay a varied assortment of fire-fighting equipment. As Bumtwig began barking out soldiers' names, Gig walked around the corner onto the square and fell in with his squad. He wore a white towelling bath robe, red slippers, and carried a towel and wash bag which hung like a handbag from his wrist. From the guardroom veranda I watched Bumtwig's thick neck stiffen as arteries bulged in anger.

"That man! How dare you come onto my parade ground dressed in that ridiculous manner."

Gig's reply was loud and clear. "But it's a fire alarm, Sir."

"What's your bloody name, soldier?"

"Ingham, Sir. Pupil Ingham."

"Right!" Bumtwig screamed, red in the face and stiff as a board. As he shouted, his body pivoted forward. "Then get yourself off my square and report to my office as soon as you've changed into uniform. In other words get yourself up to my office now!"

"It's a bloody fire drill. What am I supposed to do – bleedin' burn?"

"Get yourself off my fucking square!"

Gig broke ranks and started walking towards the accommodation. "Fucking hell," he murmured, but it was loud enough for Bumtwig to hear.

"And you jolly well march, soldier!" he screamed, pivoting on tip toes like a Picasso screeching cock. Gig's body jolted erect as if hit by an electric charge. He began marching in the silly way recruits do. An exaggerated march with his arms swinging upwards until horizontal with the plane of the ground. His torso was rigid. He marched at a light infantry pace, short and fast. One of his slippers began to come off and for several paces his foot dragged as he tried to keep it from slipping. His arms maintained their exaggerated swing. Bandsmen in the ranks began laughing. Bumtwig didn't know what to say. I don't think he'd ever seen anything like this on his square and certainly not on any Guards squares. Eventually Gig's slipper slipped off. Ignoring it, he marched with a limp. His neglected slipper lay on the edge of the square. The bandsmen's laughter echoed around the parade ground.

"Bloody well shut up," yelled Bumtwig.

When Gig went to Bumtwig's office he was given two guard duties as a punishment. He explained he'd just come off guard duty and therefore started work an hour later than first parade. He explained that he thought it had been a genuine fire alarm and acted as for real. Despite his explanations Bumtwig punished him. A few days later, after evening Orders had been posted, we read:

'Guard Duty Personnel

With immediate effect, guard personnel are not to shower after their duty. Washing and shaving, etc., are permitted. Company Commanders will ensure this rule is followed.'

From that moment onwards we were expected to complete a twelve-hour guard, have a wash and begin a day's work.

Gig became a friend and soon I gave him the secret knock to gain entry to my room. He was always getting into trouble, generally through passing insubordinate comments. Ironically, his criticisms were usually common sense rather than offensive. One sports afternoon he played football; he was in the school team. An important match was being played against another regiment and Bumtwig and Bag Puss, the Adjutant, stood on the sidelines watching. The pupils had been ordered to attend and as usual a roll call had been taken to catch anyone bunking. The match began to the bandsmen's chant of "KH, NFI". This had become our motto. Few people were interested in the game. The compulsory order to attend removed our enthusiasm. Soldiers were in groups talking. A few watched; mostly with bored faces. "KH, NFI," someone chanted. From the opposite side of the pitch a group chanted back: "KH, NFI. KH, NFI." Bumtwig and

Bag Puss stood alongside me. I could see they were puzzled. Bag Puss, who was in his uniform and wearing his officer's Sam Browne, was accompanied by his poodle. It was a little poodle that agilely kept springing up to paw his owner's knees. Bag Puss was a dumpy man with a flabby physique, heavy jowls and saggy eye-bags. With his poodle scampering around his ankles he walked towards us.

"Pupil!" he called to a Bdsm in my group. "What does 'NFI' mean? I keep hearing people chant it." The pupil was quick-witted.

"It means 'KH – New Found Interest', Sir!"

"Oh! That is encouraging."

The real meaning was 'KH – No Fucking Interest'.

During the match Gig was sent off for handling the ball. Bag Puss immediately sent a messenger to summon him to his office. His poodle was sitting as usual at his feet. Bag Puss wasn't pleased with Gig's performance, and threatened to RTU him.

"I've never seen such unsporting behaviour in all my army life. You should be ashamed of yourself!"

"It's only a bleedin' game, Sir," laughed Gig, in his normal brash manner.

"You might think it only a game, young man, but it represents the spirit of Kneller Hall. You've shamed it. I'm seriously considering having you RTU'd."

"It wouldn't bother me in the least, Sir."

"Well, I don't think your regiment would be too proud of you. Do you?"

"To be honest, Sir, I don't think they'd give a fuck. I don't think they'd judge me on being RTU'd for handling a ball in a game. They've got better things to worry about. They'd probably find it amusing and pathetic." Gig was fined forty pounds but accepted it with a sarcastic laugh. Had he not been so forthright he'd probably have escaped with a ten-pound fine.

The first few months of KH life had been bullshitty but they were going to get far worse. With the approach of the summer season, and the weekly public concerts, the pressures in our lives would steadily increase. Christmas leave was now approaching, for those of us who hadn't been detailed for holiday duties. The day before leave began we had our annual soldiers' Christmas dinner – a dinner at which the officers and SNCOs serve the soldiers and JNCOs. This is a tradition in every regiment throughout the army. Foot, for once, was in uniform as were Bag Puss, Bumtwig and students. Every soldiers' dinner was a riot; the riot itself a tradition. On our laid tables were crackers and cans of beer, bowls of nuts and oranges. The nuts were always in their shells despite there being an absence of nutcrackers. Few soldiers were interested in the meal, though they ate with gusto. It was drinking that most enjoyed. They drank themselves stupid and when the Christmas pudding had been served, the nuts, oranges and bits of food became missiles lobbed at the officers and students.

At a regimental dinner few would have dared pelt the CO with a nut or an orange, he was too respected. Foot, however, was the main target. A walnut landed heavily on the back of his neck and when he turned to face us an orange splayed square on his chest. Bumtwig started bellowing and was pelted. A few brave hearts began throwing cans of beer. Eventually, in defeat, the senior ranks ran out of the cookhouse. Such behaviour from bandsmen was highly irregular. Vulgar behaviour for most was anathema. Most of us, that day, threw nuts or oranges but wished they were stones or bricks. It was the expression of resentment, anger and frustration at a system that paid us little regard. Pupils were the system's fodder and our abilities were wasted, misguided and abused.

10

The summer concerts at KH were an established tradition. They were performed in the open with the band sat on what was known as the Rock. This was a large, whitewashed, tiered concert stand. For many years the concerts were held on a Wednesday evening but at the beginning of my course they were rescheduled for a Thursday. School rumour claimed that it was changed as Wednesday afternoon was when Foot played golf. On return from our Christmas leave we began rehearsing one concert programme a week. The rehearsals were rigorous, stressful and tiring. Our weekly routine changed and we had instrumental sections on a Monday morning. The flautists gathered in an eight-man room and together we ran through the programme. On a Tuesday we had group practice and the entire woodwind section met in one of the various practice halls. On both afternoons full band rehearsals were scheduled. On the Wednesday the full band rehearsed under the school bandmaster. Thursday morning saw a complete run through with Foot conducting the highlights and finale and generally directing the overall performance. Finally, on the Friday, the full band sight-read the following week's programme.

Towards the middle of spring, a month before the concerts were due to begin, we started another fatigue. This additional task was known as chair fatigue, and was detailed twice a week. Every Thursday morning, after we'd completed all the block jobs, each company was responsible for laying out a certain number of seats which were for the audience attending each concert. There were hundreds of them, all of which had to be dragged in stacks from under the Rock and laid out in blocks of two hundred. Each block had been marked out by the Provost Sgt beforehand. Shortly before 0830, Bumtwig appeared to inspect our work. He always found something at which to moan. A chair slightly out of line in one place, a row curved in another. His uniform and bearing were impeccable. Even though he lived in uniform, his clothes were always washed, starched and sharply pressed. His hair never seemed to grow. It was always the same length and was of a style usually associated with mental institutions. On the back of his neck it had been cut square, clipped well above his collar. His sideburns had been removed. Wearing a forage cap he didn't look silly, but on the rare occasions he took it off you noticed that apart from a band of hair across the back of his head, he was almost bald. On Fridays we stacked up the chairs and stored them away under the Rock. Whatever the weather, the chairs were laid out and put back for the next three months.

Spring Parade had been scheduled, for which there were weekly rehearsals and squad drill. The drill sessions were half-hour stints of marching around at a ridiculously fast pace, too fast to perform the movements with any grace. Bumtwig was in his element, strutting around his square, shouting out orders and terrorising us with his sarcasm.

"You in the middle, the cavalryman, you're wobbling like some pathetic jelly. Jolly well straighten up... Swing those arms, Musician Moore. You're marching as if you're in the bloody cavalry." He was especially vicious to fellow Guardsmen.

"That man in the Irish Guards!" At which point any Irish guardsman present looked at him. "Face the front, soldier! You're marching like a fucking poofda. If you march like that in your regiment you'll get a rocket up your arse." Occasionally, he ordered us into slow time, which he directed at a pace similar to a cavalry quick march. Proper slow marching can have an appealing grace to it. The arms held tight against the sides, the upper body rigid. Bumtwig yelled at us, his body twisting into knots with each bellow.

"I want to hear your bootlaces creaking as you point your toes down and out. If you march according to regulations, like the Guards do, then your bootlaces creak! Stop tottering around. Imagine you've got my pace stick stuck up your arses. I'll have you here all bloody night if you don't jolly well get it right!"

Everyone despised Bumtwig. Wherever he went he always carried his drill Sgt's pace stick. This is a wooden stick which splits into two halves and is hinged at one end. It's a big version of the JNCO's baton which some regiments stipulate carrying. The pace stick, when open, provides a gauge for the regulation distance of an army pace. In the hand of a drill Sgt it can be twirled between the fingers whilst the owner is marching, thus ensuring the regulation gauge is maintained. The stick is always carried in a military manner, either briskly with the brass tips hitting the floor in synchronisation with the opposite foot, or held under the left arm. The transition involved in moving the stick from one position to another is a smart, military manoeuvre. Drill Sgts, especially Guards Drill Sgts, have a deep affection for their pace sticks. Sticks have a power of their own that ensures their owners strut around like proud cocks in a chicken pen. On the square drill Sgts are awesome.

For the parade itself and the dress rehearsals, Bumtwig issued an order forbidding the wearing of watches, rings, wrist bracelets or necklaces. Of all the hundreds of parades I was to perform, this was the only time jewellery was ever forbidden. On occasion he even inspected bandsmen's fingernails and once gave us a talk on how to clean and cut them.

Tom and I continued to see each other after the Christmas leave but our meetings were not so regular. There were many other sexy men in the Crotchet Factory and I sorted and memorised the top twenty-five best lookers. Top of the list was a Guardsman in my squad. After we became friends, he called in my bunk every morning and gave me a kiss. He wasn't gay but if persuaded and under the right conditions, he would have succumbed. One night, we got stoned together and sat on the floor in my bunk. He leant against the wall with his long, lanky legs sprawled out across the carpet. One of my shins was tucked under his thigh and my toes busily worked away on his crotch. He ignored it; even with an erection he continued a conversation as if nothing was amiss.

Second and third on my list were two infantrymen, Liam and Mark. As I knew them both, I soon discovered they each wanted sex with one another though they never did get it together. I toyed with both of them. First it was Liam. One evening I'd gone into the NAAFI for a 'JNCOs versus Pupils' games night. These were silly affairs which messes often initiated to integrate the rank structure. Darts and carpet bowls were common, as was a boat race, skittles and snooker. They were the sort of games officers entertained themselves with when part of the Raj. A finger buffet was supplied by the cookhouse and the bar stayed open until late. Towards the end of the evening I engineered a conversation with Liam. He had a smooth complexion with fair hair that was neatly parted. He was always smartly dressed, with creases across the back of his shirts and sharp lines down the front of his barrack-dress trousers. One of his hobbies must have been ironing since everything he wore was meticulously pressed. Even the green denim pads on the elbows of his pullover were creased, and his clothes always impregnated with the refreshing smell of spray starch. Rumour had it that he was a very big boy.

When the bar closed we queued up to file out of the narrow exit. I felt very confident and by intuition suspected that something was going to happen between us, if not tonight then later. As we pushed up against each other his hand pressed into my crotch. He turned his head over his shoulder.

"I suppose a shag is out of the question?"

"Not at all. How could I turn down number two on my list?" We walked the short distance to 'A' Company accommodation and went straight into my bunk. With the door locked we got down to business. As we lay naked on my bed, our bodies were bathed in red light that shone from the lamp by my small round window. His skin glowed with a pink luminescence that highlighted the fine fair hairs on his stomach. His little, dark nipples were like two dots of blood on snow. My tongue darted over his skin until it found one; he didn't respond. I continued probing his body, searching out areas that when touched would swathe him in the intensity of the moment, annihilating all else but pleasure. The hollow at the base of his neck sent his knees twitching, tonguing his ears made his body spasm. Suddenly there was a knock on my door. We froze in each other's arms. Seconds later the visitor tried the door handle. Then another knock followed, dot dot dot dash; the rhythm to Beethoven's Fifth. "Fucking hell!" I swore under my breath.

"I know you're in there, I can hear you." It was one of the L/ Cpls in my squad. "Open up, I'm bored."

Liam began sucking my rapidly wilting cock. My head sunk back onto the pillow.

"Is it important?" I gasped.

"No! What are you doing?"

I looked at Liam and shrugged my shoulders. "Fuck off! I'm having a wank."

"Okay, I'll call back later. When you've cleaned up."

Liam's dick pressed against my arm. I turned onto my side and began playing with it. It was fat, weighty and arched. I held it round the base and slapped it onto his abdomen. When I stretched back his foreskin small strands of semen glistened on the tip. His mouth worked over my dick and his finger pressed against my bum hole. It pressed and withdrew and then pressed again, each time with increased persistence. I didn't like him doing it and kept my hole clenched shut. But it felt good. With a popping sensation his finger sunk inside me and his dick suddenly expanded in my hand. I massaged precum over his dick head with my finger tips and when it dried I spat on it. His knees moved in and out and his hips lifted gently up and down. His tongue spun over my dick in a frenzy. It sapped my energy and exploded fireworks in my head. His finger twisted and turned and hit spots that pinned me to the bed in bolts of pleasure. His dick head swelled so tight that the tiny ligature of skin that harnessed foreskin to glans was taut. It cleaved his head in two like a cheese wire. Dragging precum over it I massaged it with my finger tip. His hips lifted off the bed and his heels dug into the mattress. Around my dick his lips tightened, he moaned and a long, watery squirt of semen ejected onto his stomach and chest. His knuckles pressed into my bum as his finger sank as deep as possible. A second pump sprayed a thick stream of white spunk onto his diaphragm. My head tossed up and down on the pillow as his finger and tongue worked. A tingling sensation cascaded through my body and converged where Liam's finger pressed. Its intensity grew until I felt myself cumming into his mouth. With each muscular spasm I felt my arse clinching his finger. Gradually my body relaxed and with a sucking evacuation he withdrew. Suddenly I felt empty. Liam's chest and stomach were sticky with spunk. We lay side by side in the warm light whilst our bodies recovered. My index finger trailed across his abdomen mixing his spunk. It scented the room with a smell between freshly cut grass and swimming pools. He looked down at himself.

"Bit of a mess, isn't it? At least I cleaned you up," he laughed. "Have you got a towel or something?"

I got up from the bed and passed him some tissues. He rubbed himself down and then began getting up. His dick, still semi-erect, bounced between his thighs.

"I need a piss," he said, beginning to unlock the door.

"You can't go out there naked. Someone might see you."

"Are you bothered?"

"No. Not at all. They all know I'm gay anyway."

"So, what's the problem?"

"It's no problem. I just didn't think you'd want people to know. That's all." He went out of the room and returned, unseen, a few moments later. We got back in bed and finally fell asleep. In the morning, as is the tradition, his muted footsteps patted away into the distance. I lay alone in my rumpled bed. From the guard room Reveille sounded the start of the day's routines. My stomach churned with an ominous sensation and I knew I'd fallen in love.

I developed a friendship with Mark Aldridge, the number three best looker on my 'top twenty-five' list. It developed as a matter of course since we were both in the same company where he was a percussionist.

"Are you two in a relationship?" Mark asked one morning.

"No, Liam's far too busy getting sex everywhere. He's got no time to be bothered about relationships."

"How do you feel about that?"

"Huh! I quite fancy him. I always seem to fall for people who aren't interested in relationships."

"Well, he is a pretty boy. I would have sex with him. I've fancied him since we were in juniors but nothing has ever happened."

"Is it love?" he asked.

I sighed deeply. "I think it is but I haven't told him."

"Are you going to?"

"I don't know. I don't see much point really. He's fucking around all over the place. To be honest, sex is our only point of connection. I don't think that's a basis on which to begin a relationship. But he's fucking my head up."

"He's a great bloke but when it comes to his cock he's sex mad Don't expect too much of him, Nick."

"I don't."

"How big's his cock, then?"

"Well, if you'd like to take yours out I'll compare," I joked. In an instant he'd taken it out of his trousers.

"I haven't got a stiffy, though." My eyes bulged. "Well, what do you think?" He waggled it around a few times.

"About the same, I guess. But it's hard to say when it's soft."

"Leave it out," he laughed, tucking himself away.

One night, when we'd been boozing in Richmond we stopped in an alley way and wanked each other off.

Mark was a brilliant player who like most decent percussionists had forearms that were well developed and rippled when he twiddled his fingers. They were the result of hundreds of hours of tapping out rhythms on side drums and drum kits. He was always getting into trouble, mostly for being insubordinate. He was responsible for most of the graffiti around the barracks. On the wall outside the cookhouse he'd sprayed 'KH NFI' and on the front of 'A' Company block, 'FOG,' which stood for, 'Fuck off Graham.'

One Friday morning, just as the Company Commander and students were arriving at their office in our accommodation, news came from the offcoming guard that the front gates had been locked. From the students' office down the corridor, I could see something was happening. Huddles of pupils were gathering outside the office; some were shaking their heads and looking agitated. When I went to investigate, I discovered that someone had smashed two school trumpets in the ablutions. In the office, on the table lay two bent and twisted trumpets. Moments later, the students began shouting for us to parade. Bandsmen grabbed their berets or side hats and ran out onto the main road that divided the two sets of accommodation. I ran around my squad rooms to make sure everyone was on the move and then went outside to call the roll. From down the road we saw Bumtwig approaching. He always strutted around the school as if on a mission, but today, his gait had a greater sense of urgency. Bag Puss, with his poodle yapping at his heels, plodded along behind him. We looked straight ahead and our shoulders straightened. Whilst still on the march, Bumtwig barked out a command.

"Officer on parade!... Parade!... Par-aaa-de!... 'Shun!" Feet smashed into the ground. Birds flew out of the trees in panic. Silence followed.

Bumtwig stamped a guardsman's halt into the ground; his crashing feet echoed between the buildings. Having positioned himself to face Bag Puss, he expertly secured his pace stick under his left arm and threw up a snappy salute. Bag Puss responded with his typical officer's salute which was a casual touch to his forehead, rather like the movement you might make in tipping a hat. This lax manner of saluting was usual for officers.

"Your permission to carry on... Adjutant... Sah?" bellowed Bumtwig.

"Please, RSM," replied Bag Puss. Bumtwig marched into the centre of the two facing detachments, then turned around to survey our stony faces.

"I wonder which of you know why we are here," he said calmly. The fact that he was calm had an impact on us since he only ever shouted. Then his neck began to bulge and for an instant his body stiffened. He was like an athlete summoning every ounce of energy, fusing the mind and body into one accord. Then, in a great surge, he released himself.

"Par-aaa-de! Stand at... ease!... Par-aaa-de!... 'Shun!" He paused and looked around, possibly searching out someone to terrorise. "Par-aaa-de!... Stand at... ease!... Par-aaa-de!... 'Shun." He already had our total attention without having to make us jump up and down. "Right, before I start is there anybody here who is willing to own up to last night's despicable vandalism without wasting everybody else's time?"

No one moved.

"No. I didn't think as much. I come into my office this morning and the first thing I get is a phone call reporting damage to company... school, property. Then I've got to waste all our time with this parade in order to apprehend the culprits." His eyes slowly moved across the front of one rank. "Last night property was damaged in 'A' Company lines and in the process a sink smashed. Will the culprit, or culprits, step forward."

The parade was silent and interrupted only by the breeze and a plane passing overhead.

"I'll ask once more. It won't make the punishment any easier but I will acknowledge your admission. Now, is anybody going to step forward?" Bumtwig paced between detachments in a stiff and smart manner. In true officer tradition, Bag Puss hovered behind a back rank. He aimlessly kicked a pebble along the ground. His poodle skipped in and out of our ranks, yelping and yapping and snuffling at our legs. We ignored it.

"I see. Well then, let's look at it from a different angle. Some of you in 'A' or 'B' Company must have heard this event taking place. It makes one jolly great noise to break a sink. And to make matters worse two trumpets have been smashed up and left on the ablution floor. Two expensive school instruments, mindlessly vandalised. And you're telling me that nobody heard anything?" He looked around the parade willing the individual into admission with his glare.

"Right! Well, we'll just have to waste time here until someone owns up!"

"RSM, could I please interrupt," asked Bag Puss. He began walking to the centre of the parade. We waited.

"Gentlemen. Someone here knows something about last night's incident. Until further notice, weekend leave is cancelled and from henceforth everyone, students included, confined to barracks." Bag Puss's heavy jowls wobbled as he spoke. "RSM?" he shouted.

"Sah!" screamed Bumtwig.

"Notify me of any changes." With his poodle yapping at his heels, he left the parade.

"Right! You heard the adjutant. Nobody's going anywhere until I get the culprit." No one moved. Eventually Mark stepped forward and banged his rear foot loudly into a halt.

"Sir! I would like to own up." he shouted clearly. Before Bumtwig had time to reply, someone else stepped forward. It was one of 'B' company's clarinettists.

"Me as well, Sir!"

"Cpl Elwood?" shouted Bumtwig.

"Yes, Sir."

"Take their head dress and stable belts." I broke from my rank and collected their regimental insignia, such as is the custom when a soldier is arrested. Both stared ahead as I faced them.

"Now take them away to the Provost Sgt. Company Commanders, take over," shouted Bumtwig. A stutter of 'Sirs' followed his order and echoed into the distance. I began marching the prisoners away at the standard cavalry swagger of one hundred and twelve paces a minute. Suddenly I heard Bumtwig approaching, his ammunition marching boots crunched the tarmac. I looked over my shoulder, he was agitated and bluey-red faced.

"What the fuck are you doing, Cpl? Prisoners! Prisoners!... Halt!" His voice screeched into the soprano register. "You don't march prisoners to the Provo's prison in that lazy cavalry manner, Cpl!" He strutted up to the two men and intimidatingly put his face between theirs. "You jolly well march them at a punishing pace. Isn't that right Aldridge?"

"Yes, Sir." Bumtwig moved away from them and braced his chest.

"Prisoners! By the left! On the spot! Double march! Left, right, left, right, left, right, left! Lift those fucking knees!" Bumtwig made them double mark time for a few minutes and then ordered them to 'double march forward!' When they'd marched fifteen metres he ordered them to mark time until we'd caught up with them. At this point he ordered them forward again.

"You don't poofda around in my barracks, Cpl Elwood. We do everything here in the Guards fashion.

"Yes, Sir!"

"Do you know why that is?"

"No, Sir! I don't."

"Because I'm here and I am Guards!"

The guardroom was commanded by the school Provost Sgt, in this instance a Sgt in one of the Scottish infantry regiments. He ran the guardroom during the normal daylight working hours. The guardroom and its customary cells were his territory. He was also responsible for the general behaviour and bearing of soldiers walking about the barracks. Outside the guardroom, Bumtwig handed the prisoners over to the Provo who took his turn to verbally abuse them. Then he ordered me to accompany him and the prisoners to the local barber's. Through the little residential area we marched the prisoners. Past the old folks' home where surprised faces gawked at our entourage, past a bewildered woman pushing a pram. The prisoners ran on the spot for a bit and were then ordered forward. In the barber's, bored, waiting faces turned slowly to stare in disbelief. Being outside military jurisdiction, the Provo's prisoners sat and waited their turn in the queue.

It was a strange experience witnessing two opposed worlds coming face to face. Two worlds kept apart by fenced perimeters, sentries and military identification cards. Our escort, with its formality, uniforms, insignia, rank and mannerisms, stood in contrast to the relaxed atmosphere of the barber's. The Nolan Sisters 'I'm in the Mood for Dancing' began playing on the radio. It was Mark's turn for his haircut.

"What will it be, Sir?" asked the barber, somewhat confused by the bizarre situation.

"I'll have a short back and sides with..."

"You'll give him a fucking crew cut! The shortest one possible! I want his head as smooth as an egg!" bellowed the Provo. As the barber shore off his hair with electric clippers, Mark sang along to the song.

"I'm in the mood for dancing, romancin', I can't ever stop tonight." His face bore an inane smile.

"You fucking cut that out now, soldier!" ordered the Provo. In the wall mirror our eyes met. Both of us had smirks on our faces.

Mark would have been happy with an RTU, he hated KH, that's why they had smashed up two school trumpets. Instead of an RTU, they were given twenty-eight days in jail. During their sentence they were kept busy. Everywhere they went in the barracks was at the double. They spent their time dressed in green overalls devoid of any regimental insignia. They washed the pans in the cookhouse, weeded the gardens, etched clumps of grass from between paving stones, swept the pavements and road and cleaned all the windows of the school.

Liam and I continued to have sex though I knew that was all he wanted. Regularly he came knocking on my door asking for a shag. I never turned him down. I hid my feelings from him knowing that to expose them would scare him away. When horny he called by my room, he needed no pretext. On several occasions he asked for it during the day. If during individual practice, we sneaked into my bunk, making sure the window was shut and the curtains drawn. I never asked him for sex and seldom called up to his eight-man room. I was aware of the nature of our relationship and didn't have his confidence. Besides, he was fucking two women in Richmond and having a fling with a married student.

One night we went out with a group of mates. It was to our favourite Indian restaurant, Jolly's. It was the nearest restaurant to KH, visited by every pupil and student who had ever attended the school. After the meal, our mates decided to go into Richmond and took their leave. Liam and I stayed and ordered another bottle of wine. In a semi-drunken babble I confessed my feelings.

"There's something I've been wanting to tell you."

"My, you've gone all serious; what's wrong?"

I paused and stared into my wine glass.

"I think I'm in love with you. I've felt this way for weeks, since the night we first slept together."

"I was beginning to suspect, as every time I leave your room in the morning you sigh. And you've been avoiding me in camp."

"Have I? I wasn't aware of it."

"Besides, Mark told me not to fuck you around. He obviously knows something."

"Well, I hinted as much to him."

"It's difficult, Nick. I don't want a relationship."

"I know." The bill arrived and walked back to KH where he kissed me on the cheek and went straight to his room.

The summer concert season began. Foot was present at all rehearsals and constantly poised to unleash his authority on any erring Bdsm. If programmes weren't going well, if parts were weak, evening rehearsals were ordered. If the dress rehearsal faltered, even for a moment, further rehearsals were scheduled on afternoons. In hot weather, rehearsals on the Rock were quite unpleasant. In the afternoon the sun appeared over the top of the trees that in the morning had shaded us. It progressed from one side of the Rock to the other until eventually, by mid afternoon, the whole band were under its glare. It dazzled our eyes, made reading the music difficult and toasted our faces, neck and arms. Fair-skinned and red-haired soldiers were particularly vulnerable. We'd each signed out canvas cushions on which to sit and small stand lamps for when it was dark. Under the sun's full exposure our arses sweated and so we alternated cushion for hard concrete. Once your bum started getting too hot you pulled out the cushion and sat on the concrete. Not long after, your backside began to ache so you shoved the cushion back under. Ash was excused the first performance. Being red-haired he'd suffered sunburn. His eyes had become inflamed since we were prohibited from wearing dark glasses. When excused by the nurse, Bumtwig charged and fined him twenty pounds. His offending burn and red eyes were classified as 'self-inflicted wounds'. Evening rehearsals were cooler but we were disgruntled that they took place in our free time. That we had to wear 'respectable civvies' compounded our resentment. To resist the dictatorship that governed us, many pupils wore outlandish clothes. Shocking ties were worn and ill matched with inappropriately coloured shirts. Nonconformist pupils went to great lengths to find clothes that were outdated. One artillery musician wore a floppy panama hat, floral shirt, cravat and a white suit. School Orders stipulated: jacket, tie and slacks. No mention was made of colour or design. Wide bell-bottom trousers, platform shoes, cummerbunds, bow ties, shirts with enormous, pointed collars and hideous patterns all made regular appearances on the Rock.

Rehearsals were intense. Students conducting concert pieces were destroyed by Foot's cruel sarcasm. He ridiculed their technique, criticised their interpretation and poked fun at them given any opportunity. He made students shake with fear, sometimes anger, and on occasion brought tears to their eyes. Any mistake, great or small, was made fun of and then the perpetrator threatened with RTU or 'extra duties'. Notions of encouragement, sensitivity, nurture, development, were all anathema to him. Foot was far from perfect and his conducting left a lot to be desired. On more than one occasion he fucked up and then put the blame on someone else. No one was in a position to argue with him. His dictatorial, vindictive character, given free expression by protection of his rank, crushed us into total subjugation. On a rehearsal a percussionist was expected to put down his side-drum sticks and without pause move a few paces to his side, pick up the timpani sticks and immediately begin playing. It was a ridiculous switch and really needed two separate players. Of course, the percussionist missed his cue. Foot stopped the rehearsal, waving his hands frantically in the air as he always did.

"Who is supposed to be playing the timpani part four bars after letter B?" he asked, looking up over his reading glasses to the back tier of the Rock.

"I am, Sir! Pupil Vance."

"Well, Pupil Vance, will you kindly enter at the appropriate place in the score." We began the section again and for a second time Vance missed his entry. Foot waved his arms and halted us.

"This isn't some amateur band, Mr Vance; I demand profession-alism!"

"But, Sir! I have to make too quick a change and it's not possible to... "

"Not possible! Of course it is! You're just not trying hard enough. As for talking back to me and displaying insubordination, you can enjoy this weekend confined to barracks." He turned to Vance's Company Commander who was beside the rock with a small group of students.

"See to it, Student Levitt!"

"Yes, Sir!" he replied curtly. We ran through the section a third time and still Vance couldn't change to the timpani in time. Again, Foot halted us.

"That's another weekend confined to barracks, Vance. You're certainly learning the hard way."

Eventually, after Vance had been given five consecutive week-ends confined to barracks, a Guards percussionist was ordered to play the two instruments. He too was unable to make the change and so Foot shifted the musicians around so that both instruments had their own players. Despite this, Vance was punished and confined to camp over five consecutive weekends.

One afternoon Foot had a go at me. He began complaining about my tone.

"Cpl Elwood! If you spent as much time playing your flute as you do kicking and punching, you might improve."

"Yes, Sir!" I replied sheepishly. Foot's presence frightened me so much that I couldn't keep in tune. Paddy and I learnt to mime diffi-cult passages to avoid Foot's displeasure. We became experts at swaying our bodies in time with the music, running our fingers agilely over the keys of our instruments, and focusing concentrated expressions on our faces that reflected the mood of the music.

Paddy and I were bonded boozing buddies and members of the unofficial, nonconformist Animal Club. It always quite amazes me how politicians espouse the virtues of discipline in correcting the wayward habits of young offenders. At KH discipline was so severe, respect for our individuality so minimal, that we learnt to loathe the place. The Animal Club consisted mainly of those individuals stringently anti-KH. At the end of an evening rehearsal someone would shout, "Animal Night." Then we ran off to our rooms, changed out of our outlandish civvies and met up on the platform of Whitton Station. By the time we assembled we were armed with enough cans of beer or wine to get pissed before we reached Richmond, some ten minutes away. In town we ran rampage. In pubs we poured drink on carpets, broke hand-dryers in toilets, and someone would eat any flowers on tables. Paddy had a predilection for pissing in strange places. He pissed up the side of one-arm bandits and even on the saloon floor. On the train back to KH we tore up carriage seats, chucked whole seats out the door, pissed on the floors and broke luggage racks. We treated public property with the same insignificance as we were treated by the school authorities. The Animal Club also smashed property of the school; indeed we took great pride in this. On chair fatigues we ripped seating with pocket knives and smashed lighting equipment that had to be repaired on the afternoon of a concert. On Friday afternoons we went on regular machete hunts, vandalising property around the school with a machete. The air dome was a vulnerable target as it was usually empty. There were plenty of chairs to thrust and cut, and the metal strips of the heaters bent easily with a kick. Late one evening, one of the Animal Club shat on the floor outside Foot's office. We later discovered Bag Puss's poodle had been blamed for the mess.

At the Crotchet Factory, learning to skive was an important part of personal development and a matter of survival. Indeed the very rigour with which the school was run helped make many individuals master skivers. By wearing fatigue overalls, carrying clipboards, pushing wheelbarrows around, it was possible for bandsmen to move from point A to point B without being detailed for some menial, dirty task. Knowing where to hide during the afternoons was an advantage. Going to the school nurse with a stomach upset and telling her that you'd eaten a prawn curry at Jolly's earned a few days in bed. She sympathised, as she too knew the risk of seafood curries. To consolidate the ploy you rubbed a touch of talcum powder into your cheeks. In order to incur the right frame of mind you tickled the back of your throat with your index finger. A few noisy gags bent over a toilet bowl temporarily reminded you how it feels to have an upset gut. With a razor blade I learnt to nick the centre of my upper lip, squeeze the blood out and let it dry. Then, with a scabby lip that wasn't as bad as it looked, I'd visit the nurse claiming a split lip. It was worth it once I held the official 'Excused Blowing' chit. Whenever I was detailed for a rehearsal with the No1 band, the best band in the school which only played under Foot, I visited the nurse and was excused. In my time at the school I successfully avoided playing in No1 band.

Bandsmen tried to get themselves RTU'd but it never worked. Paddy was so eager to leave that he threw a brick through the Students' Mess window and then waited to be arrested. He was fined. A week later he smashed up the guardroom with a chair. He then received twenty-eight days in the jail of a nearby barracks. However, every Wednesday afternoon he was signed out by a student and escorted to the school football pitch where he played for the school team. After each match he was escorted back to his jail. Paddy, despite trying so hard, never achieved an RTU.

Late one Friday afternoon, just before work finished, the 'dot dot dot dash' rhythm tapped on my door. I was busy dry-knacking a score. It was Liam.

"How are you now?" he asked. I stood staring at him, shocked by his visit as I hadn't seen him for weeks.

"Hey, come in," I smiled opening the door. "I'm fine, thanks. And you?"

"I mean how do you feel about me, now?"

Embarrassed, I looked at the floor. "I'm okay. It's passed."

"Are you being honest? It's important that I know."

"Yes, I am," I lied. He stepped into my room and closed the door behind him.

"Look, Nick! The last thing I wanted to do was hurt you. I like you too much. I just thought that if I stayed away from you for awhile, well... that you'd get over it. I can't give you what you want. Fuck, I don't even know what I want. I never gave you any hint of an affair. Did I?"

"No. You didn't. It's all my fault, I should never have told you, but it has passed."

"I've wanted to come down to your room so much over the last few weeks, but didn't. I didn't want you to think I was using you."

"Look! I've known all along that we weren't going to have an affair. I could have pulled out at the very beginning. I've never thought, or felt, for one moment, that you were using me. I still fancy you, but I know, and always knew, that it was just about sex."

"Is there anything bad about that?"

"No! Not at all. If you're going to have a wank, then why not let someone else do it?"

"Do you still want to have sex with me?"

"Yes, I must admit I do."

"Would it fuck you up?"

"I know the score, Liam," I pleaded as twinges tweaked my dick in anticipation.

"So... got a spare half hour? My balls are overloaded." He winced, grabbing his crotch.

"Anything for a gentleman," I replied.

"On one condition," he added. "I come first!"

I locked the bunk door.

11

Only the constant tomfoolery made the concert season bearable. Paddy never took school life seriously and seized every opportunity to mess around, break things, or be insubordinate. On concert evenings, while the audience took their seats, we were hidden between the accommodation blocks. Then, on the command of a trumpet call, the band marched out onto the Rock in sections. First the percussionists who occupied the top tier, then the basses and trombones until finally it was the turn of the flutes. I was responsible for marching the flautists and oboists to the rock.

"Flutes and oboes!... 'Shun!" I would have to yell. Or "Flutes and oboes! Halt!" This was the way we had to do it. Then we marched towards the Rock and into view of the public, our instruments carried in a military manner – in the left hand, and held out vertical to the floor. Paddy, however, held his left forearm stiffly, pushed out his lower lip and injected the most focused look of concentration into his expression. Holding his back straight he swung his right arm higher than the rest of us. He parodied military protocol but Bag Puss and Bumtwig were too stupid to notice.

With the audience and band seated the arrival of the conductor was awaited. The fanfare trumpeters marched out towards the front of the Rock. The introductory fanfares, composed by students in turn, were all tediously alike, all boringly predictable. Every strident clash of harmony that typified twentieth-century civilian fanfares had either been censored by the student composers or edited by Foot on rehearsals.

"Oh, no!" said Foot while reviewing a student's fanfare. "Who do you think you are? Aaron Copland? Take out the seventh and second clashes before my next rehearsal. So terribly American!" The opening march, again composed by students, had likewise been censored. All originality had been suppressed and their marches reduced to insignificant, Victorian, Trumptonwick tootles. This was one of the central reasons we christened KH the Crotchet Factory.

Each concert had a student compere. Every Monday they had to take their cue cards to Foot who 'approved' them. Their jokes, their précis of the concert pieces, grammar and style were adjusted, which effectively prevented any student compering with an entertaining personality. To the audience, the relaxed manner in which Foot addressed each concert was elevated by the stifled manner of the compere. Likewise, when Foot conducted he ignored the regulations he imposed on students; he could move his feet around on the rostrum, conduct with both arms in tandem, display his emotions and contort his face in musical empathy. In contrast, the students stood with their feet riveted in one position and had to conduct in an awkward, unemotive manner. While Foot performed for the audience, eccentrically acting the conducting of pieces such as the 'Flying Dutchman' or 'William Tell' overtures, the students conducted trivial, little novelty pieces such as 'Bugler's Holiday' or 'Elizabethan Serenade'.

My relationship with Tom dwindled until I only ever saw him in passing. Liam started going out with a new girlfriend and his visits to my room became less frequent. Getting bored with the old solitary shuffle I began going to the local gay pub at weekends. The Imperial was one of the friendliest pubs I had visited and there was always someone to talk to. On a Friday visit I noticed an appealing lad at the bar. Other than casting a few glances, I ignored him. He was far too good-looking to be in my league. Last orders rang out and I squeezed to the front of the bar to order a drink. Next to me, by chance, stood the lad.

"Hi! My name's Greg. What are you doing later?"

My stomach palpitated. "I'm Nick and I suppose what I'm doing really depends on you." The gum and alcohol aided my confident reply.

"Well, we could go back to my place."

"Yes, that would be interesting."

"What do you do?"

"I'm in the army. I'm a Bdsm... at Kneller Hall."

"You look like a rugby player."

"God, no! That's much too aggressive for me. I practise karate, though."

"Really? I bet you can look after yourself."

"I suppose so. And what about you, what do you do?"

"I'm a croupier at the casino around the corner."

Just then someone pushed themselves through the crowd to our sides. It was a balding man in his fifties with a great paunchy belly that hung over his belt. He began talking to Greg. A moment later we were introduced.

"Nick, this is Roger; and Roger, this is Nick. He's coming back home with us." Suddenly there was a horrid churning sensation in my gut.

"Well, actually, I think I might have to go straight to KH as I've got a training session in the morning."

"We're only going to have a coffee," stressed Roger.

"Sorry, but I'll have to go straight back. It really is very nice of you, but I have to be up early tomorrow."

"There's really no problem," said Greg. "We can go back to our place for coffee and then drop you off at Kneller Hall."

"No, I have to go back," I insisted.

"There's nothing to be afraid of. After all, you do karate," implored Greg.

"Well, only a quick coffee and then I'll have to leave."

Through the hallway a large, spacious sitting room opened up. At the far end was their bedroom and kitchen. Roger and I sat down in armchairs while Greg went to make coffee. He took ages and when he finally appeared had changed into a bathrobe that exposed most of his lanky thighs. Placing my coffee on the table, he 'accidentally' spilt some.

"Oh, dear me," he exclaimed. "Oh, well, not to bother." Then he sat down on the sofa opposite in such a manner as to give me a comprehensive view of his genitals. After a few minutes' conversation, Greg got up and went into the bedroom. Every move they made provoked apprehensive voices in my head.

"Nick, why don't you go through to the kitchen and get us another cup of coffee?" suggested Roger. Bit by bit, I was drawn further into their ploy. Greg lay on his back on the bed, he seemed asleep but I knew he wasn't. I made a cup of coffee and took it to Roger. As I passed it to him a look of disappointment flashed across his face.

"Oh, Nick darling, sorry to be a lazy nuisance but why don't you get a cloth to mop up that spilt coffee?" This must be contingency plan number two, I thought. Greg had turned over and lay 'sleeping', his white cotton sheet seductively draped diagonally across his body. His big dick poked out from the edge of the sheet; it was fat and veiny with a swollen purple head. It was very inviting but ignoring him I went into the kitchen for a cloth. When I came out, surprise, Greg had woken.

"Come on Nick, why don't you get in bed with me?" He writhed ever so slightly. I leant against the door frame, casually chewing my gum which had lost its flavour an hour ago and holding a dish cloth in one hand. I fought to remain composed.

"The minute we get doing anything, fucking Granddad will get involved."

"No he won't. He's past it. Come on, get in beside me." He began stroking himself. Even with his fist clenched a few inches of shaft remained visible.

"I can't do it with him sat in there. He gives me the creeps."

Suddenly, Roger appeared at the bedroom door.

"What's up, Greg, is he scared?" he said with a horrible, seedy tone to his voice. The threat to my sexuality was a strategy that worked and I dropped the dish cloth and began pulling off my jeans.

"Scared," I sniggered. "No, I'm not."

We romp around on the bed together until Greg decides to fuck Roger. His dick is so big and fat he has problems trying to stick it in. Straddling Roger's buttocks he gives him a sharp dig in the kidney.

"Ugh... God!" grunts Roger, who, lying beside me, is in obvious pain. In the brief moment of tension, Greg manages to partly shove himself in. Roger's face twists and contorts as each centimetre of the invading monster slides deeper. His fingers claw agonisingly at the pillow whilst grunting like a tired, old boar. Eventually Greg's dick sinks home and Roger releases a long sigh. Propping himself up on his arms, Greg begins thrusting and with each vicious pump of his hips Roger grunts.

"What's he doing?" asks Roger, turning his face towards me. His mouth twists in pain. Tears well in his eyes as his cheeks turn bluey red. I'm not in the least aroused despite the efforts of my hand to tug my shrunken willy to erection.

"What's he doing?" asks Roger again as his bald head slaps off the headboard in a thumping rhythm. Greg pauses before resuming a series of deep stabs. As if tossed on a choppy sea, the bed springs bounce us up and down.

"What's he doing?" pleads Roger.

"He's fucking you," I reply.

"Oh... yes... get it right up there," growls Roger.

"Yer, go on Greg, shove right up his arse... hard," I say in an uncommitted tone. I can't believe Roger is actually enjoying this as his expression is one of great pain. Not one mark of pleasure occupies his face. Each series of thrusts contorts his mouth and scrunches up his eyes. Greg's rounded buttocks pump up and down, the muscles of his thighs straining with each exertion. His shiny, dark hair is matted to his forehead. In pleasure, his eyes are gently shut whilst his tongue pushes and presses against the inside of his mouth. He's making the sort of faces that are only made whilst shagging or wanking. Little beads of sweat trickle down his sides and dispel into the air the smell of sex and bodies. Huffing and puffing, the grunting boar taints the moment. The breaks between Greg's thrusts become shorter until eventually he launches his final attack. Muscles around his eyes twitch as ejaculation approaches. In a delirious toss of his head, sweat splashes onto my face and trickles across my mouth. It is warm and salty. Roger's explosive grunts turn to lengthy hisses as Greg's dick bulges bigger. Then, quite unexpectedly, Greg freezes. He's right on the brink of shooting and just a bob of Roger's enormous buttocks would be enough to trigger him. For several seconds they lie still until the ecstatic expression on Greg's face fades. With a wet slurping sound, he withdraws.

"Yah," gasps Roger who looks like he's about to suffer a massive coronary. His face is flushed with a grotesque strangulated hue. From the corner of one bloodshot eye, a tear slips onto his cheek. Knackered and wheezing he turns to face me. His eyes are glazed and droop like a sad old dog. With a sigh that sprays spittle into my face, his head flumps onto the pillow. In the instant his eyes close, Greg rolls beside me.

No matter how hard he tries, I just can't get an erection. Even when I think Roger has fallen asleep my pathetic willy doesn't stir. Greg uses his best hand and oral skills to no avail. My dick has shrunk to resemble a cherub's and in embarrassment I will it to grow. In my head voices are pleading not to let him think this is its normal size. His hot tongue probes my neck and I can feel the heat of his fat cock pressing into my thigh. It's so hard I feel it pulsing. Sliding my hand between us I grip its shaft in my hand. It feels like a length of hot, living iron. Just as Roger starts snoring, I begin to arouse. The buzzing twinkles of penile nerve endings console me that my dick is still alive. Finally, with a twitch, it begins to grow. In that instant, Greg kicks Roger's leg with the heel of his foot.

"Roger, Roger, he's getting a hard on." Roger lubbs over onto his side, his enormous gut flops onto the mattress. As quickly as I'd erected, I wilt. I feel an utter failure. When Greg motions me to turn over so he can fuck me, I oblige. It's the least I can do after my dismal performance. Greg pinches my buttock and as I tense in pain, he pushes himself into my donut. The agony of his entrance focuses my mind and forces upon me the commitment I lack – except that it is one of pain as opposed to pleasure. It sears through me and pushes me into the mattress. I am impaled into a paralysis that is so excruciating I gnaw on the pillow under my face. His rhythm is constant; a series of thrusts followed by a pause during which I glimpse heaven. I feel his entire length sliding in and out. His dick head, like a fat mushroom, drives up my arse like a snow plough. Every few thrusts, he pops out and without realignment rams himself back in. The sweat between us begins to squelch.

Suddenly, Roger wakes up and in a gruff voice, begins a running commentary. "Stick it right up... go on... give him a good, hard pumping." He moves closer, pushing his face against my cheek. His bared, yellow teeth are crooked and stained and his hot breath reeks of rot and cigars. I have to quell an urge to heave.

"What's he fucking doing to yer, soldier boy?" he gnarls, push-ing his face even closer so that our cheeks press together. His face is hot and clammy and his stubble pricks my skin.

"What's he fucking doing to yer?" His ruddy face a mass of tiny, ruptured capillaries. At such proximity, one enormous red eye rivets me. A chunk of dirty green sleep is wedged in one corner.

"What's he fucking doing to yer?" he orders with insistence.

"He's... fu... ck... ing me!" I cry through the pillow between my teeth.

"Yes, I bet you can feel every inch of his big, fat cock up your military arse. Can't you?... Can't you?"

"Yes! Yes! All of it," I cry.

"And it's a big cock too... isn't it?"

"Yes, yes... it's bleeding massive," I gasp.

"Go for it, Greg," gnarls Roger. Greg thrusts with renewed vig-our.

"Christ! Not so fucking hard will you!"

"Stop being a fucking wimp and take it like a man," says Roger baring his mangy gob in my face. Then Greg, who has started grunt-ing, pushes my head to the pillow and holds me there. He launches a final series of stabs which increase in tempo. Deep into the pillow, I cry out in pain. Greg's body stiffens and I feel his thighs tremble. Against my sweaty back, his stomach tightens. Suddenly, Roger smacks Greg's buttocks. It's a hard, crisp smack. The shock of the noise star-tles me and my body jerks. In the same instant Greg drives himself even farther and a deep moan rumbles passed his throat. I try to strug-gle but my head is pinned firmly to the bed by Greg's weight. Roger slaps Greg's arse again but swathed in pain, I feel nothing.

Moments later my head is freed. When he withdraws the vacuum almost sucks out my intestines. My ravaged bum hole feels as if it's passed a concrete shit. For several minutes the room is silent as we lie recovering. I twitch my sphincter to test if it's still there and it makes an embarrassing juicy noise.

"Righty-ho then, who's for coffee?" asks Roger.

"Yes, love. But pass me a towel first," Greg replies.

"One sugar," I mumble, exhausted, from my prostrate position. My chewing gum has stuck to the pillow under my head.

Even on the soft sofa my arse ached. Roger served us coffee and opened a packet of biscuits. Then a short while later, as promised, they drove me back to the school where I said goodbye and, with clenched buttocks, waddled passed the sentry to my bunk.

In a burst of fireworks the final grand concert concluded the season and we counted the chairs and stored them away under the Rock. Many were ripped, wrecked and even burnt on a bonfire by resentful bandsmen. At the stores we handed in our canvas bum-cushions and portable lamps. The end of the concert season was welcomed and the next event was the annual prize-giving. We had rehearsals which were scrutinised by Foot. There were many traditions to adhere to and these had to be practised. During the dress rehearsal, Foot called out random individuals from the audience and had them comply with the various formalities. We had to say 'Sir' here or 'Colonel' there and of course our drill had to be impeccable.

"And, for the first prize in kicking and punching, would Cpl Elwood please step forward," shouted Foot, in his drawling tone. From the centre of the stage he peered over the top of his glasses. I was shocked and started to blush. I got up and marched up the centre aisle to a growing chant of, "Hom, hom, hom, hom," to which a loud voice, probably Gig Ingham's, added, "He's got peculiar habits." By the time I'd marched up to Foot and halted, my face was purple. Foot motioned the chanting bandsmen to be quiet, during which Bumtwig, stood in the shadows, bellowed, "Stop that jolly ridiculous chanting at once!" His arms twitched and his body pivoted forward. "I said stop it!"

Foot handed me an imaginary certificate which I accepted. Then, I about-turned and marched back to my seat to renewed chanting. The following morning, Foot, who was out for a stroll, caught me doing sit-ups on the Rock. My punishment was to whitewash the entire bandstand. It took me the whole weekend.

Over greasy bacon sandwiches, mugs of coffee and beans on toast, the Whitton March was planned. We planned it in Bill's Café just outside the school. Folklore claimed the march was a tradition stretching back many years. It involved pupils climbing over the perimeter walls with their instruments to form up in a marching band formation which then proceeded through Whitton. The time and date were arranged, also the music to be played, and a Drum Major selected. Naturally, the students knew we were up to something and had a good idea what it was.

On the chosen lunchtime an unofficial trumpet call sounded and we clambered over the school walls. Almost three-quarters of the pupils paraded; only the nerds, bores, weak-willed and those on duties re-frained from marching. Bandsmen swapped headdress and instruments. Some wore joke noses or masks and the Drum Major, a musician from the Household Division, used a mop for a mace. It seemed a fitting emblem. We marched through the streets of Whitton and brought the High Street temporarily to a standstill. Led by the acrobatics of a mop, we returned to the school to find the main gates locked. On the far side of the black iron gates at which so many bandsmen had stood sentry, Bumtwig appeared. His face was red and angry. Behind him, like a small pack of fox hounds, stood a group of students armed with clipboards. The gates were opened and as we filed into the school our names were taken. Then we were ordered to parade on the square. As we stood in ranks, Bumtwig screamed abuse and threats at us. He waved his pace stick around like a weapon.

"You bunch of pranksters, I'd have you all jailed for this except that it would inconvenience a lot of other people. What on earth is wrong with you all? In my regiment, in the Guards, you'd have been charged. If my hands weren't tied by the School Bandmaster and rubbish of tradition, I'd have you charged and RTU'd. And do I spot NCOs on parade here?" He looked along the ranks and glared at the few Cpls amongst us. "A pathetic shamble! That's what you are. And what are you, Cpl Elwood?"

"Me, Sir?"

"Yes, you! You excuse for an NCO. Your regiment should be ashamed of you. What are you, lad?"

"Pathetic, Sir!"

"Say it again, louder!"

"Pathetic, Sir."

"Louder!"

"Jolly pathetic, Sir." I shouted. A few pupils sniggered.

"Jolly well wipe those fucking grins off your faces!" he yelled, his voice cracking on the final word. For the first time I could remember since arriving at KH, Bumtwig and the school didn't bother me. They could give us fatigues, but with only one week left it didn't matter. They could even RTU us but that would cause little inconvenience. As the end of the course drew near, the crushing power of the school dwindled towards insignificance.

The final days were filled with inspections of the entire premises: the Rock, the students' quarters, the practice rooms and our accommodation. Everything had to shine. I supervised cleaning my squad's rooms and areas and cleaned out my own room. In one swipe of bleach a collection of snail-like trails was wiped off the surface of my wall.

One evening, whilst I was packing my life away into boxes, Tom, who I hadn't talked to for ages, called into my room. He handed me a small package neatly wrapped in coloured paper.

"I wanted to give you this." I took it from his outstretched hand. "I know we haven't seen much of each other... but I'm sure you know why," he said sheepishly.

"Of course I do, but it was fun at the time."

"Yes, it was," he agreed, stepping forward and kissing me on the cheek.

"Can I open it?" I asked, waving the package at him.

"No! Open it, later otherwise I'll get all emotional." After he'd left, I opened it and found a copy of Brahms's Quintet in B minor, Opus 115. It wasn't a new score as I'd seen it on the bookshelf in his room. However, the fact it was his score made the gift all the more significant. Inscribed on the inside cover was a short message: 'It wasn't me – but I'm glad it happened. Tom. KH. 1981.'

On the last night in my bunk, emptied of all my belongings other than a suitcase, there came a knock on the door. I knew it was Liam wanting a final shag and had locked my door. I wasn't feeling horny, and besides, I had scoffed a take-away and wanked. Now I just wanted to go to sleep. He knocked for ages but I didn't give in and finally he gave up and probably went straight to the toilets for a solitary hand job.

In the morning there was no trumpet call to wake us and for the first time my squad were out of bed before me. Everyone was excited and smiling widely. Bandsmen swapped addresses, arranged future meetings and reminisced. At eight o'clock, when Bumtwig arrived in the school, the front gates were bolted shut and we were confined to camp until the course officially terminated at eleven o'clock. There was nothing else for us to do and we could easily have been allowed to leave early. However, in a final, pointless display of power, we were inconvenienced. Only after the clock on top of the guardroom chimed eleven times did Bumtwig allow the gates to be unbolted. Flung wide, the school emptied. Sometime shortly afterwards, Bumtwig ordered them locked and in doing so the course of 1979 became history.

12

Carl and I met in London and stayed at the Union Jack Club. This was a large hotel for service personnel. It was great to see him again. Sitting in the bar, we spent several hours updating each other on all that had happened in our lives since we'd parted fifteen months earlier.

For a military establishment, the gents' toilets were interesting. Through the thin walls of the cubicle doors, strategically placed peepholes had been drilled. We noticed that one hole spied onto the adjacent urinals. It quite fascinated us as its maker had gone to great lengths to ensure it was accurately placed. Carl took his dick out at the urinal whilst I peeped through the hole. Had it been drilled in any other location, his cock would have been obscured. One of the cubicle walls possessed a neatly cut glory hole. Four small screw marks suggested that the management had attempted to cover it up, but someone had subsequently removed the patch. The walls were scrawled with messages, some humorous and others sexual:

'Sailor, 22. Room 214.'
'Squaddie, 24. In bar.'
'19, slim, big cock. You 20-30, rough. Tonite, 2000 hrs.'
'Are you young, handsome and well dressed? Do you like pin stripe suits and regimental ties? Have you got a posh accent and lots of money? Are you an officer? If so, meet me here tonight and I'll kick your fucking head in.'

On the centre of one door was a large pencilled drawing of a penis. Caught in the moment of ejaculation it was the work of a talented hand. The engorged head bulged and veins pulsed whilst the balls were suspended in mid swing. Next morning, as every day, the walls were wiped clean.

Carl made use of the toilet's recreational facilities and spent intermittent periods cottaging and cruising. He quite fancied a lad in the bar and followed him to the toilets on several occasions.

"Well, did you see his dick?" I inquired when he returned.

"No, fucking wanker hid himself so I couldn't get a really good look. But it was quite a nice size."

"How do you know if you didn't see it?"

"Well I did of sorts. There was a puddle of water on the floor and I could just make out his size. Mmm, I thought, that's nice, neither too big or too small and certainly not bacon rindy. But then he is about eighteen."

"Fucking hell," I laughed. "if only hets knew that when they took a piss someone could be ogling their tackle in a pool of piss." Later that evening Carl called into one of the rooms advertised and had sex with a sailor. Then he advertised his room and received a caller. One lunchtime, just before we were going shopping down Oxford Street, he sucked some guy off through the glory hole. However, he didn't like the bloke's dick and bit it. He hurriedly left the cubicle whilst the guy was busy cussing.

I'd missed Osnabrück and the comfortable life that my band pursued in Rawlpindi Barracks. There had been many changes in my fifteen months' absence. Murray Leigh, our bandmaster, had become an important personality and under his leadership the band now enjoyed a high status within the regiment. Whether in the company of SNCOs, officers, or troopers he conducted himself in a manner that was neither patronising nor condescending. He could chat to pretentious officers about opera, tell dirty jokes in his mess, and beat squaddies at drinking pints of beer. Before his arrival we were considered poofs and ponces, now we were treated with respect and pride. He singlehandedly changed the nature of band life. On important functions we were now fitted in ceremonial uniforms, a luxury that few line bands could afford. He'd agreed with the Colonel that if he made the helmets then the regiment should fund the scarlet tunics. In his youth he had been a panel beater and so he designed and produced the most beautiful silver helmets. Each had a large regimental crest in its centre and was held on the head by a brass chin strap. From the top of each helmet, mounted on a spike, red horsehair cascaded. Our scarlets had velvet blue borders on the cuffs, a blue, high collar, and blue epaulettes. Yellow piping decorated the forearms and yellow trim each epaulette. On senior ranks the yellow piping was of fine gold thread. The big brass buttons down the front of each jacket were embossed with the regimental portcullis and motto.

Back in my band I continued training at the Song Do Kwan. I hadn't trained properly for several months. The club had moved premises from the school owned by Georg to a hall in a local amenity centre known as the Haus der Jugend. It took me several weeks to enter the club and resume training. On several occasions I packed my suit and brown belt and walked past the premises, apprehensive of entering. Through the frosted glass windows I watched the blurry images of students training. Eventually I swallowed my pride and joined the class. Georg was excited to see me and after an introduction ordered me to take my place at the front of the class where the senior student traditionally stands. The first few weeks were hard work as I fought back to fitness. However, several years of thorough sparring training had equipped me to deal with most attacks that were launched at me.

Within weeks of my return to Osnabrück, we were detailed a month's tour of duty at Tin City. In this military constructed town we supplied the 'civilian' population. It was a dreary place of several streets consisting of rows of houses built from breeze blocks. The air bit with a cold chill and icicles hung from the guttering which in the day dripped water like glass teats. The only heaters were coal stoves which never warmed the rooms sufficiently. We slept in sleeping bags on beds void of mattresses. Dirty plastic sheeting provided the window panes. Other than the beds, the stove, one downstairs light and a chair there was no other furniture. Cold, damp draughts blew through numerous cracks in the walls and under the ill-fitted front door. The floor was a permafrost of numbing concrete which was impossible to keep clean. The daily passage of coal to the stove left a trail of black dust. Upstairs, the bedroom lacked a ceiling which exposed the room to the whistling wind that whipped though wooden beams.

We were given civilian names before we left Osnabrück. Mine was Pavell White and I was a thirty-two-year-old Catholic factory worker. I was married, but my wife, in real life a WRAC, lived in another house. For a month we wore civilian clothes, the oldest, warmest ones we could find. In the frozen streets, as in the houses, the smoky smell of burning coal stained the air. It permeated our clothes, skin and hair. Apart from when detailed to take part in riots or street incidents, the entire month consisted of hanging around. Hence we developed our own routines: collecting coal for our fires in the mornings and at night and visiting other houses for tea or coffee. The highlights of each day were the meals provided in the town chip shop. Food wasn't cooked here but brought into the 'city' in hay boxes from a nearby barracks. We ate from our square mess tins and supplied our own knives and forks. In the evenings two bars opened, both run by bandsmen.

On the edge of the 'city' stood a small barracks. Situated on the brow of the hill, it rose up like a fortress. In each corner sombre observation posts were constructed. Dark slits gave the anonymous sentries surveillance of the town below. Above the barracks and between the lofty observation towers, anti-mortar fences were strung. The solid walls of breeze block were painted green and stood twenty feet high. A large iron gate gave access to the interior but it was never open long enough to glimpse inside. Hidden away behind walls and fences lived troops being trained for deployment to Northern Ireland. At various times of day armed squads squeezed past the gates and patrolled the town. Other than seeing troops on the street we had little to do with them. Sometimes gun shots rang out and we knew that one of us had been detailed to hide in a house and open fire on a passing patrol. The weapon was then smuggled out of the house and to another location by a series of runners. The troops, acting on their own initiative, had to deal with the situation. Late at night one often heard the screams of some 'civilian' feigning being kneecapped. It was always an eerie, lonely scream that mingled with the wind and rain. Every few days a riot was staged and we had to throw foam-padded lumps of plastic at the troops.

The band weren't the only civilians at Tin City. There were also an equal number of infantry squaddies. We kept a wide berth from them; they were all thick. Most had tattoos on their arses. They flashed them around when pissed. Each tattoo was identical, a small red devil on the left buttock. They were always drunk and their conversation base.

"Hey lads, we need to shag a couple a them fuckin' sleeping bags" (i.e. female soldiers).

"Oh, yeah, mate, but they're fuckin' hideous."

"Yeah, but ya don't look at the mantelpiece when yer pokin' the fuckin' fire."

"Me balls are like lead weights. I need to empty them."

"They're so fuckin' butch they're lesbo."

"Oh yeah, but lesbi sex... fuckin' lovely."

"Bet they're all lesbi-friends anyway."

"Have you heard about the lesbian who went to the doctor with a strapadichtomy?"

"No, should I?"

"A strapadichtomy, ger it?"

"No."

"Christ ya fuckin' cunt. She was wearing a strapadichtomy."

"Oh, I ger it. I was thinkin' she had some kinda disease. You mean she had a fuckin' dick strapped on."

From the edges of the bar timid bandsmen peeked at their rowdy bantering. Then the infantry squaddies began singing. They swung their glasses of beer, grinned at each other with glazed eyes and patted each other's backs.

"One white one, one green one and one with a bit a shite on.
And the hairs on her dicki di doe ran down to her knees."

A voice rose above their chorus; it chanted a simple leitmotiv.

"'B' Company, 'B' Company, 'B' Company boys. 'B' Company,

'B' Company, 'B' Company boys." The chorus began to desert and join the leitmotiv until they chanted in a raucous unison, "'B' Company, 'B' Company, 'B' Company boys." Then, with one mighty roar they shouted, "IN-FAN-TRY!" and poured their beer over their heads.

Huddled around a fire in a house, with beer cans at our feet, we mocked them.

"You seen the arse on that fuckin' bloke, mate?"

"Yeah, I'd like to knob 'im wi' me pork sword. Ha, ha ha."

"My knob's fuckin' massive. Nearly as big as my mortar. Blokes love it."

"Ha, ha, ha. Big dick, no brain. Ha, ha, ha."

Then we sang,

"Little Bo Peep has lost her sheep, and doesn't know where to find them." And someone started chanting: "Band Boys, Bad Boys, Band Boys!" And everyone joined in until with a climax we chanted, "CA-VAL-RY!" But no one tipped drink on their heads. We were cavalry bandsmen.

On one riot the squaddies decided to steal an SLR from one of the patrolling squaddies. He'd propped it against a wall while he was giving first aid to a 'wounded' comrade. The rifle was later found hidden in some bushes but only after reinforcements had been radioed. They arrived in an armoured Landrover. The observing instructors let the incident run its course but were angry that their scheme had been redirected by the action of 'civilians'. That evening we were paraded in the trainees' barrack at the edge of the 'city'. After a stern lecture by the training officer we were shown a set of slides from the aftermath of Warren Point. The devastation inflicted on the human body by a terrorist bomb was horrific; bodies twisted, burnt and blasted beyond recognition. Cardboard boxes were stacked with blackened, booted legs. Another contained a screaming skull with black, burnt-out eyes and a head smashed in two halves. We left the patrol barracks in silence. I returned to my dismal cold bedroom and wept.

Each of the garrison bands had separate identities. The most attractive band in the British Army were the Devon and Dorsets. They were barracked almost in the centre of the town and were noted amongst gay bandsmen as having a very desirable crop of sexy young men. Carl had been to KH with one of them and knew he was gay. Marc Carpenter was a petit little nineteen-year-old with fair hair and blue eyes. One night a group of us went out for a meal and Marc and I sat and felt each other up under the table. Nobody noticed apart from Marc's best friend, a horrid rat of a man nicknamed Zelda. Marc and Zelda were partners – of sorts. Zelda was short and fat and wore thick plate-glass spectacles behind which his enlarged eyes ogled. Zelda was into S&M and liked to tie Marc up in the laundry room – so we'd heard. Across the meal table Zelda watched our every move with insect-like eyes. I agreed to phone Marc the following morning so we could arrange to go out. Instead I spoke to Zelda who was brief and to the point.

"Hello, is Marc Carpenter there, please?"

"Who's calling?"

"Nick Elwood, 15th Dragoons."

"Marc doesn't want to get involved. Please don't bother him!"

"Pardon?"

"Marc doesn't want to get involved so please don't bother him."

"Well can I talk to him?"

"No, he's busy."

"Oh, okay then." And I put the phone down. Months later I discovered Marc had never given Zelda this message, though I suspected as much.

The most hideous band in the British Army was the 7th Hussars. We named them the 'ugly band' and nicknamed the most unattractive members individually. There was Fester, a short, dumpy teenager who looked as if he was suffering from carbon monoxide poisoning. His red face was swollen with the ripest of acne. He wore thick spectacles with clumsy black National Health frames. Then there was Das Ding (The Thing) whom we named after a John Carpenter horror film about a grotesque alien with mutating capabilities. He somewhat resembled Fester as he wore similar glasses and was likewise ridden with fresh and crusted acne. Both played trombone and the exertion required puffed their faces and inflamed their spots to the brink of eruption. Granny Smith was another character. His shoulders were rounded and accentuated by his skinny frame. His chin poked out and curled above it was a hooked nose. He wore little round spectacles and in profile resembled a grandmother who'd lost all her teeth. Gig, who was in their band, told me Granny Smith had a cleft palate and could poke string up his nose and retrieve it through his mouth.

A nearby infantry band had a drugs scene. There were five bandsmen and a senior rank who were into smoking pot, sniffing poppers and taking LSD. On many mornings our band bar lingered with the heady aroma of poppers that we blamed on smelly feet. The 'promise' I'd made the SIB occasionally ran through my mind when I was with them. Though their calling card was still stuck on the inside door of my locker, I hadn't the slightest intention of contacting them.

Apart from sharing an occasional joint these bandsmen never offered to supply us drugs. All five were their band's best musicians which again dispelled military 'educational' propaganda. Tripping out of their heads, they frequently went into town where they passed hours playing space invaders. One night I accompanied their trombone player, Lance, in the hope of scoring some dope at a student disco. Lance and I had developed a casual friendship based on our joint interest in classical music. On the edge of the noisy dance floor he confessed he was in love with me. His revelation was a shock and I didn't know what to say. After he'd bought his dope we went back to my barrack room to talk. Lance couldn't decide whether he was sexually attracted to me or attracted to my personality. I liked him a lot but didn't want to encourage him one way or the other. Eventually he said he needed time to sort things out and after a kiss left my room. We had sex several weeks later but a relationship never developed; he was always wanting to 'sort his head out'.

The garrison's Scottish infantry battalion band we named the 'squaddie band'. Their regiment insisted they wore squaddie-style working dress and so they suffered boots and itchy serge shirts. Every Wednesday their battalion held a gas attack drill and musical life ceased for an hour whilst they lazed around in Noddy suits and gas masks playing cards. Most of the bandsmen grew moustaches and tattoos and beer bellies were a common feature. Being a musician in a squaddie-minded battalion made their life difficult. Whatever the squaddies had to do, so did their band. Guard duties, morning runs, PT sessions and dress regulations encroached on their musical lives. Whenever we visited their band complex we realised how lucky we were.

There was always some sexual intrigue between the garrison's bands. In a nearby infantry band Carl was infatuated with one of the percussionists, a small lad named Miles. As far as we knew Miles was straight and spurned Carl's initial advances. Carl took him to a female strip club, plied him with drink and then wanked him off under the table when he got horny. After that, they were buddies and started sleeping together. Carl was rarely discreet and in this lay his downfall. His behaviour shocked the liberal singlies of the band and caused division within the factions. When sleeping with Miles, he seldom locked the door or closed the window to the room we shared. His blasé attitude and complete disregard for discretion made him the subject of criticism.

Carl had the knack of being able to have sex with almost anyone he wanted; gay, straight, bisexual, it didn't matter, in most cases he got them into bed. He had several affairs with squaddies in the regiment; often they weren't gay and probably just wanted sex or affection. Though Carl claimed he was bisexual, I never observed him with any women though many fawned over him. This was because 'bisexual' to Carl, as he often told us, meant 'men and boys'. One afternoon we went for a drink whilst out shopping. It was mid afternoon and apart from two teenagers, the bar was empty. They sat at stools in one corner of the square bar. She was perhaps eighteen and the boy slightly younger. His fingers stroked her hand and their voices were subdued. As he drank from his glass I noticed how red his lips were against his pale skin. We ordered two Pils and made ourselves comfortable. Within minutes the boy rose from his seat and walked towards the toilet. He was a pretty boy with slim, fine features and smooth skin. Carl followed him with a glint in his eye. For over twenty minutes the girl and I sat at opposite ends of the bar as if nothing was happening. We stared at the walls, peered with feigned interest at the decor and blindly glimpsed at our watches. Eventually Carl appeared from the toilet and a moment later the boy walked out behind him and innocently went to join his girlfriend.

"You didn't?" I asked Carl as he approached his seat.

"Yep," he replied with a smile. "And look, here's to prove." He pointed the toe of his shoe towards me. On the top of his foot and down the front of a trouser leg were glistening globs of spunk. Carl was very proud.

"Fuck! I don't believe it," I exclaimed.

Carl was dirty and naughty. Once, whilst staying at an infantry barracks, he got drunk. Ian discovered him in the toilets where he was masturbating whilst watching soldiers piss. We had to drag him out and put him to bed. When some army cadets visited, he gave one of the older boys a blow job in our bedroom. I walked into the room to find Carl on his knees at the boy's dick. In panic the boy grabbed his pants but couldn't pull them up in time. Besides, they were firmly in the grasp of Carl's free hand. With a little lick of his lips, Carl looked at me with a disgruntled glare.

"Fuck off! I'm busy."

Life was enjoyable and I was constantly in a state of high spirits. I felt as though my life had direction. The feeling of progression filled me with satisfaction. My black belt exam was months away and I was the best fighter in the Song Do Kwan. Training had hardened my body and improved my self-confidence. Musically, I'd become one of the better instrumentalists within the band and excelled in theory and history. I was starting to consider applying for a bandmaster's course at KH. Though I wasn't in a relationship, my friendship with Carl was a beneficial substitute. He was someone with whom I could express myself.

We regularly went into town in the afternoons or evenings where he performed comical little routines. Sometimes he fainted on a busy street and lay waiting for people to give him first aid. They were always big dramatic faints where his body swayed before his knees collapsed. In department stores he stood at displays with his trousers around his ankles or pranced around the store as if on an invisible hobby horse. With one hand on his hip and the other posed like a teapot spout he cantered between displays with an occasional nod and neigh. He was always the one that acted whilst I stood at a distance observing and laughing.

Besides our silly sense of humour there was also an artistic side to our relationship. Carl sat next to me in rehearsals and concerts where he was the band's principal clarinettist. We practised together and milked the subtleties of the more taxing music we played. Every dynamic, crescendo or sforzando was observed and we constantly moaned during rehearsals at players who ignored such marks. We particularly moaned at the cornets who sat behind us. They always played too loud and easily overpowered the woodwind section.

But Carl could be very stupid. He drank too much and on more than one marching band had stumbled or dropped his marches. On massed bands he occasionally squawked and screeched. Once we played at an international tattoo in Nijmegen. The parade and audience were silent as we played 'The Day Thou Gavest, Lord, is Ended'. Suddenly, from out of the calm, subdued music emerged a thick, reedy drone. It grew in intensity until it began to crack and squeak. I knew it was Carl, he was stood next to me and his cheeks were puffed out and his eyes bulging. In the front ranks the bandmaster's shoulders twitched and a few discreetly tried looking over their shoulders.

On most Sundays we went to a symphony concert in town. We used the Sunday concerts as an excuse to dress smartly in jackets and ties. Before each concert we treated ourselves to breakfast in a posh local hotel. We always bought a bottle of red wine to accompany our meal and make sure we felt pampered. During the interval we drank champagne and at the end of the concert walked around the ancient town wall towards the station. Our Sunday trip to the station always ended with a half hour's play on the Space Invaders and Asteroid video games at which we were expert. Then, after a quick loiter around the toilets, we went for a coffee or lemon tea before taking the bus back to Rawlpindi.

Railway stations in Germany, though usually aesthetically pleasing, have a seedy side to them. Their toilets are notorious gay cruising areas and the station environs are rarely far from a red light district.

We always checked for gays loitering around the toilet entrance and usually met Benno, a middle-aged man whom we knew. Benno was an eccentric little fat man who always dressed as if modelling himself on Gustav von Aschenbach from Mann's *Death in Venice*. Often he wore spats and he always carried a little polished cane. He had a collection of chequered, brightly coloured and fawn blazers and a matching collection of silk bow-ties. He usually covered his balding head with a boater. Benno had developed a crush on me and began following the band to local concerts where he indiscreetly photographed me with a cheap Instamatic camera. My comrades made light of his appearances in the audience.

"Where is he?" bandsmen asked.

"There he is!"

"Fuck! Would you look at what he's wearing."

"He got his cane with him, and a lardy bow tie."

"Oh wait for it, hand in pocket... and out comes the camera."

"Hey! It's Andy Warhol."

"Watch out Nick, he's after you."

Once Benno asked Carl and me to his home for afternoon tea. He had a quaint little flat behind the town centre. On arrival he handed us each a present. Wrapped carefully in floral paper were a delicate bone china cup and saucer. He said they had been his mother's. The framed photos in his front room, of him, a woman and girl, prompted us to ask questions. He had been married for twelve years and had a daughter who was nine years old. He had known all his life he was gay but for many years assumed a heterosexual identity. It was a mistake, he told us. He should have acted on his impulses whilst still a young man instead of hiding his true nature. Eventually, he confessed to his wife, after which she and his daughter left him. I felt sorry for Benno. He was on a doomed mission to recapture his lost youth. He haunted the station and gay bars in search of the adolescent boy of his dreams but only ever found tawdry rent boys and those prepared to take advantage of his pathetic kindness.

13

1982 was the year that dreams came true and then went wrong. I was at the pinnacle of physical fitness. My black belt exam had been set for April 3rd and Murray had recommended me for a bandmaster's course. On my innocent excursions to the station, where I caught the bus back to camp after training, I attracted the attention of several men cruising. I considered earning some extra money as a hustler and decided that on a future date I'd visit the station and look for some trade. In my new diary I made a note of my plan by writing the abbreviation 'MP' (male prostitute) on the entry for February 3rd. It wasn't that I needed money or sex but was more a test of my ability to attract men and improve my self-confidence.

That evening I put on my best clothes and went and loitered in the large foyer. It was a busy station with several Schnell Imbiss fast-food stands, a bar, restaurant, newsagent, florist and an amusement arcade. I paced between the toilets and the station entrance and noticed other men doing the same except that their patch was between the toilets and escalator or toilets and Imbiss. Like territorial animals we each had a path that we marked. Of course they could have been waiting for friends but all too often they glanced at the toilets or leered at passing men.

There's an art to loitering. It consists of anxiously looking at clocks or displayed arrival times and browsing in shop windows where you track the reflection of potential trade. Spotting other loiterers passes the time. Perhaps they glance too often at the toilet entrance or overact their anxiety. I continued pacing; browsing in one window, checking the arrivals board and glancing at my watch. Every few minutes I deviated from my path to walk onto someone else's patch. It was a tactic that hopefully made them perceive my motives as nonsexual. They were ugly, middle-aged men, probably married and after a quick fuck. All wore drab het clothes: dreary-coloured shirts and socks, shapeless jeans that either bulged or hung from their arses and tasteless chain-store jackets. Their eyes were vacant and their faces draped in destitution. Competing for a quick shag in a public toilet was the lowest to which they could sink. Apart from Benno, punters from the Gentleman were rarely seen at the station and probably went out of town to cottage and cruise in fashionable clothes, shaved faces and aftershave.

A sexy boy left the bar and headed for the toilets. I'd seen him exit from the reflection in the florist's window but had to turn to evaluate his looks. Suddenly I noticed four men hurriedly converging on the toilets from various directions. Two were the middle-aged men I'd noticed earlier. The rivalry of the situation dampened my urge to compete. I felt sorry for the boy and hoped he would use a cubicle rather than let a gaggle of frustrated straights leer at him pissing into the urinal. The thought of joining them in the hunt turned my stomach. It was far too early to go to the Gentleman and after a brief browse in a nearby porn shop I decided to return to barracks and have a wank.

Carl was my now best friend and I moved into a room with him and gave up my single-room entitlement. We passed books to each other and shared our appraisals of them. Our favourites were historical novels by Mary Renault, in particular *The Last of the Wine* and Plato's *Symposium*. In *The Last of the Wine*, we revelled in a world that reflected our ideology. It valued 'homosexual' relationships, knowledge, platonic friendship and honour. The values missing in our military lives and society were romanticised and exalted in her pages. I began composing a symphonic poem based on it. Seventeen minutes, influenced by the symphonic works of Shostakovitch and Mahler. This took only a few weeks to complete, but dry-knacking the full score and individual instrumental parts took months. Under the small lamp on my table, I scribbled away until the early hours of the morning. In the silent hours I was accompanied by Carl snoring in the background. Devotedly, he made me cups of coffee and slices of toast, collected my shopping from the NAAFI, and even brought me meals from the cookhouse. We discussed all the standard philosophical subjects: the nature of time, life after death, the concept of infinity and the like. Carl was intelligent; he had five O-levels. He could argue about all sorts of things and easily beat me in disagreements. I loved him and wanted his company all the time. Sometimes he felt squashed by my attention and became moody and secluded but generally we did everything together. Many bandsmen didn't believe our relationship was platonic.

Carl and I always shared our band bar duties. Such an arrangement meant that we weren't individually tied to duties for a week. With two gays working the bar, our clients were guaranteed good quality, clean service. At break times we served coffee and biscuits and in the evenings provided novelty snacks such as samosas or onion bahjis. We bought bottles of liqueur which the SNCOs considered 'unmanly'. Our main problem, however, was the cockroaches that infiltrated the bar when it closed. There were two cockroach colonies in our accommodation. German cockroaches occupied the bar, and fat Oriental roaches the boiler room. Both species were distinct. The

German were narrow and light brown; the Oriental ones squat, of rosewood appearance, with two little cerci protruding from the rear of their abdomen. Visiting the toilet barefooted in the dark incurred crunching them into the floor. Orientals were crunchier underfoot than were their German neighbours. Regardless of colony, we hated them all. There were thousands of them. They hid in the cracks of walls and behind the wooden panelling that encased the radiators. Spilt beer and Coke, crumbs from crisps and food made the bar a cockroach paradise. I don't know if cockroaches have ever been assessed for intelligence, but they knew at what time the bar officially closed, and crawled from their hiding holes in anticipation. Most hid waiting in the rafters where the bar spotlights caught their waving antennae and magnified them like alien monsters. It was pointless waging a war against individual roaches. There were too many of them to make any difference. Once I severed one in half with a combat knife; it dragged itself away and left its lower abdomen twitching on the wall.

On a day that we'd taken over the bar for a week's duty, Carl decided we should get rid of our unwanted guests. Buying some insect spray in a German supermarket, we waited until the bar closed and then set about spraying their hiding places. As it was past closing time they were already out and waiting, silently twitching from behind rafters or the racks of beer glasses. A few scuttled bravely across open spaces and usually escaped before we could squash them. Some of the females dropped their ootheca in their flight across the bar top. These were small, shiny brown sacks that pulsated with life. The spray stank and seemed to have no effect at all. The following morning, however, when we went to clean up from the previous night's drinking, we found the bar top and floors covered in roaches. Worse, they weren't dead but seemingly paralysed. Most lay on their backs, their disgusting legs and antennae clawing the air. They festooned the floor, they had dropped in empty beer glasses and even fell upon us from the rafters as we worked. We swept hundreds into pint glasses and lined them up on the bar, where we watched them twitching around in brown clumps.

"Let's put them in the microwave," Carl suggested. "Just a short enough blast to scramble their brains." He placed the glasses in the microwave, handling them as if phials of acid. I reached for the dial.

"How long for?"

"Let's try a thirty-second blast." The machine hummed into action and pinged when the cooking time expired. Carl opened the door.

"Christ, what a fucking stench," he complained putting a hand over his mouth. Reaching in, he carefully removed a glass between finger and thumb. Steam wafted above the brown mass of frazzled exoskeletons. He positioned it on the pristine bar top. A horrid, sweet roasting smell assailed my nostrils.

"Fuck, that's gross," I agreed and quickly buried my nose in my arm pit. Some had popped and others twitched spasmodically. When we opened in the evening a new batch, on their backs and twitching, covered the bar surfaces. They continued falling for most of the evening. We never did rid the bar of cockroaches. When sprayed by the lethal mist of official fumigators they simply escaped into our rooms, hid themselves behind our lockers and furniture, and then returned to the bar a few days later.

Carl was fussy about everything, how tidy his room was, his clarinet playing, his clothes and his food. He liked his coffee cup filled to the brim and the crusts cut off his toast, and insisted on unsalted Danish butter. On toast or bread he liked expensive preserves rather than cheap jam, which if a British brand, was considered too working-class. He always shopped in delicatessens for the best wine, fresh coffee, preserves, tea and olives. He was quick to complain in a restaurant if the food wasn't hot or to his liking. One afternoon a squaddie was busy trimming the hedges that fronted our accommodation. It was a cold, wet day and the squaddie, whom we both recognised and admired, was soaking wet. Carl opened our window and asked him if he'd like a cup of tea. In our bunk the squaddie sat in our sofa whilst I put on Beethoven's 'Appassionata' and Carl brewed Earl Grey. Then we served him buttered toast with cherry preserve and tea in Benno's bone china cup and saucer. In our little sophisticated boudoir, amongst the chinks of saucer against tea cup, we sat and made trivial conversation. I wonder what the squaddie told his mates about band life.

Carl was my leching buddy. In the town, from one end to the other, we leered at sexy boys until we were mentally and physically exhausted. Sometimes we might pass one and make little clicking noises. They grinned, looked bewildered or ignored us. Once, after clicking and winking at a passing boy, he stopped and turned around. I turned to face him as he raised his fists. Standing my ground I readied myself in a fighting position. He stopped in his steps, threw up his arms and called me 'schwul'. Then he turned and walked off down the street. We even leched during marching band. We employed a primitive body language to communicate. Carl and I stood on opposite sides of the back rank and looked out for any sexy boy on either side of the band. A nod of the head and bulge of the eyes signalled an approaching victim, whom we would then subject to our intense scrutiny. If feeling particularly daring, we winked at them.

Bands dread military exercises. In March we began a three-week exercise in a desolate, lonely location. Bitterly cold and with constant damp in the air, the mornings were typified by a thick mist that clung between the trees of the forest. It was a constant battle to keep warm and dry while we slept. Squaddies lived for an exercise, claiming them as the reason for joining. This was an interesting admission as recruitment magazines certainly never highlighted the rigours of exercise life. The regimental squaddies lived in their tanks which were hard and uncomfortable and ice-box cold inside. We rarely accompanied our regiment and instead were attached to the RAMC as medics.

I was posted to a Dressing Station that moved location frequently. We lived under tents in damp forests or on occasion in barns. My duties were to navigate an ambulance to and fro between battle locations and the station. My driver was an old Polish man who spoke no English and only a little German. At a battle location I had to administer first aid and assess those needing immediate evacuation. The casualties were usually mock ones but occasionally they had minor injuries or ailments such as upset stomachs or injured feet. Mock casualties had all manner of injuries which were realistically created.

Casualties were supplied by units known as Cas Sim. The wounds created were works of art: eyeballs hanging from sockets, intestines spilling out of stomachs, broken limbs, missing arms and grotesque bruises. I treated one casualty who had a sheep's eye attached to his face with plasticine. Compound fractures were modelled from purple plasticine with a bloody gash from which protruded a chicken's thigh bone. At the juncture where plasticine met skin, appropriately coloured creams created bruising. Many casualties deserved their Equity cards. On the battlefield they hollered and writhed or lay unconscious and when treated they hissed, complained or moaned. Having been briefed on the symptoms of their injury they were able to provide clues helpful in diagnosis. Unusual cases were thrown in to test us: mental breakdowns, shell shock, piles, buttock wounds, bodies pierced or impaled.

It's fascinating how the human body quickly adapts to the discomforts of exercise life. Cold and damp were a constant problem but the lack of regular sleep was soon overcome. After a few days I could sit down anywhere and sink straight into sleep. Then, when I had to get up and move into action, I snapped awake, grabbed my equipment and was ready to go. For most of an exercise in the field, that was how it was. Sleep was snatched in short bursts with the occasional snooze of several hours. I slept in the ambulance with the Polish driver who stunk of garlic that he ate raw. There I kept warm by covering myself with a pile of blankets carried for casualties.

Even under imaginary missile attack we casually counted, folded and packed in a procedure that took several hours. We counted out tent pegs, neatly folded canvas, coiled up guy lines and picked up litter. Meanwhile, the planes that bombed us had returned to their bases unloaded of all their sophisticated projectiles. The British had spent so many years training their troops by simulation it had now become a game.

Bunking was our right; it was the equivalent of the perks that officers gave themselves. It was considered an honourable pursuit, especially if one did so with flair. We never took exercises seriously and used every opportunity to skive or ridicule the seriousness of the medics. When packing tents and equipment or setting them up, bandsmen and NCOs disappeared into the forest while the medics enthusiastically laboured. To avoid work, we hid ourselves inside our tents or in ambulances where we slept amongst blankets. On the road, pretending to be lost allowed you time to eat at an Imbiss or have a decent crap. The officer in charge of our unit had an iron bed and mattress in his spacious, heated tent. Outside the opening stood a crate of chilled Pils. Whenever he moved, officers' mess staff loaded his perks on to the wagon and packed his tent away. One afternoon, when I complained to him how tired and cold I was, he let me sleep on his bed. In warmth and comfort I quickly fell asleep.

Exercises had grand names such as Crusader and Lion Heart. It always intrigued me who chose the manoeuvre title. Probably some crusty old Major-General who had no active service experience and little knowledge of what went on in the ranks. The army was full of contradictions.

Together with another student, Heinz, I took my black belt on April 3rd. He is now a fourth-degree black belt, still teaching in Osnabrück. Heinz was a flashy technician but lacked any power or sparring ability. He always starched his suits so that every kick and punch sounded as they do in cheap kung fu films. He had a glass eye and when I sparred him it was easy to land blows on his blind side. The grading took an afternoon during which we performed all our patterns including the one for black belt which was Chung Moo. We smashed boards of wood with combination techniques, defended ourselves against armed opponents and were questioned on first aid and teaching methods. We were examined by a panel of four black belts including Georg and Lütz. The exam was a formality; years of training separated me from the novice white belt that I once was. I knew I'd earned the right to dye my belt black. It was irrelevant whether I passed or failed. I had already become what I'd set out to be – a martial artist.

That evening, when I went back to my barracks, I carried a black belt which Georg had presented. On one end, in gold thread, was my name in both English and Korean, and on the other Korean characters for Taekwon-do. Lütz presented me with General Choi's *Taekwon-do*, a book commonly referred to by Taekwon-do practitioners as the 'Bible'. Written on the inside page was an inscription: 'To Nick. April 3rd, 1982. Lütz.' I'd taken my black belt one month after the fifth anniversary of my first lesson. In that time gaining my dan grade had become increasingly less of a goal until eventually the object of training was in the never-ending quest for perfection of technique, physical and mental harmony and development of power. For each black belt the Song Do Kwan nurtured, a hundred students had given up training. I knew that over half the students who made dan grade ceased training within a year of attaining their black belt.

One Sunday evening Carl and I argued and fell out. It was his fault; he never could control his drinking. We'd gone to visit our old BSM who had recently been commissioned as a lieutenant in the regiment. Jim and Samantha Elster had been good mates of mine since I had joined the regiment. Like all young bandsmen I'd been press-ganged into baby-sitting for pads. I hadn't minded baby-sitting for this couple as they were down to earth and enjoyed a good laugh. They didn't scrimp on the food. I continued baby-sitting until their son was a teenager. When promoted, Jim's family moved from their married pad in a concrete block estate to a spacious house in a wood. Officers' houses were in secluded locations and had large gardens.

Neither of them were going to change their ways now that they had officer status. They were too proud of their non-officer background. Of course, with the passage of time they both came to act in an upper-class way and adopted mannerisms as prescribed in the *Sloane Ranger Handbook*. We failed to realise the ability of the institution to mould you into its professional identity. Ironically, SNCOs promoted as officers were never given the same credibility by their peers as those who'd joined as officers and trained at Sandhurst. In the officers' mess, the Elsters were outsiders. They came from state schools, from council estates, had regional accents and lacked 'proper' education. However successful Jim would become, he'd always be an example of the working-class boy made good and used to proclaim the 'meritocracy' of the system.

Officers didn't have wives; such a term was common and denoted the spouses of 'other ranks'. In both official documents and verbally, there existed a clear distinction between 'wives' and 'ladies'.

A 'lady' was an officer's wife and was given the same privileges. Troops were expected to salute the CO's lady, though whether this was part of Queen's Regulations or not, I don't know. If ever I saw her approaching I avoided her. There was no way I was going to salute a civilian. By the *Sloane Ranger* dictates, ladies were supposed to drink gin and tonic. When they went to the bar for a drink, they never had to order it. A cold gin and tonic with a slice of lemon was automatically handed them. Sam always sent it back and ordered a vodka and lime. The other officers' wives looked down their noses at her, or giggled and guffawed as if she were committing a terribly naughty crime. They couldn't hide who they were, that Jim was a mere ex-NCO; he had tattoos on his arms and no proper officers bore such a working-class brand. To have mimicked the mannerisms of the mess would have been shallow. It would have been a patronising insult to their sophisticated and cultured lifestyle where such normalities as olives, smoked salmon, caviar and Pimm's are tastes cultivated from birth. So Jim and Sam flaunted their proletarian upbringing and the officers' wives tittered in exaggerated shock. But gradually, bit by bit, they assimilated into their new status. They drank Pimm's in the garden and gin indoors. (One must never be seen drinking Pimm's indoors.) They bought a horse, wore waxed Barbour jackets and green welly boots.

At Jim's, we drank lots of beer whilst ridiculing and laughing at the officers. By the time we came to leave Carl was staggering and boisterous. We walked down the darkened road with big black trees looming up out of officers' gardens. Carl started shouting. "You fucking wankers! You stuck-up fucking lardies."

"Carl! Keep your bloody voice down," I whispered insistently but he continued his barrage.

"You fucking scum. Look at you! Up here in your posh fucking houses with your stuck-up fucking Pimm's and Barbours. Oh, yaa and one must simply do this, darling."

"For fuck sake shut up! You're going to get us into trouble."

We passed the Colonel's house; it lay at the end of the street. Their front bedroom light was on. I was beginning to feel uneasy as Carl's behaviour would reflect badly on Jim and Sam. For a moment Carl was silent and I relaxed. However, he staggered to a halt and began shouting up at their bedroom window.

"Oh, Colonel Devon-Hunt, your Lordship. Oh yaa, my horsey didn't jump so well today. What, by golly, yaa! One must simply sample these delightful marinated olives. They go so well with the cucumber and mint in my Pimm's."

"Right! That's it. I'm off. He'll have the RP up here if you don't stop," I snarled.

"Piss off, Nick. I'll do what I bloody well like! Colonel," he shouted as if affectionately calling a dog. "Colonel! Oh, Colonel." Then he let out a ripping burp that echoed around nearby houses. "Colonel! You stuck-up old fart."

I quickly walked out the end of the street onto a small dirt track that led to the main road on which Rawlpindi Barracks lay. The track passed through a wood with stood an old farmyard where George I had allegedly been born. Once in the cover of the bushes I turned back and watched Carl. He passed the end of the Colonel's house. At their bedroom window the curtains moved as if someone had been peeping out into the street. I stood waiting for Carl who began stumbling over the rough track.

"You sodding idiot. They were looking out of their bedroom window. Jim'll probably getting a bollocking and fuck knows what Hunt will do to us. I can't believe how stupid you can be!"

"Stop whining on like a faggot. He won't know it was me. Besides, you didn't do anything except hide in the bushes."

"You can be a real idiot!"

"Fucking belt up and stop telling me what to do."

"No!" I exclaimed turning to face him. We stopped and confronted each other. "You fucking belt up. I don't want to get myself or my mates into trouble because of your selfish, drunken childishness."

"I'm getting tired of your moaning," he shouted as he swung a fist at me. It came as a surprise and in an instant my temper flared. I stepped back and side-kicked him in the chest. He stumbled, regained his balance and then lurched forward. My turning kick caught him on the temple but apart from a slight jar, it was an ineffective kick. My tight trousers had taken most of the power out of the technique. With a loud rip I felt them tear along the seam. In a moment's lack of concentration, Carl closed the distance between us and attacked me with a flurry of rabbit punches. I wanted to laugh; it was as if he were trying to pat me to death. I dodged them though one glanced off my jaw. Side-stepping his attack I swung my foot high in the air and brought my heel down onto his chest. Though I pulled the kick it winded him. I could tell he was hurt. He screamed loudly and advanced towards me in a rage, his arms madly flailing the air like cloth helicopter rotors. I grabbed his lead arm and pivoting my body swung my hip into his stomach. His body curled over my back and with the momentum he landed on his back. As I threw him he grasped my shirt, its buttons popped off as he fell to the ground. Before he landed, I raised my knee and positioned my heel over his face, ready to drive my foot onto his ugly phisog but something stopped me and I ran off towards the barracks. The cool evening air brushed against my naked chest and I felt the strange sensation of my arse hanging out of my trousers. I couldn't walk past the sentry in such a mess. Instead, I climbed over the perimeter fence and made my way back to the band block. That night I slept in a corner of the band practice room with a pair of rice flails beside me. In the morning, when I went for a wash, Carl was at a sink. He ignored me but busily hummed loudly. It was an annoying hum, as if to say, "Ha, ha, you don't bother me." It agitated me but when I saw his reflection in the mirror and the big yellowy blue bruise on his chest, I felt satisfied.

As I was in charge of the accommodation, I moved out of our room and into a single bunk which was my entitlement as a JNCO. I made sure that someone Carl didn't like moved in with him. I put Dave Black in his room. He complained about having to move but I callously pulled rank and made my request an order. Carl ignored me and I estimated that I would have to wait several weeks before we could patch up our relationship.

I met Andreas exactly a week after my black belt grading. On an evening warmed by spring sunshine, Ash and I walked to the 'Gentleman'. He was soon to be married to a woman he'd met at KH. Though a busy Saturday night we managed to acquire a table in front of the bar. Behind us a vase of fresh daffodils gently scented the air reminding us it was spring. In the orange glow from the lamp on our table they were the colour of rich egg yolk. Browsing the crowd in front of us, I noticed an attractive boy of perhaps nineteen or twenty. He stood with his back to us at the edge of the bar, close enough for me to hear the odd word from his conversation. He wore dark-coloured cotton trousers that clung seductively to his arse. One pocket flap stuck up giving his neatness a casual air. The legs of his trousers were loose and hid the shape of his legs. His T-shirt was striped and just the right fit to be neither tight nor loose. As his lithe body moved it shimmered over his skin highlighting the contours of his back. Every so often, when he turned his body, I caught him in profile. His hair was short, just longer than military length, and his features sharp.

The boy preoccupied me and sent pangs of desire through my stomach that sucked at my strength and weakened me. It wasn't lust but rather a desire to give myself to someone else, to share intimacy, to experience love. Bolts of longing exposed my inadequacies and made me quiver and swoon. The wine had gone to my head and I wanted a cigarette, a sure sign that I was either tipsy or stressed; tonight it was both. I never bought cigarettes and instead scrounged them off other people. Besides, I only had a couple of fags a year. A passer-by obliged my request and gave me a one without stopping to offer me a light. Taking it, I resumed my observation of the boy whilst maintaining a minimal concentration on Ash's gossip; just enough to be able to nod in the right place or interject with 'yes' or 'no'. Ash caught me unaware.

"What do you think?" he asked.

"Yes," I replied with a nod.

"You're not listening to me at all, are you?"

"Sorry! What did you say? The music's too loud."

"I said, you're not listening to me. You haven't heard a word I've said! Who are you ogling at?" He surveyed the crowd of people stood before us. "The young one stood there," he said nodding his head towards the boy. "I can spot your type straight away, Gay Boy." I put the cigarette to my lips and began searching for a light I didn't have.

"Yes," I confirmed. "He's got a nice arse, hasn't he?"

Suddenly, the boy turned around. "I beg your pardon?" he asked in perfect English.

I gawked in astonishment. "I'm sorry, what did you say?"

"Have you got a light for my cigarette?" I improvised. He took a lighter from his pocket and flicked me a flame. I leant forward and lit my cigarette. He began laughing and then sat himself on a seat at our table. I took a long drag from my fag.

"I thought you said I've got a nice arse," he said smiling. "Sorry, I must have mis-heard you."

The introduction unfolded before us as if scripted and rehearsed. How he had heard my comment, I am not sure. He must have strained his ears to catch our conversation. His name was Andreas and he was a student at a private college near Rhine. He was visiting the Gentleman with two priests from his school. He was relaxed, and joked and laughed with confident ease. He showed us a trick with a packet of Camel cigarettes. Lining up two full beer glasses, he placed it behind them. Through the glasses the camel appears in reverse. Camel cigarettes and their distinctive packet have never seemed the same since. He asked us if we were likely to be affected by the Falklands conflict which had recently begun.

"I'm not going," I said. "It's got fuck all to do with me. It's thousands of miles around the other side of the world."

"But it's part of your country, isn't it?"

"How can a place thousands of miles from British territory be part of Britain? We pinched it off the Argentineans in 1833!"

"But it's part of your empire."

"Well, the history of empire is the history of slavery and exploitation. Every country we've invaded in the name of empire has resulted in the suffering of natives."

"Me and my wife's bags are packed ready to run away," interjected Ash.

"So are mine," I added.

"But you're in the army. You're supposed to do as you're told."

"True," said Ash. "But when it comes to my life I make the choices, not the army."

"If it was a cause I believed in, like fighting for the end of apartheid in South Africa, then I'd go. Just because I'm a soldier doesn't mean that the government has the right to waste my life as it chooses. Anyway, why should I die for their so-called democracy when the democratic right to my sexuality is denied? If you ask me, we need a war for democracy in Britain."

"Calm down, Nick otherwise you'll start a war in here," laughed Ash.

"What do you think?" I asked.

"Oh, I agree with you. I've never liked the nature of British imperialism."

"Thank God for that," sighed Ash. "I was half expecting a punch-up."

How could I know my chance meeting with Andreas was to escalate into a passionate romance. Love, infatuation – what's the difference? Love is merely infatuation plus experience and familiarity. Looking back across fifteen years, I can say with all certainty that I loved him. Even today I am still in love with the memory of him.

I met Andreas again at the Gentleman. I didn't dress specially and actually arrived late to meet him. Despite my apparent casualness, I was excited and nervous. We promised to write to each other over the next week and to meet the following Saturday. He asked if I could find him somewhere to sleep so that we could spend the weekend together. Ash lived only a few minutes away and owed me favours. On Tuesday morning a letter arrived. Behind the closed door of my new bunk, I eagerly opened it. The paper matched the mauve envelope and in one corner was printed a black tree.

Dear Nick,

As I promised here is my letter and hope that I too will receive one from you shortly. Life at Handrup is boring and waiting for mail is the most exciting time of day. You can probably imagine what it is like for me here, it must be similar to the army. Many priests are gay but it's not mentioned. Only one of my friends knows I am also so it is difficult sometimes.

I spend all my time living a lie. You must have experienced this too? I had a great night with you at the Gentleman. You really make me laugh. Make sure you tell me in your letter how you are getting on with Carl. You really admire him and I'm waiting to meeting him sometime.

I hope you will be able to arrange for me to stay at Ash's over the weekend. You will need to phone my mother and tell her lies so she will let me stay with you rather than go home.

I've told her all about you and she says she would like to meet you sometime. Of course, she doesn't know I'm gay but she suspects. You can tell her that you want me to translate at a karate competition. I'm sure, if you think it's worth it, that you can make a good lie.

Do you ever listen to ABBA? I'm going to send you a tape in my next letter. They are my favourite group. I haven't eaten all day; something seems to have taken my appetite away. Mum cooked me some pizza but I pushed my plate aside. She's worried that I'm coming down with the flu or something. I had to insist I felt okay in case she kept me away from school.

At the moment I'm sitting in my room at Handrup, I share it with another student. His name's Marcus, he's good company. I've only been back in school half an hour and writing to you was my priority. Anyway, please write back soon and let's plan the weekend.

Yours, Andreas.

I _ _ _ _ Yo _

Every morning that week and for weeks to follow, I received a letter from him. It always arrived in a tasteful envelope that contained matching paper. In the evenings, I sat down and replied. Each letter became braver and more revealing.

Dear Andreas, couldn't you find yourself a more romantic name? "Andreas" is so hard and teutonic. But then nothing could be more unromantic than "Ich liebe dich". Yuk, where is the German spirit of passion?

Carl isn't talking to me and he's still got a bruise on his chest. He can be such an idiot but I know if I wait long enough we will get back together again. Ash has said it is fine for you to stay at his house. I could stay there as well, if you still want me to? Just to keep you company!

Why haven't you been eating? Are you ill? I have been feeling strange this week. I don't know what it is. I can't seem to concentrate on my work. Anyway, I will phone your mum up on Thursday and spin a few lies to her.

I've been listening to some ABBA but would welcome a tape from you. Write again very soon, like right now!

Yours, Nick

I L_ _ _   Yo _

Nick, I've just been sat studying some Latin exercises. Do you read any Latin? I just can't concentrate and something is taking up all my mind. Perhaps we both suffer from the same illness. Do you know what it is? I'm thinking it's a case of "Hals über Köpf". Thanks for phoning my mother, now we can certainly meet on Friday. My train arrives at Osnabrück at 1800. Can you meet me there?

I suppose I best tell you that I'm sixteen – and only just. I avoided telling you how old I was when you asked and felt flattered that you thought I looked twenty-something. I didn't want to tell you in case you felt it might affect our friendship but you'd have found out anyway. I should have told you two weeks ago but didn't and now I have changed, I realise 'I've been waiting for you' (ABBA). So as you can probably gather I'm really at a school rather than a college. If you are upset by this then don't reply. I don't want to get any sicker and then find out... Well, I hope you understand.

I hope you enjoy the cassette which I have included in my letter. It's got most of my favourite ABBA songs on it. Maybe you'll think of me when you listen to it. Sorry my letter is so short but I have a lot of work to do and am finding it very difficult. I really hope you will reply. "Andante, Andante. Please don't let me down."

Yours, Andreas

I Lo _ _   Yo _

Dear Andreas, I was surprised to discover your age though I can understand why you didn't tell me. The fact you are sixteen doesn't bother me – perhaps it should – but then there is only ten years' age difference between us and we could easily both be in the same old folks' home when we're older. Besides it's only friendship. Of course if ever we get caught I'll be the one who gets the blame.

I have been listening to the ABBA tape you sent me. (Thank you.) Yes, very romantic indeed! I notice you inscribed it with a Latin phrase, "Amo Te" and should warn you I have a

Latin dictionary. I am even sicker today than I was yesterday. However, I think it will pass when the weekend arrives.

Band life is no longer important and other things have been occupying my mind. I think you know what I mean. Anyway, I won't go on. "I've seen it on your face, tells me more than any worn old phrase."

Nick

I L_ _ _ Yo _

Suddenly the twice daily mail call became an exciting event. Eagerly I awaited every delivery. I could see where our correspondence was headed. The references to ABBA and the obvious spaces for the words at the end of our letters, symptoms of our 'illness'. Neither of us committed ourselves but the innuendoes were clear. On the Friday afternoon I received his final letter of the week. Holding the envelope preciously in my hand, I closed my bunk door. I waited for a moment to compose myself and indulge in the experience. To add a suitable atmosphere I put Andreas's ABBA tape on my stereo. Today's envelope was green, as was the matching paper. I opened it slowly and threw the top strip in the bin. Then I took a deep breath and opened it.

One of us had to take the plunge and diagnose our illness, or perhaps just my illness at least. I've known what's been wrong for the last two weeks; in fact since the night I first met you. Of course it takes courage to write in case I have misread your letters – but I don't think so. I hope, after you have read this, that you will still meet me at the station.

I can't stop thinking about you. You're in my every thought and in all my dreams. I can't eat and when I'm alone I sit and day dream about you. My 'illness' is simple. I'm falling in love with you. Is this how quickly it happens?

In Spe, Andreas

I Love You.

The music from ABBA's 'I let the music speak' swooned over me and I filled with warm contentment. I had just arrived at a destination for which I'd searched all my life. I was reckless to have continued a potentially gay relationship with someone so young. But no thought of terminating our friendship crossed my mind and indeed I encouraged it. I questioned my feelings; were they of love or infatuation? Only the passage of time could answer that question. The chance of reciprocal love was rare in an army environment and I seized the moment.

In an old cigar box, I numbered each of his letters and stored them safely away. As the months passed the ABBA cassette reflected the state of our emotions. Some songs had an immediate significance; others would have to wait until further developments assimilated them into a context. I kept his letters for a long time until the moment arrived when I tearfully threw them into a dustbin. Sometimes, when I want to feel the heat of one of those moments we shared, I wish I'd not been so impetuous.

14

In my red holdall I neatly folded a freshly scented, starched, white sheet on top of which I packed a pillow slip – not for sleeping on but to mop up any tell-tale signs of sexual passion. Then, on top of this a pair of jeans, a T-shirt, some underwear, a bottle of wine and two glasses. When I stepped out into the bright sunshine and walked down our little path between the silver birch trees, I became aware of how beautiful everything was, as if nature had manifested itself anew for our rendezvous. Birds chirped in the trees and the bows of the birches were heavily laden with mustard-coloured flowers. The air was scented with the smell of fresh cut grass. In my stomach I felt the knots of anxiety and excitement, in my dick the urge to have sex, and in my mind love and lust. A buzzing cocktail of emotions put a skip into my heels and made me walk tall.

I met Andreas at the station and we walked the short distance to Ash's house. He lived in a flat at the back of the railway shunting. His fiancée Dawn was a big woman of twenty-two with a very lively and outgoing personality. Like many of the bandsmen's wives and friends she had a nickname; hers was Melon Tits. She was the only woman with whom I'd ever come close to having sex. She declared it her solemn duty to either persuade or coax me to have sex with a female. I politely and wittily parried her advances but one evening, whilst she was sat in my lap and being suggestive, I developed an erection – it went no further. I don't think Ash would have minded if anything happened between us. He was convinced of the sincerity of my gayness and would have seen any sexual activity between us as a mere experiment. Dawn was an infant school teacher who brought her schoolmarm mannerisms into her social life. She loved being the centre of attraction and always performed well with an audience. Ash and Dawn were to be married in June and they'd asked me to be their best man.

Dawn cooked Andreas and me a meal and we sat and ate around their small table. Andreas impressed them. He talked to Ash about politics and stood his ground when disagreed with. Then Andreas had a conversation with Dawn in French. His French was as fluent as his English. Meanwhile, Ash showed me how to pull their sofa down into a bed. Several bandsmen had used it with their boyfriends or girlfriends. Ash and Dawn saw themselves as matchmakers and were always trying to partner couples and offering them their sofa. With their key securely in my pocket, Andreas and I went to the Gentleman.

It was a busy evening and the drag queens were out in force. We had to push past them to get to the tables at the back of the bar. They all wore exaggerated wigs, flouncy, sequinned tops, jeans and trainers. In a crowd their swirling wigs were as lethal as their flying wrists. We found ourselves a table in the back of the club. I'd never sat in this part of the bar before; it always seemed the exclusive domain of couples. Some sat immersed in conversation, their hands clasped across the table. Others snuggled up and petted. They were drawn to this part of the bar as it was quiet and secluded, the orange lighting so low that from the bar you couldn't see the tables. After much initial polite conversation we circumnavigated to the subject of emotions.

"But you've found it hard working at school?" I asked.

"Yes, of course. You're all I've thought about all week. I have to say it. Were you mad at my letter?"

"No! Not at all."

"I think about you when I get up in the morning and when I go to bed at night. I dream about you and keep saying your name over and over in my head. I'm completely 'Hals über Kopf' with you."

"I've been feeling the same way too. I really can't believe this is happening; it seems so unreal, so unexpected."

"Me too." He paused and looked at me. His big brown eyes were dilated; they were beautiful. Tingles ran down my spine and the tiny hairs on the back of my neck strained. I scrutinised his features like an artist does his model. The curve of his eyebrows, the symmetry of his nose, the shape of his lips, the downy, faint hair on his upper lip that caught the glow of the orange lamp. His eyes drew me into them like a whirlpool. I felt his hand clasp mine and our damp fingers intertwined. We swam in each other's eyes. For a moment he broke out of his trance and sipped some Coke. Tiny droplets beaded his upper lip; the tip of his tongue swiftly brushed them away. Slowly, across the table, our heads moved closer.

Our first kiss seared into eternity. Our lips met and our tongues probed. He jetted a cold stream of Coke through my teeth. The gum I was chewing hardened. A sucking passionate kiss made us breathless and sent bright carousels whirling on the inside of my eyelids. Like moles our tongues burrowed, feeling out the contours of teeth, the fullness and warmth of wet lips and the probing of the other's agile and pliant tongue. Gently, we knocked our teeth together. The chink of tooth on tooth sent pleasant, muted vibrations through my skull. His cheek was soft, hot and subtly scented with aftershave. Fine hair brushed across my forehead as his lips found my neck and nuzzled my ear. His scent invaded my nostrils and made my erection strain even harder against my jeans. We found each other's lips and began biting. Gently his hot breath surged over my face and shot shivers down my neck and shoulders. His eyes stared into me and sucked me into him. I willed myself into him, longing to capture his experiences, his hopes and fears, to capture his essence. We kissed for most of the night, taking pauses to rejuvenate ourselves by going for a piss or dancing to a slow tune.

A prolonged passion took its painful toll on our balls. Mine felt so engorged that they stabbed spasms of pain into my guts. We decided to have one more dance and then go home. Andreas rested his clammy forehead on the nape of my neck and relaxed for the first time all evening. His body was wet with perspiration, it was cold against the inside of my arms. His T-shirt clung to his body and I could feel a warm, damp aura around him. His racing heart pounded against my chest. I looked up, for the first time in hours I became aware of the mass of people around me. The drag queens delicately dabbing sweat from their foreheads, the old bald guy who always dressed as a sailor, the macho moustached men in their chequered lumberjack shirts. On the edge of the disco stood a chubby young man. He had an expression of total dejection on his face. His big, empty eyes stared at the world but were ignored. He looked as if he were staring into a world in which he played no part and across which there could be no communication. His face poured out sadness and loneliness. My arms tightened around Andreas's body and he tenderly kissed my neck. A solitary, significant kiss. Amongst the faces at the bar sat Benno. As usual, he was on his own. He stared blankly at me. His lower lip had curled out and his face collapsed around it in surrender. He too seemed to be in another world. I couldn't believe that I stood here now and held a beautiful boy in my arms. For a fleeting moment I could feel their anguish, their loneliness, their self-pity. I have been there, I thought. I too have looked and longed at the life of this alien world. Yesterday I was looking in and pining, today I'm part of the action. I pitied them and felt how part of my romance had filled them with painful thoughts that for us the club was just a prelude to the evening. They would lie lonely in their beds and we'd be vigorously shagging away. I felt my cock deflate and as it slipped down in my pants, cold, slimy strands squelched over its end.

We left the glittery, hectic Gentleman into a dark and lonely street. The air cold against our bodies reminded us how sweaty we were. Moisture was evaporating from my forearms. The soft bass beat coming from the Gentleman disappeared into the distance. Far away the city softly buzzed. The mournful hum of lone cars, the early birds, told us morning was about to break. Our footsteps echoed into the quietly humming drone of Osnabrück. We walked in silence; there was no need to talk. I could feel a slight trepidation working its way into my stomach. Little anxieties intermingled with excited anticipation. Thoughts raced and flashed across my mind. What if we don't get on in bed? How big is his cock? Or thoughts about exploring his body or what he looked like naked. We found our way into Ash's flat. Inside we fumbled in the darkness and began to pull down the sofa. He went to the toilet whilst I spread the white sheet on the bed and opened the bottle of wine. Knowing we would have plenty to drink in the meantime I moved the wine and glasses out of the way of potentially flailing limbs.

He was lying on the bed beside me, still dressed. In the morning chill the perspiration dried off our clothes. Our hands began eagerly exploring each other's torso. Through his T-shirt, silkily slipping over his skin, I feel his rib cage, the firm curves of pert pectorals and the slight undulations of muscles across his back. His roaming hands brush against my nipples and in a surge of passion I squeeze him against me. My fingers, pressing gently into his kidneys, search out a strand of muscle that when trailed will make him swoon. Gradually we play each other to the brink of oblivion, all the time moving our hands closer to each other's groin and intensifying our probing of erogenous zones. Running fingers under waistbands we brush buttocks and slip under T-shirts. He sits astride my stomach, his face illuminated by the light through the window. Hair falls down over one eye and his lips and eyes twitch and twist in response to my fingers. I run my hands under his T-shirt, over his stomach, up the sides of his ribs, in towards his pectorals and across to his armpits. My hands follow the contours of his body from one muscle group to another. As my arms rise his shirt pulls upwards. In a swift motion he slips it over his head and discards it. Before it flops to the floor my hand follows his muscle map down to his waistband. With one fluid flick I pop open his trouser button. It was almost time for our dicks to make their grand entrance. Dropping himself slightly backwards his body arches towards my feet. With one hand supporting, the other busies itself undoing my flies. The skin on his stomach stretches taut so each ridge of abdominal muscle can be traced. In the invading light I see a bulge in his pants. Verging away from the centre of his body it points to one shoulder. I run my palm across it, careful not to squash his balls. A little sticky patch appears at the top of his trousers. I press my hand harder, squashing his helmet into his lower abdomen. Dropping his jaw with a gasp his eyes close. His head falls backwards until only the point of his chin is visible. His breathing is erratic and gasping and each inhalation sends tiny ripples across his abdomen. His burrowing fingers find their way inside my flies and begin pressing themselves into my dick.

The next best thing to watching someone's freddy pop out for its first appearance is getting your hands on it, preferably when it's still clothed in pants or boxers. The floating feel of hot balls being cupped, the way they bob up and down and twitch when you pass a particularly sensitive spot. Inside an excited pair of pants is one of the most divine places for a fumbling hand to be. I juggled with his nuts and squeezed my forefinger and thumb around the swollen base of his cock. Andreas's dick boinged out and quivered briefly. Moments later mine followed and we whipped our pants off.

"Don't you dare come yet," I gasped.

"I don't intend to. I want this to last as long as possible," he whispered between clenched teeth. In the cool morning air our hot bodies sweated. With every swish of his tongue on my dick a surge of pleasure pressed me into him. It was an engulfing pleasure that fused into one my physical and mental being. Subdued Sunday sounds floated through the window: the bang of a distant door, the shunting of a train, a passing car. Eventually in synchronisation we came into each other's sucking mouths. His rigid dick drenched my tonsils in thick spunk. Unable to close my mouth I had to force my throat to swallow. Then I too felt ejaculatory tremors but before reaching my peak my dick began squirting. Several pumps later the full intensity of ejaculation hit me; with an aggressive jerk that jackknifed my body, a renewed splurge blasted into his mouth.

"Fuckin' hell," I moaned as another jerk suckled him. I collapsed into the mattress with Andreas slurping my final emissions.

A clock, somewhere in the room, ticked loudly. We lay at each other's feet recovering and re-entering our one-dimensional world. The draught from the window chilled my skin and raised goose bumps on my limbs. Along the sides of my tongue was a creamy, saline taste. Andreas positioned himself alongside me. His warm aura enveloped me in security. Propped on one elbow he kissed my lips and squirted my spent ejaculate through his teeth and into my unsuspecting mouth. It sprayed onto the roof of my mouth pooling at the back of my throat. As I swallowed, his spray continued. I hadn't realised just how much I'd come. I heard a muffled fizzle as frothy dregs flopped onto the tip of my tongue. He lay down beside me and I swallowed quickly as if taking a dose of horrible medicine. For a while we lay in each other's arms, listening to the sounds of the city and our hearts and savouring physical closeness. Andreas turned over and opened the bar of chocolate. Needing to rinse my mouth, I poured the warm wine. Beside the bottle I noticed the unused pillow-slip. I passed him a glass, lay back down and ate the chocolate he handed me, swirling the wine over my teeth and around my mouth and refreshing my palate.

"Fuck, what do we do now?" I sighed. Andreas's head lay on my chest. His soft hair, smelling of apples, brushed my chin and neck. He angled his head towards me.

"What do you mean?"

"Just that. What do we do now? Where do we go from here? What do we do after having sex like that?"

His palm stroked across my stomach. "Are you upset about something?"

"No, not at all. I've just had the most exciting night of my life. Most people I've had sex with either just lay there or haven't really been into it. Most of them were never really gay. Any that were I met in passing." He snuggled closer, his hand gently massaged my chest whilst my fingers toyed strands of his hair. "How inconsequential having sex with you, being with you, has made my life... and maybe all that is to follow. Part of me wants to stop it all now before we get into anything deeper."

"Is that what you really want, Nick?"

"No! Of course not. But you're sixteen and I'm twenty-six. I'm in the army and you're still at school. Then there's your parents. Before we even start so much is in our way."

"We can do whatever we want."

"Maybe so, but it would be difficult."

"If we really wanted to we could."

"I want to, there's no way I wouldn't want to see you again. It's just the hatred and bigotry we have to put up with. I often want to be in love and then when I am I realise the pain it causes. It's like I've been blind all my life and suddenly I've been allowed to see paradise. I don't know how long you'll be here for, whether or not we can work things out, whether I'll feel like this over a longer period... whether you will. Neither of us can say. But my biggest fear is that at some point I'll be blind again, or you'll be blind, and it will all be one painful memory. That's the problem with relationships, they're terminal. At some stage a partner suffers."

"So the only remedy is to avoid all situations that make you happy. That would make life very boring."

"Yes, I know."

"We can only take one step at a time. Whatever happens in the future will happen. Maybe we will end – who knows, but we should enjoy ourselves in the meantime. Anyway, you shouldn't be such a pessimist, it's bad for your health."

Two weeks after my bust-up with Carl, during which he constantly ignored me, an event occurred which permanently changed the nature of our friendship. Drunk in the band bar, he decided to take his new car for a spin around the town. In the early morning we heard that he'd had an accident and was seriously injured. The band block awoke and we huddled in rooms or milled aimlessly around the building. It reminded me of Kieran's death. Murray arrived and sat in his office making phone calls. No one did their block jobs that morning and all our rehearsals were cancelled. Before NAAFI break we were informed that Carl was in the local hospital, in a coma and with a poor chance of survival. He'd broken his thigh in thirteen places and was possibly blind in one eye. His mother flew to Germany and was accommodated with a pad. For five days Carl lay in a coma before finally regaining consciousness. He had always been lucky, but sadly, his luck was running out. He was transferred to the British Military Hospital in Rinteln. A leading eye surgeon visited to perform micro-surgery and saved his sight.

Carl's wrecked car was dumped at the back of our band block. That he survived was a miracle. The car had veered off a main road, knocked down a small tree and ploughed straight through a pub wall. The front of the vehicle had concertina'd, pushing the steering wheel backwards. In the violence of impact the seats had twisted out of shape. The windscreen lay smashed in a million pieces over the seats and floor. By the foot pedals one of his shoes lay pathetically covered in chunks of glass. Splats of blood stained the dashboard.

I've often wondered if the events before his accident played any part in it. If we hadn't gone to Jim and Sam's that night, if I hadn't argued and hit him, would we still be friends? Would he now be in hospital? He had so much going for him. He was an excellent musician, had been promoted to L/Cpl and was bright, a thinker. He was my idée fixe, the source from which I drew inspiration. Part of me had become Carl. He influenced the way I looked at the world. Before I met him I didn't have opinions or ideas. It was only recently I had come to realise that I had the potential to do things, to direct my life. I had self-confidence and was aware that I was sometimes more than equal to my comrades. In Carl's sexuality I found security, familiarity and empathy.

I was only able to visit him once before he was sent back to the UK for treatment and physiotherapy on his plated leg. He lay in traction wearing an eye patch. Naked from the waist up, his chest and face covered in small abrasions that had been dabbed with purple iodine.

"Nick," he whispered.

"God, what a fucking mess you're in."

"Yeah, you could say that," he winced.

"Are you in a lot of pain?"

"Some, they've got me on morphine but the worst part is being stuck in one position all the time. My arse aches like mad." I sat down beside his bed.

"So, how's the band?" he asked.

"Oh, the usual, you know, messes, messes and more messes and the same shit music. Still, I suppose I shouldn't complain, should I?"

"And how's your love life?"

"Oh, it's okay," I lied.

I left the hospital and didn't see him again for almost seven months. Carl's body survived the accident, but the Carl I knew and loved didn't. Apart from a few glimpses of his ghost I've not seen him since. His doctor told me that the brain is like a blancmange. His head had been dashed against the windscreen and we had to hope it would eventually fall back into place. I'm still waiting, still hoping it might.

Carl lay in a hospital bed in the UK and I was selfishly preoccupied with my own life. I didn't give him much thought during those months. As if he was dead, I packed away the contents of his room. I was packing a friend away for ever and though I didn't yet know it this was the closest there would be in terms of a funeral. In his room were his little treasures: his record collection, his clarinets – one pitched in A, the other in B flat – his expensive aftershave, his clothes. They all went into cardboard boxes that were subsequently sealed and packed away in our box cupboard which was the neutral zone between the German and oriental roach colonies. There they would remain until he either returned or they were forwarded to wherever he went. For protection I forced myself to hate him. I hated him because he'd abused our friendship, because he wasn't here when I needed him. I hated him because I loved him.

The cigar box in which I kept Andreas's letters, all numbered and in chronological order, filled up and I had to find a new one. In a corner of my white suitcase locker on top of my wardrobe, I hid them from prying eyes, each box secured by a blue elastic band. We wrote to each other most weekdays and he visited me at weekends when we stayed either at Ash and Dawn's or at a hotel. Twice a week, he called me from his school. He always phoned at one o'clock when I sat in the BM's office waiting. Sitting in the BM's seat, using the military phone line to talk to a gay lover, gave me a pleasurable sense of satisfaction. It was two fingers up at the homophobic institution.

My romantic disposition affected my playing. One Friday morning, before we finished work for the weekend, we rehearsed an overture of which I have forgotten the title. It was a difficult piece with a romantic, lyrical flute solo written into the middle section. That morning my flute sung like never before. My tone was fat and warm and pulsed with a subtle vibrato. Even Murray cast me a surprised glance. Then he hunched his shoulders, held one arm against his stomach and gagged as if he were going to be sick. His other arm continued conducting. I raised my eyebrows at his little joke; he couldn't faze me. Then he directed the first performance of my composition, 'Last of the Wine'. I had finished copying the parts several weeks earlier, just before I met Andreas. I was thrilled and only one wrong note marred the thousands I'd copied. When finished, the band applauded.

"Nick, that was fucking great, well done!" Hands slapped me on my back and Jim shook my hand.

"Excellent, mate. You should be proud of it."

"Not bad, Nick," said Murray without managing to look at me. "A sort of combination of Ravel and Wagner. But a good attempt. A few too many suspended thirds but you could work them out."

"Might be an ideal piece to play on a mass bands concert?" suggested Jim.

"No," said Murray, turning his back towards us and picking up his scores. "It's not dramatic enough." He began leaving the room. "Well, have a good weekend," he added on his way out.

I needed space and went and stood in the entrance alcove. Busily bandsmen packed away their equipment. It was a bright sunny day and light streamed into the doorway, a warm light that tingled my skin. I felt fulfilled. Murray's criticism didn't perturb me. He disliked my interest in music theory, composition and conducting. He secretly considered these within the sacred domain of bandmasters. I threatened his status. It was a ridiculous attitude to adopt since he was a superb conductor, theorist and flautist. The kind of musician that can put his instrument down for a couple of years and then pick it up and play as if he'd never ceased practice. He'd taught and encouraged me and should have taken pride in our achievements.

Andreas was a dirty bugger. I was the first person whom he'd had sex with but he had an exercised imagination. We tied each other up, pissed on each other, undressed seductively and indulged in a bit of pain. Used at the correct moment, aftershave on bollocks opened the gates of the twilight zone. Timing was important as the lotion took several seconds before stinging the sensitive sac. He liked to catch our spunk in a wine glass. Then we'd drink it whilst kissing. It wasn't my favourite habit but one he liked. Even if consumed fairly shortly after mixing, it would have gone cold and started to congeal. It dangled between our chins like heavily dewed cobwebs and stuck to our jowls. In the glass it was like white egg custard which had to be sucked more than sipped.

Spunk is something you drink fresh. Taking it afterwards, when cold, is rather like going to a party, pouring a decent whisky and taking it home with you. But spunk isn't whisky; it's actually quite unpleasant. Pheromones drive humans to enjoy orifices and secretions which without passion would turn stomachs. Eel 'n' mash and caviar divide us horizontally; samosas and chips divide vertically. Yet all of us, black, white, monarch and tramp are epicureans of pallid spunk, sweaty bum holes and stagnant crotches. The gentleman licks out his scullery maid's unwashed vagina with more commitment, passion and vigour than he ever experiences a glass of his expensive champagne. What does the universal love of bodily secretions and orifices say about the presumed superiority of smoked salmon or truffles?

Andreas and I rarely fucked. There were a host of other pleasures to enjoy. Like all lovers we soon discovered the right buttons to press on each other's bodies; the exact points which when played correctly coursed urges of passion through our veins and muscles. I bought him his first razor and over Ash's kitchen sink I taught him to shave. He insisted on keeping his downy moustache. With a smooth jaw he splashed on Paco Rabanne aftershave he'd bought. We'd already used over half of it on each other's balls.

Weekend engagements were a hindrance. Sometimes we were away for the whole weekend, at others for an afternoon or evening. The most regular weekend engagement was an officers' mess. We usually arrived back in barracks around midnight. It was always an anxious journey where delays, or the driver not driving fast enough, raised my blood pressure and started me cursing under my breath.

"Fucking hell, what's wrong with him? Can't he go any faster than this? I could walk back quicker. What's that silly bag doing in front? There should be a law banning crusties from driving slowly."

Back in the barracks I frantically showered, shaved and rushed into town to meet Andreas at a prearranged destination. When I was away for whole weekends, we had to forego our meetings, in which case we wrote extra letters. We'd been seeing each other about five weeks when he revealed something that was to shape the nature of our relationship. We were spending the weekend at Ash's. On our return from the Gentleman we pulled out the sofa. The little grunts and contented noises told us Ash and Dawn were asleep. By now Andreas and I had developed our own familiar routine. I spread the white sheet over the bed, tucking the corners in a military style. Andreas took the wine and chocolate from the fridge and fetched glasses. I puffed up our pillows and hid the Paco Rabanne, Vaseline and wank rag in the discreet space between the bed and the wall. By now, the wank rag resembled a giant crisp. Then we took a shower and soaped each other as we pissed over each other's legs. Dry and clean we went to bed. His body always smelt fresh, his hair scented by apple shampoo and his neck from Paco Rabanne. Even when sweaty, his arm pits smelt beautiful.

It was a particularly warm evening for early May. We'd left the Gentleman early though it was still dark and morning was some time away. The window above the mattress was open and a cool draught puffed over our sweaty limbs. Outside, the lonely clanging and banging of freight trains on the shunting obscured the buzz of the city. Inside, the house hummed with life, the creakings of wood, the gentle drone of the refrigerator. Houses are rarely silent. I laid my head on his chest, listening to our hearts. Nuzzling my cheek against his skin I felt the clamminess of our bodies. Our cheeks brushed and I became aware of a warm wetness on my face. I moved my hand and felt his cheek, then sat up on one arm.

"You're crying." He was silent.

"Yes, I know." His chest heaved and I felt him release a stifled sob.

"What's wrong?" I pleaded.

"There's something I've been wanting to tell you. I should have told you weeks ago, on the first night we slept together, but I didn't. I was afraid you wouldn't want to continue seeing me."

"Is it that bad?"

"Yes, it's very bad." His voice was nasal. I soothed his face with the back of my hand and waited. "I might have a place to study at a school in America in September," he sobbed.

"For how long?"

"A year. A whole year! I've been hoping for months that I might get a place but since meeting you I don't know what to do. I want to get accepted but I also want to cancel it." I hid my shock.

"Well, all we can do is wait and see. Let fate decide for us. You can't cancel it. You'd be losing too great an opportunity and I'd feel guilty."

"If you want to stop seeing me, either until I find out or permanently, I'd understand."

"Is that what you want?"

"Of course not. But inside there's a fire raging and you're the only one who can put it out. Make it go away for a short time, any-

190

way."

"Then perhaps we should just take things as they come. A little at a time and not worry about what the future might bring. After all, it was you that said we should enjoy the moment. Being a pessimist isn't good for you." He lay still and looked up at the ceiling. I cuddled up close and we pulled ourselves into each others' arms. He cried quietly; I didn't speak.

Andreas wouldn't go, I persuaded myself. Then the letter arrived offering him a place in Muskegon, Michigan. The reality of the situation struck home but I felt determined that if Andreas felt as I did, our relationship could continue by post until he returned the following year. From that day onwards our lives developed a sense of urgency. We wrote to each other continually and often had letters to give each other when we parted on a Sunday afternoon. However, our happiness was now tinged with sadness and despondency, as if we both faced a terminal illness.

On several occasions I travelled to his home in Lingen on the Ems canal. His mother, Rosie, was a very attractive woman in her forties. She took to me straight away and we enjoyed each other's company. I don't know if she suspected anything but she certainly encouraged our friendship and seemed to perceive it as beneficial to Andreas. He hated his father and I could see why: he was a grumpy, miserable bloke who seldom spoke and rarely smiled. Years later he and Rosie separated.

The intensity of our relationship turned me into a scheming liar. I fibbed my way out of the odd working engagement with stories about going to a wedding or funeral. I even phoned the BM's office from a local phone box and pretended to be a US army officer.

"Hello," I said in a casual American accent. I deliberately chewed gum to invest myself with a laid-back drawl. "I'd like to speak to a Bandmaster Leigh. Have I got the name right?"

"Yes, you've got the right place. This is Mr Leigh speaking. Can I help you?"

"Good morning, Sir. This is Colonel Wanesskii from the United States 4th Brigade Education Unit at Baden-Baden. Do you have a Cpl Elwood stationed in your band?"

"Yes, we do, Sir. He's our flautist but I don't think he's here at the moment."

"Well, he applied to sit some examinations with us and the entries have been confirmed. I have the dates here."

"Okay. Go ahead."

"June the 11th and 12th. I'd appreciate it if you could give him time off but of course, that's your prerogative, Sir."

191

"Well, I'll have to check my calendar but I don't think there'll be any problem, Sir. I'll pass on your message when I see him."

"Much obliged to you, Sir."

I left the phone box with a big grin on my face and spat my gum into a bin. My theatrical accent seemed to have fooled him. When I returned, the BM handed me the exam dates and gave me four days off. Nothing could be allowed to stay in the way of our few months together. Even when I contracted a muscular virus that incapacitated me for a week, I managed to struggle to Lingen for an afternoon and spend a few hours in Andreas's company. We walked from his house to the canal where the warm sun invigorated my weak muscles. A large graveyard and church stood beside the bank along which we strolled. We entered the cemetery by a rickety, wooden gate encrusted in moss and lichen. Walking between the tombstones we became solemn and reflective.

"This is what it's all about," I said. "Life and then death. People of all walks of life, the rich and poor of all ages and across generations laid out together. In death we are united."

"Graveyards always make me thoughtful," he added. "It's our final destination. But it's not death that's important. We can't escape it. It's what you've done in between birth and arriving at death that matters. It's the fun and happiness you've found that's really important."

"Yes, you're right. We can't take anything with us. It's only life that matters."

"I don't want anything to happen to you," he said looking at me. "I would rather it happened to me than you. If you were killed, or something, I couldn't stand living without you. It would be a nightmare. Of course, that's very selfish of me. I couldn't stand the pain; it would be unbearable."

"The same here," I replied.

"But if I was killed, then I'd like to be buried here. It's a beautiful cemetery. Then when you visit you'd remember our conversation today and hopefully you'd remember the good times we've had. You could be buried here too." His hand knocked against my thigh and clasped my fingers.

"Yes, I'd want that. But who knows? Perhaps we'll both end up being buried here as old men." We walked slowly between the tombs hand in hand, between rows of families, couples, through rows of people that may have been neighbours, kin or enemies. What did it matter now? Through sturdy tombstones that marked the remains of the insignificant, we walked. For a while we were silent. I pondered the span of time that separated us from death. The rows of dead highlighted my mortality. I felt the burden of all those years' pressures that we'd have to overcome: our year apart, coming out to our families and friends, my career, the upheaval of redefining social relationships, the constant uphill struggle of living under a heterosexual dictatorship. I don't know what Andreas thought about in those moments of heavy silence. My concern was the approaching death of our physical relationship and its consequences.

In him I found respite. When I snuggled up against his body and slid my hands between his thighs, drained by sex and becoming sleepy, I felt as if I were home. Nothing else mattered; there was nothing else. I was complete.

15

Murray, a prolific drinker, had accepted as many Schützenfests as possible. Such engagements were well paid and gave us extra money. Often they were in tiny obscure hamlets. Then there were the regular messes which we had to perform.

It had become a recent trend for the junior officers to conduct their respective marches at the end of a mess. The marches were shortened and we took our cue from the beat of the bass drum whilst the BM stood in the wings. In one mess we played 36 consecutive marches. The fourth was the REME quick march, 'Lillibulero'. The young officer conducting thought himself a comedian and began cantering up and down the front of the band as if riding a horse. He held his palm up high to represent the horse's head, and his legs strutted out to mimic its legs. With his free hand he smacked the conductor's baton off his arse. The officer audience thought the whole act hilarious and cheered and clapped. Then, out of the wings, stepped Murray, his face red and angry. He walked straight up to the officer, snatched the baton from his hand, grabbed him by the collar and kneed him swiftly in the bollocks. With the officer bent double in pain, Murray turned around to face the band and picked up the beat with his baton. He expected to be arrested but instead received a personal apology from the messes' CO. The offending officer received fourteen extra duties.

On German civilian engagements we were well looked after and paid. The easiest engagements that summer were a succession of supermarket openings in various towns. We usually played in stints of forty-five minutes and then took a break. On such engagements we were accompanied by a couple of adults dressed as Disney characters. They entertained the children by handing out sweets, waddling their inflated heads and performing stupid walks. At some stage we'd have to march around the store in one long conga. The Disney characters skipped alongside and threw sweets indiscriminately. We marched all over the store; up escalators, around neat mannequins and between the frozen food cabinets. We nicknamed such engagements 'frozen chicken jobs'. The managers provided us plenty of alcohol, probably to numb our sense of reality. A regiment that had charged in the Light Brigade and fought at Dettingen was now reduced to meandering between peas and frozen chickens while flanked by cartoon characters. As well as alcohol, we were also given a meal which was often in a nearby restaurant though occasionally in the complex's board room. When we ate as a band, it had become custom to toast the Queen. Ian Moore, who was now a L/Cpl, was always the toast master. Undoing his flies under the table, he pulled out his bollocks and stood to attention with his dick tucked inside his trousers. If nobody else were around he pulled his tunic to one side so we could see his balls. Then holding aloft his glass of Pils, he turned to face me.

"Gentlemen, The Queen," he said in a stately voice.

"The Queen," chanted the rest of the band in a loud chorus. They nodded their glasses and drank. I wasn't in the least a queen but it was very amusing. Ian had become a good mate. He was married now, but every morning when coming into work he called in to give me a hug. I still found him attractive but knew nothing would ever happen between us; time had mellowed my feelings.

Letters from Andreas arrived every day and I was into my third cigar box. With him I had broadened my cultural perspective. Together we'd visited the city's art galleries, museums, the zoo and every coffee shop and ice cream parlour the town had to offer. The latter were one of my favourite destinations. They sold all sorts of exotic ices, often covered in fruit and laced with liqueur. Most were run by Italians and their delicious ice cream was home-made. It was in our favourite parlour that Andreas suggested we become engaged. At first I thought it a silly idea since we'd never be able to marry. He cast aside my criticisms and argued it would help us to cope with the test we'd face when he left for the USA. I eventually agreed and over a cup of hot chocolate we decided to do so as soon as possible.

Ash and Dawn volunteered to host a party at their house and Dawn, in her typical schoolmarm fashion, designed little invitation cards which she sent out to our extended faction. The engagement was planned for a Friday evening so that afternoon Andreas and I went to buy rings. A young woman served us. We didn't want anything expensive or flashy and quickly found a pair we both liked. They were simple rings lacking any embellishment and made of white gold. I tried several on until I found one that fitted. To negate a rather embarrassing predicament, I spun the woman a yarn that Andreas's finger was the same size as my girlfriend's. She measured it.

"She has big fingers... for a woman?"

"Yes," replied Andreas. "She's a farmer." When I paid for them we received a free bottle of cheap champagne.

I remember poignant events and each year there will be a few occasions when I wear a black tie. But if there's one event of which I wish I could recall the date, then it is the day Andreas and I were engaged. As if searching to find an unmarked grave, I survey the months of June and July and wonder on which day it fell. All my close mates attended. No one was the least bothered that it was a gay engagement and that apart from Andreas we were in the military. They gave us congratulatory cards and even presents. Someone gave us socks, someone else a bottle of wine and Ash and Dawn a boxed set of ABBA records. In the middle of the party, when the alcohol had livened the company, we exchanged rings. Our fingers lingered gently as we eased them onto each other's finger.

"You need some Vaseline to help you," laughed Ash. Then we kissed as my mates cheered. They were a blur. The centre of my attention was Andreas, his brown eyes, the soft touch of his lips and the erotic scent of Paco Rabanne. We kissed. "In spe," he whispered in my ear.

Despite wives being present, Ian took his balls out and toasted 'the queens'.

I wore Andreas's ring on the third finger of my right hand from that night onwards. It felt strange and I continually played with it. Whenever I felt lonesome I twiddled it around. Some SNCOs asked why I suddenly had it on my finger. Most of them knew what it represented. "It's a ring, silly!" I replied.

I fucked him for the first time on his parents' bed when we stayed there the weekend after our engagement. His parents were away and it was an obvious place to stay. The second night we slept in his bed so we could christen it. Towards the end of July, when he'd finished school, we spent a week at a campsite near my barracks. As his departure drew near, every farewell was increasingly difficult. My hands became clammy, a knot formed in my stomach and a lump which stole and stifled my words welled in my throat. With each farewell the horrid sensations increased.

Eventually the end of August arrived and as if planning a funeral, we arranged our last weekend together. We had chosen to spend our final Sunday night at a small, plush hotel near the Johannestorwall Kirche. It was a weighty day from which neither of us could draw enjoyment. That evening the Gentleman was lively. We sat in a darkened corner and tried our best not to dwell on the morning. On the dance floor we held each other tight. We had planned the entire execution of events even to our final gut-wrenching farewell. In the hotel room we had sex but it wasn't enjoyable and we gave up and just lay entwined. Everything was for the last time: the last undressing, the last of daylight and the final communion of our bodies. We drifted in and out of a fitful sleep until the sounds of the morning heralded an ominous dawn. Finally, we had our last un-rushed, intimate embrace before we painfully tore ourselves apart.

It was still early when we left the hotel. The sky was crystal blue and the air cool and fragrant with the smell of baking bread. We took a bus to my barracks but alighted a few stops from the camp entrance. Opposite the married quarters lay a cemetery. Immense spruce trees, tended lawns and gardens fronted the large entrance. The grass was soft underfoot and coated in dew. Behind a tree that obscured us from the view of the houses, we held each other for the last time. In his hair, still damp from showering, I smelt fresh apples. Our breathing was laboured and our hearts rushed. He looked up with brown eyes; a small tear had formed in a corner of one eye. In the morning sunlight it glistened like a polished pearl.

"Don't cry. If you start, then I will," I whispered. The lump in my throat choked my words.

"I won't," he sniffed, wiping his eye. I kissed his cheek and tasted his salty tear.

"Promise you'll write to me regularly," I asked.

"Of course. You don't need to ask that." In my stomach my guts were a raging fire, twisting and stretching around as if trying to rip me in two. Though the air was cool I could feel sweat oozing from my palms and armpits. For a final moment we held each other in silence. Our bodies sucked every sensation from the experience: the touch of hand on skin, of tears on lips, of fragrance and beauty. He spoke quietly, in a voice that for the first time since I'd known him, was trembling, scared and insecure.

"This is so difficult, Nick."

"A year isn't long. It will be painful, but it will make us stronger."

"Yes, it will." Then he kissed my lips softly and floated out of my arms for ever. Between us, I was aware of our separation: now a few feet, in moments yards and soon thousands of miles.

"I love you. I'll keep every promise I've made, Nick." No one had ever said my name as he did that morning. The tone and pitch of his voice, the sad, pained expression on his face. He said it with genuine love, with awesome affection and meaning.

"Please go, before I start to cry, or you do." Then, bravely, he walked away. As if suspended in water, he drifted across the road. It was as if those brief parting moments were stretched out in time. I walked in the opposite direction, turned and looked over my shoulder, waved and called after him., "Amo te."

"Amo te," he replied. Then he turned the corner and was gone. A giant sob burst out of my tightened throat and tears began to fall from my cheek. The tears fell and fell, tears that had been welling for the last twenty-four hours. The nightmare had begun.

Half an hour later, I placed my white baseball boots, socks, pants, jeans and semen-stained white T-shirt in a carrier bag. In my sad box, a small tin of significant objects, I placed one of his cigarettes and a few strips of chewing gum that remained from a packet he'd bought.

With Andreas in America, I immersed myself in training, the most strenuous training I'd ever undertaken. The pain and exertion temporarily obliterated him from my thoughts. In the evenings I ran around the sports field until I could go no farther. Sometimes tears ran down my cheek as I ran. On an old typewriter I typed a list of the days that separated us; a total of approximately 330. I stuck the chart on my wall and every morning I religiously crossed out the previous day. I filled my spare time studying and decided to sit O-levels in music, biology and English. Despite my best efforts it was impossible for me to forget him. The letters we wrote kept the fire inside me raging. When I wasn't training or studying, I locked myself in my room and became a recluse. At night, when it was quiet, I lay and cried myself to sleep. I had never experienced crying like that. A consuming cry that shook my body, filled me with self-pity, and sent tears streaming down my face to soak my pillow.

I rented a small flat not far from the barracks with a view to living there when he returned. It was a positive move which made me feel good and boosted my frame of mind. It was a cheap, dingy flat in a building occupied by Turkish workers. There was no hot water, shower or heating. I'd recently made friends with Archie, a man who in the evenings ran a Schnell Imbiss wagon outside our barracks. He sent a plumber to my flat and for two hundred cigarettes a small heater was fitted into the bathroom. I spent several weeks engrossed in decorating every room. Past the guardroom I carried bits of furniture, a heater, bed, table, chairs and a sofa. I hadn't been given permission to take such items but no one challenged me at the guardroom. By the end of three weeks the flat looked grand. The kitchen was decorated in various shades of white and blue, my bedroom in brown and orange, the study in lime green and the tiny hallway in black and white. Army officialdom insisted I still paid for a room in Rawlpindi and so I had the luxury of two bedrooms.

In early November Andreas's letters stopped. At first, I concocted excuses for their absence. Perhaps he was busy or they'd gone missing in the post. Eventually I realised that something had happened and in my correspondence I implored his reply. He remained silent and in increasing frustration I phoned him one Sunday afternoon from a telephone kiosk outside the main gate. It was a horrid day filled with the sombreness of Sunday and accompanied by a claustrophobic, dark grey sky. Rain splashed heavily to the ground. I dialled his number and visualised his telephone ringing in distant Michigan. In the earpiece, the dialling tone sounded as if a wad of cotton wool separated the small amplifier from my ear. It was a diffuse, hazy, ring but I recognised his voice.

"Hello, Andreas Bic."

"Andreas, Andreas!"

"I can't hear you, could you speak up."

"It's me, Nick."

"Nick! Why are you phoning me?"

"I wanted to know why you haven't written. I haven't had a letter from you in over ten days. Is something wrong? It's been really hard for me."

"Yes, and it's been really hard for me, too."

"So why haven't you written?"

"I think we need to cool down. I think that will be for the best."

"Cool down! You've got to be fucking joking! I haven't stopped thinking about you since the day you left..."

"And I haven't stopped thinking about you, but it's just too painful. We really have to calm down."

"But you could have written and told me. We could work it out together."

"Look, Nick, I really can't discuss this over the phone. People are in the house."

"Andreas... Andreas." Then our brief contact was severed as the line went dead. Emptily it hummed at me.

I carried on writing to him for months but eventually realised that he wasn't going to reply. I hadn't received an explanation and thought we might patch things up when he returned. So I continued buying little things for our flat and struck out every day that passed on my calendar. There was no one I could turn to for comfort. I stopped going out and became a solitary gay.

In mid November I went home to my parents for a week. Like most young gays I had learnt out of necessity to keep my private life to myself. I came out to my mother and father on separate occasions. When my father was at work I confided in my mother and burst into tears on her shoulder. She told me that she'd suspected I was gay since I only ever brought men home. Though she did her best to comfort me, I sensed she didn't understand. She seemed to find it impossible to comprehend that what I felt for a lover was no different from that which she'd experienced with my dad. I told my father during an argument.

"I'm gay." My father looked shocked.

"You mean you're a fucking poof?"

"No!" I said. "I'm gay."

"I never thought I'd have a son who was one of them!" he shouted angrily.

I've always envied the relationship straight children have with their parents. The way they are encouraged to have partners, and can generally bring them home to become part of the family. All my partners or potential partners have been 'friends', my gay life with all its joy and pains a complete enigma to my parents. Little of my gay life was validated by them. It is as though I failed them by not being straight. They worried about what neighbours or relatives might think, worried about my contracting HIV and secretly waited for me to turn straight and take a girlfriend. We should never be happy with our parents until they are prepared to stand against bigoted society alongside us.

Christmas came and with it a card from Andreas. It didn't answer my questions and simply read 'Have a good Christmas'. My mates tried to convince me that he'd used me, that he was young and naive, that he was a wanker. At times I tried hard to hate him but if ever I did I was only fooling myself. Then Carl returned. I was in my flat one evening just before starting back at work after the holiday when my doorbell rang. He was wearing a fancy cashmere coat, a flat, fawn coloured cap, burgundy trousers and matching shoes. In his hand he carried an expensive walking stick. I invited him in and made a pot of tea. Then we sat and talked. He asked me about my love life but I told him little about Andreas. Our conversation was strained and neither of us felt easy in one another's company. I sensed the real purpose of his visit was to flaunt his new clothes and convince me he was doing well. When he left, I noticed how bad his limp was.

In spring Andreas's mother Rosie invited me to Sunday lunch. Ian volunteered to drive me the hour's journey to their home in Lingen. Their house, its fragrant odour and photos on the walls brought memories of him back from where I'd hidden them. Over the meal Rosie produced photos he'd sent her from Michigan. When she passed me them my throat constricted. Tears welled in my eyes as I looked at him in his new life, with his new friends and possible partners. I had to make witty and inane comments about each one.

"Oh! Isn't that a nice shirt he's wearing... Isn't that typical, Andreas's grumpy look?... God! Look at those icicles. It must be freezing." I wanted to run away. He was having fun and had forgotten me and the relationship we'd had. He hadn't even bothered to give me a full explanation why he'd remained silent all these months. Most painful of all, I noticed that he wasn't wearing his ring.

Within the band there was one Cpl who resented me progressing in

Taekwon-do. For years Anthony Kitchin had made me the brunt of his ridicule. "You should learn to box; learn to use your hands properly instead of in that stupid kung fu fashion... God! You're so slow. You could see that kick coming a mile away... You're too big to do kung fu. The Chinese are small and kung fu's meant for small people."

"There's more to kicking than speed," I argued. "If launched at the right moment your speed is unimportant; you're going to hit them. I might look slow from thirty feet but in front of me you wouldn't know what's coming."

"Yeah, yeah! I can't see how someone who can't kick a football can kick someone in the head." He taunted me so much that eventually I asked Georg what I should do. He suggested that next time he ridiculed me I should launch a back fist to his face but just miss. Weeks later, I did as suggested and as my fist recoiled from the surface of his skin he blocked me.

"See! I stopped it," he laughed proudly.

"No you didn't! It would have struck you."

"Can't you even tell if you hit me or not?"

Then we launched into a petty argument about whether he'd been hit. His micky-taking continued and on a subsequent occasion I sent an axe kick over the top of his head. I swung my leg up and crashed it downwards. Normally its target, struck with the heel, is the opponent's head, shoulder or chest. Instead, I brought my heel down past his shoulders. It would clearly have been a connecting technique but he chose to ignore its implication. Kitchin was our resident band socialist. Though there were one or two others who took up politics as a form of protest, Kitchin was staunchest in his views. He was also the band's biggest moaner and complained, on a regular basis, about the officers, the monarchy or our 'corrupt' SNCOs. Little everyday incidents, often caused by bad man management, he moaned about as they occurred. Often, when our morale was low, perhaps when on exercise, or when we were delayed returning from an engagement, his moaning served to lift our spirits and make us laugh. His needling intensified and he took every opportunity to criticise. I knew that eventually I would actually have to hit him.

A few weeks later the band had its annual exercise. It was still cold and as always we were sent to a bleak and desolate corner of Germany. We were attached to a TA Field Ambulance and like most territorial soldiers, they enjoyed every minute of the experience's discomfort. We loathed exercises; they took us away from our regular routine, away from our warm barracks and cosy beds. For the Territorials, they were a holiday that broke the monotony of their civilian jobs and marriages and provided an opportunity to play at soldiers. At nights we fought the cold and damp. My sleeping bag wasn't long enough so I either curled up or lay with my shoulders exposed. The food was awful: tinned stews where meat had disintegrated into individual strands, greasy fried eggs that looked as if they'd been varnished and stewed tea with a thick texture due to the use of evaporated milk. The toilets were thunder boxes, wooden seats with canvas walls. I only visited them once. When I walked through the canvas door I was confronted by soldiers conversing and shitting. I don't know why they'd erected thunder boxes as more soldiers seemed to shit in the forest.

It was on this exercise that Kitchin and I finally came to blows. We found ourselves engaged in a trivial disagreement when he unexpectedly threw a punch. It would have missed had I not stepped back into a pile of cow shit. In the soft pat my foot slipped and I fell onto one knee. In the loss of balance my head came forward and his knuckles glanced off my forehead. Looking up, Kitchin adopted a boxing posture and was busy ducking and weaving.

"Come on then," he goaded. My temper flared; I sprung forward and in one movement pulled his head onto my rising knee. He staggered back with blood streaming down his face and oozing between his fingers.

"I'm fed up with your sodding piss-taking." I shouted. A Bdsm tried to console him but Kitchin pushed him away and bent down to pick up a weapon. It was a mere twig a few inches long and would have easily snapped had he hit me with it. Holding his bloody head with one hand and the stick in the other, he advanced. My low kick thrust onto his advancing leg and made him stumble. A second kick, launched without placing my attacking foot back on the ground, thumped into his midriff and sent him sprawling.

"You've fuckin' had it," he yelled, still holding his bloody head.

"Piss off!" Then I turned and walked into the large tent behind me. But Kitchin hadn't given up. With the pathetic little stick still in hand he angrily ran towards me. In his rage he didn't see the camouflage scrim which hung down to head height from the tent's roof. It caught him in the face but still he advanced until the scrim was taut over his skin.

"You fucking bastard! I'm going to fucking kill you."

"What, with that little twig? Piss off and leave me alone before I smack you again." He struggled to free himself from the scrim which pressed into his face and squashed his nose flat. Flailing, he became thoroughly entwined. Scrim caught the buttons of his combats and ensnared his stick. Blood ran down his manic face. Eventually some bandsmen encouraged him to calm down and escorted him to the ambulance station. Kitchin was a racist and wasn't pleased when he was given stitches by a Pakistani doctor. After this he began to treat me with respect and we became mates. Whenever he overstepped the mark, I reminded him of the scar on his forehead though he never forgave me for having his head stitched by a Pakistani doctor.

The end of an exercise always caused a great deal of excitement. We anticipated it during the hours of boredom. It only took a couple of days' deprivation from the comforts of life for us to begin reminiscing.

"What I wouldn't do for a warm, dry room?"

"God, someone remind me what real food tastes like."

"Imagine if you could have a plate of chicken and chips, now."

"Chicken and chips! Oooh!"

"With thick clods of mayonnaise."

"And the chicken skin crispy and sprinkled with paprika."

"And a good dollop of potato salad."

"And a proper bog to shit in."

"Oh, fuck, yeah. A decent bog!"

Rations the consistency of baby food and a lack of proper toilets led to this topic occurring regularly. When we returned to barracks after an exercise we ran to a toilet or shower. As normal, you claimed ownership by throwing your towel or beret over a door and then went to unpack and find your washing kit. Once, desperately needing a shit, I waited to use the toilets. With pressing spasms bending my legs and squeezing my arse cheeks, I hobbled to my room. In desperation I shat into a carrier bag. It was a most wonderful shit, splodging instantly into the bag, tingling my body pleasurably and making my eyes water. I wiped my arse on some blotting paper and twirled the bag shut. I was quite surprised by its weight and mass. I'd never felt the weight of a shit before and it easily weighed over three Sunday dinners' worth. I prodded the dark mass which resembled the consistency of porridge. I felt the heat it emanated on the back of my hand. In the front of our barrack, behind the tank hangers, was a massive ditch with a dead tunnel. Rumour claimed that the SS had at one time built a series of passages under the camp. They were blocked off at some point to deny entry. Swinging the bag in my hand, I flung it deep into the bowels of the tunnel.

16

Since Andreas left I'd watched the silver birch trees outside our block shed their leaves in the wintry wind. For a spring and summer we'd lived in happiness in their shade, and in sadness I now watched each puff of wind disseminate them across the ground. Throughout winter I watched their barren branches willing them to bud. Eventually spring encouraged the growth of tiny shoots. Their leaves opened in the warmer weather and a green canopy began to block out the hot sun. Summer was here and under the new foliage I would find answers to my questions. The 330 days on my wall had almost all been etched out. After almost a year, a letter arrived from Andreas asking if he could stay at my flat over the weekend.

On the Friday afternoon, I took the carrier bag from inside my locker. One by one I lifted out the bag's contents. I lifted out my white T-shirt and ran my fingers over the material. I lifted it to my face and could smell the faint scent of his aftershave around the shirt's neck and shoulders. The smell evoked a flood of memories that swirled around in my mind: his face, his voice, his brown eyes, his soft, gentle words and lyrics from ABBA songs – 'I've been dreaming of you', 'Kisses of Fire,' 'The winner takes it all'. Songs I hadn't been able to listen to for a year. Pangs of anxiety and anticipation pulled at my stomach. I didn't know what to expect from our meeting. Deep down I hoped that when he returned we could pick up where we'd left off; that his silence had been born out of his necessity for survival, that the only way for him to cope had been to forget me. But I also knew that he could well be bringing me bad news, just tying up old ends and settling old scores before moving on.

I laid the T-shirt carefully on my bed, as if handling a precious object. Beside it I placed my white baseball boots, T-shirt, pants and jeans. Now I felt only despondency. There was a flicker of hope in my heart but it was barely alive. "In spe," I said aloud in a tone of wretched resignation. Picking up a pen I scribbled out the last days on my calendar. For a moment I was transfixed by the number of days I'd crossed out. Each one had been filled with thoughts of him. Then I showered, shaved and dressed in clothes I'd last worn on a distant day in August. Once ready I picked up my sad box in which I'd placed significant reminders of our last night together: a cigarette, some strips of chewing gum and my ring. I slipped the ring on my finger; it felt strange, alien. Then I put the tin in my pocket. Like old times, I took bus 63 to the railway station. Benno was still busy cruising outside the gents' toilets searching for his elusive dream. Like always he was immaculately dressed, this time in a yellow suit, tan Panama hat and wearing a red silk bow-tie. He carried his carved walking cane in one hand. We said hello to each other and chatted for a few minutes. He wanted to know where I'd been and where Andreas was. We'd both been missed at the Gentleman. I divulged little and skirted his questions with white lies. We parted and I took the escalator to platform six where Andreas and I had rendezvoused on so many occasions.

The large white clock suspended from the station roof loudly ticked away the seconds. Relentlessly it ticked and clunked the final minutes that brought him steadily closer. Far in the distance, where the tracks merged into a unity a dark speck appeared. The last mile of distance, the last minutes were approaching zero. Eventually the train rumbled slowly to a halt and a circle was completed. It was a green train... green, the colour of hope. Then he stepped out onto the platform. We smiled broadly and shook hands as if old acquaintances rather than lovers. He'd changed, his shoulders had broadened and he had grown taller. We took the bus to my flat and all the time he talked, about his flight, his friends in Michigan, about American television. He didn't stop talking the whole journey.

That night Ash, Dawn, Ian and Carl visited me for a drink. Carl, who'd never met Andreas, busily eyed him up as if he were the first man he'd ever seen. You fucking wanker, I thought. I felt an urge to leap up and punch him. Andreas was full of Americanisms that soon began to grate on my nerves.

"Hi, you guys... what are you guys doin'... that's so cool... that's darned good," and "that's so gross". For a second time I heard all his stories about his year away, about his bloody American family, his frigging brilliant friends and the fucking great times he'd had. Eventually I suggested we go for a walk. We left the party and ambled down the road towards the cemetery: through the wooded entrance, past the tree where we'd said our last farewell and into the vast field. It was a beautiful evening for whatever was going to happen. For a while we slowly strolled in silence. Then he took a deep breath.

"So, Nick, tell me, how have you been this past year?"

"Why didn't you write to me?"

"Ah! Here we go."

"What's that supposed to mean?"

"I've been anticipating this conversation. You know it was very difficult for me, Nick. I had a new life, an exciting life full of new experiences. Memories of you and our relationship upset me and stopped me enjoying the moment. I know we made promises but things change. I've changed; you'll have changed. We all change. That's life!"

"How profound. In what way have you changed?"

"Probably in many ways... but I think you know what I mean."

"You could have told me. Do you know what a shit year I've had? Not a day has gone past without me thinking about you. Three hundred and thirty days of you in my head. I didn't know why you stopped writing or if ever we'd get back together again. Whilst you were out having fun, I was being torn apart."

"I dealt with it the best way I could. I thought at the time that it might have made it easier for you."

"Easier for you, more like."

"That's not fair. Maybe I was wrong. Maybe I should have told you but I didn't mean to hurt you. Neither you or I are to blame for what is said and done."

"ABBA!" I spat. "I haven't been able to listen to them since you left. When you stopped writing you tainted all those brilliant memories for me. I haven't been able to think about them without fucking crying." We walked in silence, the living between the rows of the dead and the occasional bunch of flowers that commemorated them. It was a fitting location to share last rites.

"And what would you have told me? I need to hear it from you so I can finally put out the flames and get on with my life."

"That it's over between us. I don't know why. Without you there in America something died. Now all we can do is try to remember all the good times we had."

"Yes, well that's all very easy for you. You've had a year to work out what's what in your head. I've had a year of not knowing one way or the other. Besides, you're the winner."

"The winner?"

"More ABBA. You know... The winner takes it all, the loser has to fall."

"Maybe so, but that's not my fault, is it? It's no one's fault. We had so much fun, Nick. I've got such darned good memories of you and Ash and Dawn. We can still be friends, I hope?"

"That's just the easiest thing for someone in your position to say. I don't know if I can just yet. I've hated you, blamed you, cursed you and throughout all I've loved you. Fuck! I loved you so much; it was never infatuation. Now you're asking me for us to be just friends. That may take some time. Right now I feel awful, like my guts have just fallen out."

"I loved you too. I really did... something changed. I couldn't help it. I can say I'm sorry but I can't be blamed."

We headed back to my flat in a strained silence. Suddenly I was alone, my dreams finally shattered by words I wished I'd heard months ago. I wasn't in a party mood but nonetheless agreed to go to the Gentleman with Andreas, Ash and Carl. Theo was excited to see me: "Nick, mein Liebling, we've missed you. Where have you been all this time?" He put his arms around me and gave me an extra big, sluggy kiss. His thick moustache felt like a doormat. He'd put on weight which I felt cushioning my stomach.

"I've been busy. You are looking very well, Theo."

"Ja, too much cognac," he replied patting his portly belly. "And I see Ash and Carl with you." As was his manner, he kissed them each in turn.

"Oh, and Andreas too?" he said, kissing him on the cheek.

The bar was fairly full; it always was on a weekend. Amongst the crowd huddled around the small bar were faces I recognised. Benno sat at his usual spot. He smiled at me and made a fleeting contact with the world before quickly resuming his saggy, sad face. Stood against the jukebox was the chubby chap, still looking, still searching. He nodded at me in recognition. Most of the drag queens were on the dance floor busy trying to outdo each other with their practised routines. We pushed our way through the crowded bar and sat at a table in the back of the club close to where we'd first sat eighteen months ago.

It was a traumatic evening during which I concealed my anguish. I wasn't in a mood for socialising and stayed put in my seat most of the time. Ash and Ian floated around the bar talking to people they knew. Carl and Andreas frequented the dance floor. It was through misty eyes that I watched them embrace and kiss. I knew Andreas didn't fancy Carl but sensed this was his way of pressing home to me that our relationship was finished. As for Carl, well, as far as his cock was concerned he had no scruples. I was half expecting them to disappear to the toilets.

That night Andreas slept in the study of my flat while I slept in the bedroom. It was a restless night where I drifted in and out of a shallow sleep tormented by vivid, reminiscent dreams. Getting up early, I began to clean up the mess from the party. Beside my tape player lay a cassette that caught my attention. Picking it up I recognised it was one I'd sent Andreas before he left for Michigan. The tape was a compilation of pop songs relevant to our relationship and on which I'd written the words 'I Love You'. The words, having since been rubbed out, were barely visible. I recalled that he'd put the tape on the night before and that it had been a recording of a Michigan radio station. He'd insisted we listened to some of the adverts which he found very amusing. It had meant so much when I sent it to him. I had recorded all the tracks with care and affection; he had chosen to eradicate all memory of our time together.

In the morning he returned to Lingen. He made his own way to the bus stop and I watched him disappearing into the distance. The feeling that 'I am losing him for ever, without really entering his world.' Of course I felt like shit but a weight had been lifted from my shoulders. I'd confronted my worst nightmare, asked my most dreaded question and been given an answer for which I'd been prepared. I cleaned up the flat and then washed my year-old clothes, washing away a year of anguish. My bottle of Paco Rabanne was emptied down the sink and discarded into the pedal bin. From my bedside table, I lifted three cigar boxes full of letters, took them to the communal bins at the back of my flat and threw them away. I forced myself to let them fall amongst the rubbish and resisted the temptation to go back and rescue them.

Not a letter, postcard or phone call passed between us. I know I loved him, that I wasn't just infatuated, because for years I thought of him. At first it was every day, then every few days, eventually just on special occasions such as his birthday. He has become a dead soul commemorated on April 8th, who occasionally haunts my thoughts and sends me crashing back through time to a place where life was a cocktail of contradictory emotions.

A new recruit joined us from JLR. Lee Purvis was an unfortunate character; at eighteen, he was in the middle of a teenage explosion. His face and hair were greasy, he had a runaway acne problem and was short and chubby with little piggy eyes in a permanent squint. As if to confirm his unattractiveness, he was given two nicknames, Peanut Cluster and Toad Eye – because of the skin tags hanging off his back and one small one on his eyelid which you only ever noticed if he was asleep. He was incredibly clumsy. In marching displays he was a liability, either dropping his march cards or making a wrong manoeuvre. On another occasion, rather than ask the BM to stop the bus, he shat his pants. On the trombone, however, he was a virtuoso. His tone was strong and his interpretation precise. He attracted envy from a few Cpls and SNCOs who weren't pleased with his combination of musical ability and youth. When playing, his fat, exploded face puffed up and his piggy eyes closed almost completely. That such a beautiful sound was the product of one so young and unattractive was hard to believe.

As usual, we were detailed for an exercise as soon as the bitter German winter set in. The annual medical competition was between teams from garrison bands, each headed by a SNCO. I was put in command of our 'sink group' – the established failures. Lee, Alan Shearing, David Black, Ash Brown and others, the bandsmen who were guaranteed to throw our chances down the drain.

I wasn't looking forward to it, the night escape and evasion manoeuvre, the casualty simulation tests, the firing range and the gas chamber. I didn't detail tasks but let team members volunteer. David proficiently treated a head wound and Ash dealt with a resuscitation. Alan chose map reading and led us to checkpoints over dark, treacherous countryside with absolute precision. We hit a river where a wooden bridge should have stood. It had collapsed and lay broken in the water. Unsure what to do I asked him where else we could cross. In that instant, Ash shouted, "Fuck the bridge," and jumped, machine gun above head, into the icy water. The rest of us followed and his short cut saved us a twenty-minute march. By the end of the first day Lee and David had the most bloody blisters on their heels. They had stupidly worn new boots and their heels were gnawed raw. But they finished the fifteen-mile night march with hardly a complaint. We found someone suitable for every task. After two days of exhausting tests and three nights with little sleep the final event was the battle run. We dreaded it. Set in a large sand crater with fiendishly steep banks the entire ordeal was executed with tactical regard to a hostile enemy. The casualties were lying at the bottom of the pit, obscured by undergrowth as were the trip-wires and snipers.

Armed with SMGs and one stretcher we plunged down the bank. Thunder flares pounded our heads and threw sand and dirt high into the air. The cloying, dusty fog encrusted our hair and skin. We reached a burnt-out tank with its injured crew. A soldier walked in circles muttering to himself, another had his guts hanging out, another a broken arm. We rushed to treat them as a sniper opened fire. Lee and Alan deployed to a ditch and covered us. David strapped the stomach wound, knees up and torso propped, onto a stretcher. He was practically sitting upright. I knew it would make the stretcher harder to handle but we couldn't lie him flat. With covering fire we pulled out. Ploughing through undergrowth with our heads bowed, the stomach wound shielding his face with one arm to avoid the whipping branches. The stretcher bearers' slung weapons jerked precariously close to the casualty's head. I didn't have to shout orders, there was no need. Alan caught us up and slickly relieved Ash on the front of the stretcher. Ash dropped to the rear to provide covering fire as Lee appeared to replace the rear bearer. Suddenly, to our sides several thunder flashes exploded and sprayed us in dust.

"Fucking hell!"

"Keep going, we're almost clear," Ash yelled. Our legs were already wobbling, our breathing laboured and our faces twisted by effort. We stopped and assembled in the final cover, before us loomed the enormous sand bank.

"Christ, I'm fucked," gasped Lee.

I slapped him on the back. "One big push and we're home. Right, let's get the walking wounded to the top. Alan, Geoff, get one each and don't let them go. I'll go with you as cover. The rest of you stay here and give covering fire. When you get to the top stay there and cover us. I'll come back down to help with the stretcher. Saddle up, let's go."

I dashed out from the cover of bushes and began bounding up the hill. My feet sank in sand and frustrated my efforts. For every two steps I gained one. A thunderflash exploded and chucked up a screen of dirt. I threw myself into a small ditch, cocked the SMG and laid down covering fire. I didn't aim, it was pointless, there were no visible targets and my chest heaved so much that the barrel rose up and down aimlessly. It jerked in my grip as it fired and spent cartridges spat onto the dirt beside me. Through the haze of sand Alan and Geoff appeared with their casualties.

"Fucking run!" I screamed. Geoff's face was purple. He was finding it difficult to sustain his energy.

"C'mon, push it. We're nearly there." I looked above me, the ridge of the bank was only twenty metres away. Jumping out of my hole I struggled upwards. Stopping short of the top I found cover and resumed firing. Geoff was straggling, hindered by his shell-shocked casualty. Alan passed me, looking as if he were crying in pain. He had one hand on his casualty's back and was shoving him along.

"Go for it Al, you're nearly there." Then I turned to Geoff, he was only half way up the bank and his casualty wasn't co-operating. He kept trying to sit down and had obviously been detailed to be awkward. As Alan disappeared over the top of the hill I jumped out of my recess and bounded towards Geoff.

"Fuck this," Geoff wheezed. "I'm gonna have a fuckin' coronary." I jumped between them and grabbing the casualty by his combat jacket I violently jerked him towards me. His head bounced of my chest and for a moment a frightened, shocked expression flitted across his face.

"Fucking move it, Soldier, before I loose my temper. I don't care what your fucking orders are."

"Only doing my job, Cpl. No need to get violent."

"I'm not being violent; not yet. Now get fucking moving!" Geoff grabbed him by the arm and dragged him up the hill. He was exhausted and for a moment I thought he might actually be about to collapse.

"Get him to the top Geoff and stay there!" I ordered. Then I ran down to the edge of the undergrowth where the stretcher team held out. Above us Alan had found himself a suitable ditch. On my signal he opened fire. We broke cover, dashed towards the foot of the hill, and pushed straight into the slope. The stomach wound grabbed at the stretcher sides as he tilted backwards. Lee at the rear was arched back precariously and I could see he couldn't hold out.

"Dave!" I yelled, "Get on the front and help pull. Ash, cover us!" I slung my SMG over my shoulder and pushed in beside Lee on the rear of the stretcher. "Right, get ready to lift. One, two, three, lift!" The stretcher teetered almost tipping over.

"Fucking hell, if you drop me I'm suing," complained the stomach wound.

"Shut up and keep your guts in," snapped Lee who was fighting to keep his side of the stretcher level. We pushed ahead a few meters with Lee almost on tiptoes. Neck arteries surged as we screamed at each other. Only one steep pitch separated us from the finishing line. A crowd of faces craned over the edge shouting to us.

"Come on lads, you're almost finished!"

"Fucking go for it!" Alan hefted in behind us, propping up Lee's straining torso.

"One last push lads. On my count." One, two, three and the stretcher lurched forwards. With a massive burst we reached the top of the sand crater and collapsed at the finishing post.

Lying on my back, trees and sky swirled above me. In my chest my heart beat violently and blood rushed in my ears.

"You got the best time," someone shouted and a hand patted my shoulder. "By a clear two minutes ten seconds."

"It was inevitable," I gasped cockily. "Well done lads!" I looked to my side at my exhausted comrades. They lay prone around me.

"Is someone going to untie me?" complained the trussed-up stomach wound.

We paraded in the garrison gymnasium where the top three teams were awarded medals. Our team had gained a clear first place. Winning had been a team effort and teamwork our strength. In other teams the section commanders delegated tasks and led from the front. They hogged the map regardless of how skilful or not they were, and during the battle run shouted orders and avoided strenuous tasks. After all, that's what leaders are supposed to do. One by one we marched up to the presenting officer, saluted and were awarded our medal and certificate. Lee, his usual self, marched out to the front of the parade, banged his feet into the slippery, polished gym floor and fell backwards onto his arse. To hoots of laughter from bandsmen, he saluted from where he sat.

The celebrations that afternoon were curtailed as the following day our regiment had to undergo an ARU inspection. A team of high-ranking officers arrived and we prepared to carry out whatever task or tasks they deemed necessary. There were two tasks we feared, one was the inconvenience of being crashed out of barracks as this involved us having to load tons of ammunition onto three-ton trucks. The other was the BFT. That year we were given two hours to put together a dancing show. Murray ran through our library catalogue and selected Scottish dancing music. With no experience, the BSM choreographed the formation dancers. The inspection team sat themselves down in the band practice room ready to watch the performance. We began with a snappy reel and after a few bars' introduction the practice room doors swung open and two rows of squaddies skipped in holding hands. They'd dressed themselves in red PT vests and green army towels were wrapped around their hips. The towels were held in place by green and yellow stable belts. They skipped around in circles and then performed figure-of-eight formations. Two clumsy soldiers, red-faced and embarrassed, attempted a sword dance and then to a final set of circles they skipped from the room. The regiment passed the test which deemed us fit for a combatant role.

Since Carl's return to band duties I had wanted to make amends but though we warmed to each other our old friendship never regained its intensity. He'd developed a cutting, spiteful disposition and would strike out indiscriminately. One morning I called in his room, he was sat reading a book.

"Carl, do you know there's a Mahler concert at the Stadthalle on Sunday?"

He continued reading.

"Hey, Carl. There's a Mahler concert at the Stadthalle." I waited for a response knowing that he'd heard me.

"Carl! I'm talking to you."

He licked his thin lips nonchalantly before raising his eyes as if confronted by an annoying child.

"Do you have to bother me with trivia? Can't you see I'm reading?"

"Fuck you!" I muttered as I stormed from his room.

For a few weeks he went straight and claimed he had a girlfriend. Though we never met her, he talked about her incessantly and was zealous in his efforts to assert his heterosexuality.

"Of course, I've never really been properly gay," he told me one evening. "It was trendy, the in thing. Life's so much more optimistic without all that homo palaver. Now I can think about a bright future, about getting married, having kids, settling down. You should try it, Nick. It sure beats those soulless fumblings."

"Well, I'm very pleased for you," I replied. I wasn't going to let him bait me.

Several weeks later, pissed, he staggered past the guardroom sentry shouting, "Be camp in camp." The guard had to escort him to his bunk. On the odd occasion we went to a Sunday concert or to the Gentleman. Something had happened to him. He had lost the spark that used to brighten our lives. He could still be funny and the centre of a party but one minute he was his old self, the next venomous and sarcastic. Over the period of his convalescence he had saved a substantial sum of money. He bought himself a whole new wardrobe of clothes, a computer, a 'tea's maid' and a video. He flitted his money away and then started buying on credit. On this he bought a television, clarinet and electronic organ. He was still paying off the loan on his wretched car and when he couldn't keep up the payments he was taken to court. Meanwhile, I waited for his brain to settle down into its old mould.

Late one afternoon Carl and I were about to set off into town when an internal message was delivered to my room. From the writing on the brown OHMS envelope, I could tell it was from Murray. I opened it:

> Come to my office this evening at 1930 hr's. Destroy this letter when you have read it! ML.

We read the short message with worried faces and then burnt it in my bin. We didn't cancel our plans to visit the town or to take a squaddie whom we'd befriended along with us. We had made Steve's acquaintance in the cookhouse. His youthful good looks had spurned us to engineer an introduction. The opportunity arose one lunchtime when he was sat alone at a table. Carl and I joined him. He was an interesting lad with an open mind and good sense of humour and so we introduced him to the band bar. For several weeks he was in our company most evenings and even began to listen to Mahler symphonies with us. We hadn't told him we were gay and from our conversations deduced he was probably straight. He mentioned women far too many times to be interested in men. On the bus ride into town Carl and I ran through all the possible explanations for Murray's clandestine letter. All the time, Steve tried to console us.

"You've got nothing to worry about. You're both JNCOs. What

could you have possibly done that's bad?"

"A lot," I muttered under my breath, beginning to lose my patience.

"It's nothing; you wait and see. It'll be something really trivial. I don't know what you could be worried about. Maybe you're both getting promoted or something."

"We're fucking gay!" I snapped, tired of his prattle.

His eyes bulged. "Both of you?"

"Yes, both of us," I replied. The bus was on the outskirts of town but without checking, he blindly stabbed at the 'next stop' button. When the bus pulled up, he hurriedly made his exit.

Carl looked at me. "You fucking wanker," he said licking his lips like a lizard.

"Well he was beginning to fucking annoy me."

In town we drank coffee and pondered over our future, both certain we were at the threshold of an SIB investigation. Carl wasn't bothered one way or the other but I was terrified. We returned to camp in time to go straight to Murray's office where we found him already waiting. He was sat at his desk, still in uniform and with a stern look upon his face.

"Smack on time," he said looking at his watch. "Well, come in and close the door." We obeyed. "Right! I'll make it short and to the point. The SIB are coming tomorrow to search your rooms. The Colonel has told me to pass on this information so you can get rid of any knickers or women's clothing that you might have hidden away."

Carl and I stared at him in horror. "Women's' clothing?" I asked inquisitively.

"Yes, I'm sure I needn't say anymore."

"What are we supposed to have done, Sir?" I asked.

"I haven't a clue. I've no idea what you two get up to off duty – though I have my suspicions. The Colonel said it was an investigation into charges of homosexuality. Of course, I told him I was surprised. I can't imagine either of you dressed as women! Anyway, we've never had this conversation. Have we?"

"No, Sir!" we muttered simultaneously.

That evening we scoured our rooms for anything that might incriminate us. We threw away magazines and books and sifted meticulously through our letters and personal drawers. From other straight bandsmen we borrowed dog-eared heterosexual porn magazines and copies of *Penthouse* and *Mayfair*. These we stuffed randomly between our clothes and books.

Two SIB investigators arrived early next morning and struck terror into my guts. They wore identical suits, carried identical briefcases and were swathed in an air of officialdom. I hadn't forgotten the previous visit. Immediately they began to comb through our belongings, first in Carl's room and then in mine. They wouldn't tell us what they were looking for or what we'd been accused of. From my room they took my joss sticks, a combat knife and all the straight magazines they found. From Carl's they took a selection of magazines and a photo of him taken while he was at Junior Leaders. We accompanied them to their barracks. For over half an hour they left us in a deserted corridor before calling us into separate offices for interrogation. I found it incredibly difficult to lie about something I did not see as wrong. As under my previous interrogation I admitted my 'crimes'. Though frightened, I felt stronger than when they'd previously interrogated me. If they wanted to kick me out that was fine but I wasn't going to deny my sexuality in its entirety. However, the Sgt who questioned me discussed the nature of homosexuality and even confessed he thought its illegality absurd, creating more problems than it solved. He was quite aware that there was an extensive network of gays in the forces. I asked him why we were under investigation and he told me they had caught a soldier 'in the act'. When interrogated, he claimed Carl and I had gone to gay bars with him. The soldier was Jamie Forbes of the Parachute Regiment.

It was obvious that the investigation uncovered little with which they could charge us. Besides, someone at the top was pulling strings and my investigator seemed positively pro-gay. When we returned to Rawlpindi we were immediately sent for by the RSM. Both he and the Provost Sgt were new to their appointment and had set about reorganising the Regiment within the spheres of their jurisdiction. Sgt Fuller, the Provo Sgt supervised his prisoners whilst they painted the camp entrance curb stones in the regimental colours. They were painted alternately in green and yellow. Outside the guardroom entrance, on the veranda he installed a decorated regimental bass drum and two large brass shells flanked the doorway. On his feet, to announce his presence, he wore steel-studded ammunition boots that crunched the ground as he walked. The RSM insisted on a strict civilian dress code and outlawed all earrings, white socks, trainers and 'weird' hairstyles even if off duty. Of course, he didn't outlaw tattoos on soldiers' hands or necks. They unofficially denoted the non-officer class. He ordered 'no parking' zones around the barracks and detailed the Regimental Police to begin traffic warden duties. He even booked his own wife for illegally parking their car outside RHQ.

The RSM stood in his tiny office in the Regimental Headquarters. He stood back to us, his hands clasped behind him. We stood at attention in front of his desk. Like all RSMs it was a desk that was permanently on parade. Though he heard us enter he stood silently staring out of his office window. Then he braced himself and took a deep breath.

"So! You've been frequenting queer bars in the town have you?"

"Occasionally, Sir," replied Carl.

"Why on earth would two soldiers in a distinguished army regiment want to hang around gay bars? I mean, I know you're bandsmen, but tell me that's just a rumour?"

"They're fun, Sir," I replied evading the second part of his question.

He turned to face us. "What do you mean, they're fun? Eh! Cpl. Elwood."

"There's never any hassle, any fights or aggression."

"Well, I'm not really surprised, are you? I mean, they're faggots, aren't they? They're not able to fight or stand up for themselves. Too busy copping off with each other and practising their sordid sex acts."

"Alexander the Great was a faggot, sir," I added.

"Who? Faggots never make good soldiers. They're not men for a start."

"One of the ancient Greeks' best squadrons were faggots," I insisted. I could feel myself wanting an argument with him. He was a stupid oaf with little wit or intellect. Like Bumtwig at KH, he had a thick neck and an expression permanently pained with concentration, as if to maintain a cognitive state demanded immense will power.

"The ancient Greeks," he laughed. "They're obsolete and that's probably why."

"Well what about Col Baden Powell. He wasn't quite on the level," said Carl. "And he's a national hero now."

"And Edward II and James I. They were too," I added.

"You're not here so we can discuss whether or not faggots make leaders or soldiers. It's illegal and that's all there is to it." He paused. "So are you two faggots, then?"

"No, Sir," I said clearly. "We are not faggots!"

"No, Sir!" added Carl.

"Well, then, why are you going to faggot bars; eh! Cpl Powell?"

"Same reason, Sir. They're fun and friendly." The RSM turned his back and resumed surveying the barrack road outside. Suddenly he threw open his window and began bellowing at a passing Tpr.

"You there! Yes! You! Get a bloody haircut, Tpr. Or else I'll have you on extra duties for the next month." Pulling his window shut he muttered to himself. "Bloody slouchy, slovenly behaviour." He placed his hands behind his back and pulled himself to his full height, which wasn't very tall. The satisfaction of both his rank and power were obvious. Behind his thick Neanderthal skull, he was deep in thought.

"And what about this Paratrooper, Cpl Elwood? This man, for lack of a better word, Forbes. What's he got to do with this?" Out of the corner of my eye Carl cocked a limp wrist at the RSM's back. For a moment I lost my concentration.

"Well?"

"He was just a mate, Sir. We sometimes went with him to the gay club in town." This time Carl cocked his limp wrist, put his hand on his hip, collapsed the tension in one knee and blew him a kiss.

"Was he gay?" I seductively gave my crotch a quick rub and Carl mimed having a wank.

"I don't know, Sir. I never asked him."

"And how did you know this man?"

I stuck up two fingers at him. "He was a Bdsm, Sir. We knew him through his band."

Carl blew him another kiss just as he began turning back towards us. We quickly pulled ourselves to attention and wiped the grins from our faces.

"Well, you know this doesn't look good to the regiment. We can't have soldiers, or even bandsmen come to that, frequenting gay bars. No matter for what reason you might go there. They might be friendly but given half a chance they'll pounce on you. One night you'll get drunk and wake up with a sore arse and it's just the sort of behaviour that newspapers love. We can't risk that."

"But it's not illegal for us to go in a gay bar, Sir. Just cause someone drinks in a gay bar it doesn't mean they're gay," said Carl.

"Oh, Cpl Powell, but it is illegal because I've just said it is, so from now on I'm ordering you to stay out of queer clubs. Is that understood?"

"Yes, Sir!" we replied in unison. We left RHQ is high spirits and walked back to the band block.

"Well, we didn't have to lie, did we?" asked Carl.

"No! I mean, I never did ask Jamie if he was gay. Especially after seeing him snogging you on the back of that green grollie. There was no need."

"And anyway," continued Carl. "What's the point of asking someone if they're queer when they're in a gay bar with their tongue down your throat?"

"Yeah! You could have probably boned the RSM over his desk and when he realised what was going on he'd have asked if you were gay. Then you could have said, no, of course not."

"Yeah," laughed Carl. "And he'd have said, 'Oh, well then, carry on'."

"And we're not faggots are we," I said confidently. "Gay, yes; but not faggots."

"'Oh RSM'," mimicked Carl. "'Alexander the Great was a faggot.' I was half expecting you to quote Plato." We continued joking all the way to the band block and for a few minutes I felt close to him again.

"I wonder what happened to Jamie?" I asked Carl as we entered the band alcove.

We ignored the RSM's order and within two weeks were back at the Gentleman. We knew the Military Police surveyed the premises to report erring soldiers. The problem was that the woman officer detailed to survey the club was lesbian herself and used her official duty to chat up women and socialise. Somehow she never found anyone to report.

17

Carl's behaviour within the regiment wasn't doing him favours. He started employing the services of the regimental prostitute, a Tpr Baden. I first heard of this service through Steve the squaddie. Initially sceptical about such a rumour, I overheard two squaddies talking about him at the Imbiss. He had supplied his young lips to relieve one of the squadron Sgts and so Baden, though relatively new to the regiment, was nonetheless infamous. After each leave he failed to return and was classified AWOL. Either the military police returned him to barracks or he arrived at our gates days late. He became virtually a permanent inmate in the regimental prison. He told Carl he really wanted to leave the army but that whatever he did they wouldn't let him go. He insisted his prostitution had nothing to do with attempting a discharge. Carl paid him fifty marks, his standard fee for a blow job. It crossed my mind to make use of his services; he was a sexy looking lad, who always had a naughty grin and rosy red cheeks. Carl's nocturnal activities with Baden quickly became regimental gossip.

Every evening, outside Rawlpindi Barracks, a Schnell Imbiss wagon parked. They sold chips, bratwürst sausages, grilled chicken, hamburgers and beer. I had become good friends with the family who ran the business and often passed an evening at their wagon. It improved my German immensely. Archie was the owner of several wagons which his wife, three sons and two daughters worked between them.

It was Michel, Archie's son, who told me that Carl had passed by the wagon dressed as a woman. He'd seen him that very evening and was incredibly excited about it.

"I couldn't believe it. He wore these gold high-heel shoes and was wearing a wig. It was so funny. He even had a matching gold handbag. He just walked straight out past the guardroom and sentry. He looked just like a woman." Michel laughed and tears streamed down his sweaty face. "Just like a woman," he repeated, rubbing his eyes.

"Are you sure it was him?"

"Of course I am! I spoke to him. He asked for a can of beer. At first I didn't recognise him, her, but then he winked at me and I realised it was him. 'Carl?' I said. 'What are you doing?' He said he was going to a party. He was wearing lipstick and eye shadow."

"He must be going to a fancy dress party. Was anyone with him?"

"Yes! He was with some squaddies. They got into a taxi over the road."

"Were they drunk?"

"Oh, a bit I suppose. But Carl was wobbling in those high heels. He looked so lady-like. Do you think his accident has turned him into a transvestite?"

"I don't know what's wrong. He's been upsetting a lot of people and doing lots of strange things. If he's not careful there's going to be trouble."

"And you know," he whispered, leaning towards me. "He's been here with that prostitute boy?"

"Well, that's what I mean. He's not really discreet about it, is he?"

Michel thought to himself and resumed laughing. "Oh, Nick. You should have seen him. He was perfect. Those gold shoes and his little gold handbag swinging off his arm. The British Army," he chuckled.

For several days Carl's drag act was the talk of various factions. The squaddies who frequented our bar told us how their mates had met him in a club. They sat with him most of the evening and bought him drinks. They thought he was hilarious. The squaddies didn't find his behaviour odd and naively assumed he was doing it for a laugh. Next he began an affair with a Bdsm named Shaun from the neighbouring band. We heard the rumours before Carl decided to tell us. Most of us tried telling Carl that'd he'd better be careful but his response to our advice was scathing sarcasm and rejection. The band began to lose patience with his behaviour. He found himself excluded from our bitchy factions and when his back turned we viciously slated his character. Carl's luck finally ran out shortly after we returned from Christmas leave. Amongst his five O-levels was one in German language. He spoke it well had been accepted on an advanced German course that entailed a month away from the band. On a Sunday morning he departed for Rinteln, a garrison town several hours away. He returned to barracks the following day, handcuffed and under an MP escort. On his arrival an icebreaker party welcomed course members. The blasé way in which he flaunted his sexuality finally backfired. He made a pass at another pupil, feeling the guy's crotch. Unfortunately the object of his lust was an MP. Carl was subsequently arrested and RTU'd in disgrace.

Had he not overstepped the mark and made enemies the whole incident would have been quelled. However, the hierarchy failed to support him and he was given the choice, accept a discharge or face a court martial. Few of us wanted to see him leave; he was an established personality. We stabbed him to death behind his back but this was done to anyone worth talking about. Factions could whip up immense support or dislike of an individual and in my years of service I had learnt to manipulate opinion to my advantage. I could shred someone to ribbons one moment and easily be their best mate the next. Much of the animosity generated towards Carl was initiated by me but I didn't intend it to result in his demise.

Carl accepted discharge and remained with us whilst the bureaucracy formalised his documentation. We threw a big party during his last week. From a collection we bought him a bronze statuette of a regimental dragoon that we dressed in a Barbie doll outfit. It was difficult fitting the dress over the rigid dragoon so I ripped it and re-sewed the back seam. At the party Murray presented Carl with his dragoon and we laughed as he held it aloft. It was strange that his leaving marked the only occasion at which knowledge of his sexuality wasn't officially a secret. Soldiers raised glasses and shook his hand and laughed at the coutured dragoon. For a solitary evening in his ten-year service he was unofficially permitted equality.

I wasn't paying attention to Carl as Shaun had been invited and I fancied him. His gay inclinations were recent news and I'd decided to strike while the iron was hot. Throughout the evening Carl continually looked at him and took every opportunity to sit at his side. I was envious; like a mountie Carl always got his man. However, Shaun had noticed my cursory glances and suddenly smiled back at me. It was a big white grin with eyes that flashed wickedly. If I could only get Carl out of the competition I'd be in with a chance. Amongst the crowd was a squaddie whom he fancied. He was a small lad with dark hair and a little snub nose for which Carl had a predilection. It was when Carl went to the toilet that I ordered a pint of mixed spirits from the bar. I gave it to the dark-haired lad and asked him to offer it to Carl as a farewell drink. When Carl returned the lad stood up.

"Can I have quiet, please. Excuse me! Can I have quiet." Faces turned in his direction and talking ceased. "I'd just like to present Carl with a drink on behalf of the boys of A Squadron."

"Oh, thanks," said Carl with a smile.

"You have to drink it in one," the lad grinned. I laughed to myself; Carl wouldn't refuse such a challenge. Even if it made him retch he'd finish it to impress the boy. Several individuals cheered.

"Go on, Carl. Go for it."

"Woow, Carl, you can do it." All attention focused upon him and provided him an audience for whom he couldn't resist performing. Lifting his glass he focused himself on its contents. Like a martial artist psychologically preparing themselves to smash a brick, he concentrated. His face was intent. The party stood, silently waiting. When almost ready, he took a few deep breaths and then began gulping. Drink ran down the sides of his mouth and spilled onto his chest. His face contorted and his eyes squeezed shut. With several gulps remaining the bar began to cheer and clap.

"Yeah! Nearly there."

"One last mouthful! Go on!"

Carl snatched the drained glass from his mouth and stood immobilised as he strained to suppress the urge to vomit. Give it a few minutes, I thought, and he'll be legless. Murray, sat at a table of SNCOs and an officer, was already drunk and ate a candle for a joke. The officer, commissioned from the ranks, went a step further. It was an action that happened so fluidly it seemed to exist between the cracks of the party. Murray sat laughing as the final chunk of candle popped into his mouth and he began chewing. He smiled, sensing victory at the dare he'd just accomplished. It was a game he often played and always won. Suddenly, on the window ledge to the side of the officer, I noticed a scurrying cockroach. Without taking his eyes from Murray, the officer's fist shot to the side and as if using a hammer squashed it flat. Murray continued chewing, unaware of the officer's crashing fist. Still looking at Murray, the officer picked up the twitching roach and held it to his parted lips. Mortally injured, its antennae quivered. Murray's eyes strained and he stopped chewing. An instant later and the roach disappeared into the officer's mouth. Next, Murray ate a daffodil that stood on the windowsill but it was a vain attempt to win a lost cause.

Carl was drunk and had already retched alcoholic bile into the sick bucket. Ash suggested we go into town and continue the party. Shaun agreed. Leaving, we took a taxi to a nearby bar. Unfortunately, Carl staggered along behind us. In the back of the cab he fawned over Shaun and tried petting him. Thankfully, Shaun pushed him away with a laugh.

"Get off, Carl. Your breath smells of sick!" Then he looked at me and winked. Next to the bar was a striptease club where Carl had taken straight lads he wanted to seduce. It was empty. Piped music played from the wall speakers. We sat at a table in front of the small stage on which lay a shaggy feather boa.

"Were the hell is everyone?" asked Ash.

"Maybe everyone's busy shagging in the back rooms," said Shaun. It was a plush bar and from the ample lighting I assumed the artistes to be of healthy complexion. Carl staggered to the stage and began trying to dance seductively. He managed to pick up the red feather boa and threw it around his neck. Lurching over the stage he caressed his chest and crotch and rubbed the boa over his face. Under the table Shaun's knee pressed against my thigh. Carl began unbuttoning his shirt and trousers and pushed one end of the boa down the front of his pants. At that moment, just as Shaun's palm slipped onto my leg, a scantily dressed artiste appeared and began scolding Carl. In red suspenders bordered with frilly black lace, she wrestled the boa from his grip. In the brief struggle, he staggered and fell onto his backside.

"We'd better get him out of here," suggested Ash. "Before she phones the MPs."

"I'm gonna be sick!" mumbled Carl. Picking him up we left the club and dragged him into the pub next door. Shaun went to hail a taxi.

Old German pubs, such as the one we were in, often had purpose-built vomit bowls in the toilets. They're a convenient public house facility which I've never seen in Britain. A sturdy porcelain sink with a deep conical bowl on either side of which are large steel handles. The top of the bowl is fixed at average chest height. Once you've had to use one their utilitarian value becomes evident. A sink or toilet bowl is no good to a drunken man who can hardly stagger in its direction let alone direct a jet of vomit in its vicinity. Besides, when drunk, the distance between mouth and target might as well be a thousand miles. An old German vomit bowl is a drunk's salvation. They call out like sirens to the staggering pisshead. Their solid size and height give a drunk something on which to collapse and their cold stone sides help focus the mind on the distant world of reality. The vomit bowl sanitises the act of puking. We led Carl to its handles and with his head deep in the bowl, he retched loudly. Grotesque, prolonged vowels gurgled past his throat and were amplified by the bowl. We stood beside him though the handles provided all the support he needed.

"Waaaaaa," he boomed.

"Hey, I'm gonna go back with Shaun in a bit. Do you mind making your own way home?" I asked Ash.

"Urrrrrrr," gagged Carl.

"No, that's fine. I'm tired anyway. Are you going to take him home with you?" Ash responded.

"Yaaaar," went Carl as if trying to reply. Ash patted him on the back.

"Yes," I said as if speaking to a child. "Shaun and I will take you home before we go on to shag. You just be sick in there like a good boy before I go and blow Shaun's lovely fat cock," I taunted. Ash laughed.

"Ya wha?" blurted Carl. He turned his head towards me and a

stringy strand of bile dangled from his chin. His eyes tried to focus but seemed to stare way past me. He gave up and turned back into the bowl.

"Ya wha?"

"You drank a whole pint of spirits, Carl. How do you feel?" I asked. Ash joined in the piss taking.

"No way you can shag tonight, Carl, you're far too drunk."

"Urrrrrr."

"We're going for bratty, chips and mayonnaise. You wanna come?" I asked.

"We're cruel," laughed Ash.

"Give over. He's been a fucking pain for the last few weeks. He deserves it. Hey, Carl. We're going for bratty and chips. You wanna come?"

"Wha?" he blabbed, his face very grey.

"Bratty and chips," repeated Ash. Carl's mind gave in, his eyes swirled and the vortex in his head swept him into its current. His head fell forward, his knuckles turned white on the handles and in a violent jerk he churned his stomach into the bowl.

"Waaaaa! Ughhhh!"

"Go for it, Carl!" encouraged Ash.

Outside Shaun had hailed a taxi. We said goodbye to Ash and put Carl in the front seat. At first, his near-vomiting state attracted the driver's attention. German taxi drivers pride themselves on clean, comfortable vehicles and many refuse to carry drunks. It didn't take the driver long to notice that Shaun and I were busy wanking and kissing in the back seats.

"Rawlpindi Kaserne?" he asked as if to confirm our military identity.

"Ja, stimmt!" I replied between kisses. Meanwhile my hand vigorously rubbed Shaun's swollen dick.

"We're gay soldiers," muttered Shaun against my face. He was smirking.

"Dirty schwuler," I added.

"Fucking perverted homos," said Shaun.

"Give us yer sons!" I grunted. We laughed as we kissed. From the front seat, Carl, who'd been silent, moaned. The driver looked at him and then back at the road ahead. He met my eyes in the driving mirror.

"You are no problem. But I am hoping your friend will not be sick," he said in English.

Outside our barracks we coaxed Carl into paying the bill. He took money from his pocket that we passed to the driver. We left

Carl lying on the ground outside the main gate and walked hand in hand to my flat.

In a flat intended for a lover, I fucked an acquaintance to a Beethoven piano concerto. He was nice, his body firm and smooth. I sunk into his sucking butt and lost myself in pleasure. The back of his knees bounced against my biceps whilst his palm slid up and down his veiny cock. With each lunge his balls bobbed up and down. A few times I poked him hard just to wipe the vacant expression from his face. He was enjoying himself but I felt like hurting him just a little. With a forceful thrust I made his mouth blow bubbles and his eyes shut out the world. Each time his head rolled, his free hand clawed the mattress. Meanwhile his wanking hand pounded his dick. It was the first and last time I ever had sex in my flat. Soon after it was demolished.

Carl left the band a few days later. I said goodbye to him in the entrance alcove. It was a subdued farewell considering the friendship and closeness we'd shared. I wasn't upset to see him go. I had never forgiven his lack of consideration the night he tongue-sandwiched Andreas. Part of me wanted rid of my dependence on his companionship. We shook hands, wished each other luck and promised to keep in contact. Then he disappeared down our little path wearing his burgundy-coloured trousers and flat cap. Carl left a hole in the band's ranks, despite our casualness at his departure we missed him. He had been a personality that made us laugh, he was someone with whom you could have a decent conversation and whose musicianship enthused us. Many bandsmen could not believe that Carl and I had never slept together or that we hadn't been in a relationship. For years we reminisced about his outrageous exploits. His presence enriched and enlivened the band's oral history and I'm sure, even today, he hasn't been forgotten.

Band life was becoming tedious. I'd visited most places I was likely to and become bored playing the SOS. The 'Regimental March' and 'God Save the Queen' could be played with mind-numbing detachment and the bulk of the programmes, medleys from musicals, compilations of the classics and novelty pieces, could all be rattled off on auto-pilot. Since Carl's departure I'd felt isolated. He had been one of the only musicians in the band who had any appreciation of music. If I didn't go on a bandmaster's course I'd eventually be promoted to Sgt and from there possibly reach BSM. However, the frustrations of having to perform a conductor's interpretation of music, of really only being a senior Bdsm, would never disappear. The bandmaster's course was an escape from familiarity and boredom. It was an escape from the incompetent musical morons who, despite rehearsals, frequently marred performances with ridiculous blunders. I sent my composition, 'The Last of the Wine', to Foot at KH and he wrote back recommending me to apply for the 1985 bandmaster's course.

When the time came for me to attend auditions I had a change of heart. I managed to suppress the doubts but gradually, as the auditions drew closer, they emerged. First I had to consider my sexuality and the problems this might cause as a bandmaster. I'd have to go back into the closet and adhere to a strict code that limited fraternisation between the ranks. I'd have sexy musicians in my band and have to hide feelings towards them. Knowledge of my sexuality would have preceded me and would become a malignant rumour to be manipulated as need arose. I would be in a position where I'd be unable to defend myself from gossip and there would be no one in whom to confide or express myself. My life as a gay man would have to end or in the least be conducted in a highly clandestine manner. If that wasn't enough to dissuade me, I began to recall the way students had been treated at KH. The hours they spent transposing some symphonic movement from orchestra to military band, or the way they were humiliated and destroyed whilst conducting. Then there was the culture within the students' mess: quasi public-school initiation ceremonies and inter-mess rank structures. Three to four years' struggle for a qualification that in Civvie Street held little value. It was a qualification that said more about the owner's deferential character than their musical ability. Three to four years of carrying out pointless activities designed to ensure your obedience whilst learning little. I was committed to studying but didn't know if KH was the right place to do so. Reaching a conclusion, I withdrew my entry and remained one of the army's most qualified bandsmen.

Eventually our MFO crates were brought out from their dusty cupboard in no man's land between the German and Oriental cockroach colonies. Gradually we began to pack away our belongings. From the inside of my wooden military locker, I removed the SIB's calling card which I'd kept stuck on the doors of various lockers I'd occupied over the years. Before I threw it in the bin, I held it between thumb and forefinger. The edges had curled up and the bamboo texture had become grimy to touch. The blue and red cap badge blurred and beyond a jumble of colours and letters, images flashed: Jamie and our relationship, the occasional crushes I'd had and of course, Andreas. Then it fluttered down into my rubbish bin. "Forever Onwards," I muttered.

With our equipment and most personal belongings crated we began scrubbing and polishing the entire building. On my final evening

in Osnabrück garrison I went for a drink with Georg. At the end of
the meeting he drove me to Rawlpindi Barracks and there, opposite
the regimental motto we said farewell. As red tail lights twinkled out
of sight, I bowed. It was a bow full of respect, humility and meaning.
I walked the short distance down the hill to the cemetery entrance
where Andreas and I had said our final goodbye. Since he'd returned,
the tree under which we'd embraced had twice shed leaves. I plucked
a few leaves, almond-shaped with serrated edges, put them in my wallet. Back in Rawlpindi, I placed them inside in my sad box alongside
strips of chewing gum, my ring and a cigarette.

18

Tidworth, my next posting, was a bleak little garrison on Salisbury plain. Apart from barracks there was little other than a NAAFI, Chinese take-away, bank and newsagent. Tidworth was an army town. The vast open plains around it were rolling and desolate. Tough grass covered the landscape, interrupted here and there by small woods which keeled in the direction of the wind that swept the plain. The hawthorn bushes which grew in abundance were black and gnarled. The garrison was neat and vast expanses of tended grass separated its buildings. Grass which, since the spawning of the RSM, had only ever been trodden by the brave. By the time I arrived with the main party the guardroom had already been decorated with the regimental bass drum and two brass shells, which, as usual, stood on either side of the entrance. The regimental flag flew beside the Union Jack above the RHQ and squadron flags flew outside their respective lines. Within days of the advance party's arrival, Kanpur Barracks looked as if it'd had no other owner than the 15th Regiment of Dragoons.

Shortly after my arrival in Tidworth I was promoted to Sgt with the appointment of T/M. As with my previous promotions, it happened very quickly. Our S/Sgt had accepted a post as an instructor at JLR. The promotion, though a surprise, did not come as a shock since I was next in line and well qualified. The day it became official it was posted in Regimental Orders and I moved into the WOs and Sgts' Mess, a grand Edwardian building designed as an officers' mess. On the right-hand sleeve of my khaki jumper I wore the prestigious crossed trumpets above four inverted chevrons. When in shirtsleeve order, the small brass trumpets were mounted on a leather wrist band. My nickname for this was the Bangle of Gondor as sight of it caused passing soldiers to stiffen their shoulders and call me 'Sir'. The appointment didn't require this but many mistakenly considered me a WO. My new duties included rehearsing the fanfare team, which consisted of eight fanfare trumpeters and a timpanist. On engagements I was expected to conduct them as I did every morning at eight-thirty when we marched to RHQ to play Stables.

My room in the Sgts' mess was massive and could be divided into a bedroom and study area. Two large bay windows looked out over the fields and woods that lay beyond the building. It was situated on the edge of the barracks and surrounded by woods, fields and horse paddocks. The mess entrance contained a fine mosaic floor. Door knobs were brass and the carpets thick and springy. That evening, as was the usual military tradition, I went to the mess bar for my promotion party. As was the custom I paid the bill for the first round of drinks. SNCOs slapped me on my back and shook my hand whilst congratulating me.

"Well done, Nick."

"Yes, congratulations. You're one of us now."

"Thank you, Sir," I replied shaking a hand.

"Oh, no, call me Dave now. All first-name terms in the mess." And the WO slapped me on the shoulder. I struggled to say the names of those who had made my life shit. Wearing an extra chevron suddenly made me one of them. As if until my promotion, I hadn't been worth talking to.

Mess life was wonderful and the privileges conferred on SNCOs welcome. Now I could walk around Kanpur barracks without constantly being on my guard in case I was doing something wrong. Suddenly the barracks were rid of most of the predators that preyed on me as a lower rank and pulled me up for needing a haircut, having sideburns that were too long or not walking in a military fashion. Once I'd been overheard swearing in a conversation which had taken place at the Imbiss wagon in Osnabrück. The WO who heard me sent for me the following morning and gave me a roasting. It made no odds to him that two army wives at the Imbiss had themselves been swearing. He accused me of bringing the army into disrepute. My BM wouldn't defend me as the WO was one of his drinking pals. On another occasion a WO screamed at me for sucking a Polo mint whilst walking around the barracks. A few days later I saw him leaving one building and entering another with a lit cigarette discreetly hidden in the curled palm of his hand. Now I was being bought drinks and being called 'mate' and 'pal'. As a Sgt I had access all over Kanpur. Doors that were once barred to me were now open. Any favour I needed, buckshee clothing, an extra long sleeping bag or rations from the mess, was gratefully granted.

Life was luxurious. Oil paintings of historic regimental figures and battles adorned the walls of the breakfast room, bar, dining room and corridors. Humorous military cartoons hung in frames over the urinals and the sinks always had soap by them. Silver statuettes and candelabras decorated our solid oak dining tables. There were regimental place mats and silver cutlery. We were waited upon at the dining table and selected from a wide menu. Gone were the roasted chickens that looked like sparrows; now they were big fat birds. Gone were the variations on corned beef: the fritters, salad, hash and even sweet and sour corned beef; now it was beef wellington, chicken Kiev and pork cordon bleu. Now I ate three courses at dinner instead of the cookhouse two. When my parents visited, I arranged for a mess waiter to bring tea and sandwiches to my room. They were little triangular sandwiches with the crusts trimmed off.

I enjoyed mess life and for several months quite fancied myself as a country squire. I had my shoes heeled and toed with metal caps so that my presence was announced by a clip-clop noise. I wore cavalry twill or striped shirts, cord trousers and a Barbour jacket. My ties were made of silk and a matching handkerchief hung from the breast pocket of my jacket. Sometimes a naive squaddie saluted me, side-stepped my path or held a door open. In the garrison banks, till staff were polite and courteous and shop assistants gave me extra attention. Barbour jackets were the in thing amongst the officers. After all, they had been listed in the *Sloane Ranger* book as a vital possession for the 'well to do', and the Queen was always wearing them at horse shows. Despite army regulations, cavalry officers wore waxed jackets when in uniform. It didn't really matter as they flouted Queen's Regulations all the time with maroon socks, long hair and sloppy, unmilitary salutes. One officer always returned my salute as a casual slap with the back of his hand against forehead. I began saluting him in the same manner.

On Saturdays I took the bus into Salisbury and ate lunch in an old coach-house restaurant. As if some middle-aged country gent, I sat in front of the warm, sparkling log fire dressed in my clippy-cloppy clothes. I ate pâté and toast or ripe pheasant, sipped sherry and read a novel, perhaps Dickens's *Hard Times* or Hardy's *The Trumpet Major*.

A new Bdsm joined our band from Catterick; his name was Matt Walsh. One afternoon, a few days after our arrival, I sent him a note. It was an unusual form of communication within a unit but its pretentiousness appealed to me:

> Matt. I wondered if you'd like to go out to dinner
> tonight. I know a really quaint restaurant in Salisbury. If
> you do, come smart and meet me at the bus stop at 1900.
> Yours, Nick. (T/M)

That evening I put on my posh clothes and clip-clopped through the paddocks to the bus stop. A silk handkerchief sprung from my breast pocket and I wore a tweed flat cap which was the rage amongst officers. Of course, I was attracted to Matt. It was the start of another infatuation and close friendship.

Promotions always caused grievances amongst certain soldiers who thought themselves or someone else better. When I was promoted to Sgt some bandsmen started moaning. My sexuality had become an attribute to criticise. Their homophobia quite astonished me since I hadn't suspected it would arouse concern – it had rarely done so in the past. On the bus one afternoon someone called me a 'queer' and later, from the back row, someone shouted 'bum boy'. Their comments weren't meant malignantly but with the BM on the front seat they made me uneasy. For a moment I was sure I saw the back of his neck stiffen. In his presence I didn't like the subject of my sexuality paraded in such a mocking manner. Factions were busy working behind my back and their infectious propaganda was gaining ground. The following morning a complaint was lodged with the BSM objecting to the fact that as a homosexual, I'd been promoted to Sgt. Even my best mates succumbed to the lobby against me. They argued that though they liked me and I did my job well, it just wasn't fair to have someone who broke Queen's Regulations promoted as a SNCO.

"So it's okay for me to be gay and a Cpl, then? Is that what you're trying to say?"

"Yes, well, no. A gay Cpl isn't as bad as a gay Sgt."

"What if I was in the closet. Would that make a difference?"

"Yes, I suppose it would."

"But if I do the same job in the closet as out what difference does it make?"

"It's against army law. That's the difference!"

"But that's just discrimination. Do you agree with that?"

"It's just not right."

"Oh! So you do."

"It's not natural. Sex with the opposite sex. That's natural."

"Why?"

"Because it's about having babies."

"Oh, so you are unnatural then?"

"No, of course not."

"Well are you a virgin?"

"No!"

"So you've had penetrative sex, then?"

"What do you mean?"

"You stuck your dick in them?"

"Yes! Of course I have."

"But you've got no kids and you've had sex. By your own definition you've had unnatural sex." And so the arguing continued. I knew I had to diffuse their trivial attack swiftly. Cpl Horton (whose affair with a salt cellar was still largely a secret) and L/Cpl Mercer were the instigators. Both of them were crap musicians and Mercer was so unattractive he probably envied me for at least being able to have sex –

even if it was with men. The BSM, Martin Hoe, whom we called Bungle, knew I was gay and didn't seem too concerned by the allegations. He suggested leaving the issue to fizzle out of its own accord. Such a solution didn't agree with me. If I lay low and appeared silenced by their complaints they'd sense victory and my sexuality would be a weapon to use in the future. That some of my closest mates were party to the accusation required a deadly and successful counter-attack. One that prevented then from ever plotting against me again. In short, I had to stamp on them to ensure respect. My offensive was obvious. I'd had it in my possession for years. It had lain waiting for the necessity of events to activate it.

That evening I visited the cookhouse and sat myself down at the table where the malicious faction was busy eating. They were easy to spot as they only ever came together when faced by a potential threat. Around a block of tables, separated by sauces, spilt food and cellars, they rallied to debate their grievances. I sat at a spare seat amongst them. A few gave me uncomfortable looks and probably thought I had come to either concede or do battle. For my attack to strike deep I had to hit whilst they were unguarded.

"Hi!" I said.

Heads turned towards me, all busy feeding on horrible cookhouse food: greasy little chops of fat, sparrow-sized chickens, mutated clods of potato and most popular – chips. Squaddies and bandsmen all loved chips. With mouthfuls of food they mumbled hello and sheepishly looked back at their meals, cautious of engaging eye contact.

"Don't mind me. I've just popped over to see if you trumpeters are ready for the job tomorrow?"

The eight members of the fanfare team sat around the table; some looked up.

"No problem, Nick," said Andy. "All our kit's bulled and our trumpets and banners packed."

He was a mate yet I felt an immense desire to order him to call me by rank.

"I just wanted to check. We don't want the RSM making any complaints, he might think I can't do my job."

"I've done it hundreds of times," stressed Leon Mercer, his enormous nose poking out so far he found it difficult to drink the final mouthfuls of tea without craning his neck back.

On my right sat Tim who hadn't spoken to me during the outbreak of accusations. He was fighting to drag little bits of meat from the awkward recess of a bare chop. The thick rind of fat on the edge of his plate lay discarded.

"You okay, Tim? I haven't seen you much in the last few days."

"Yes, I've been rather busy," he replied with a mouthful of chips.

"I suppose you have. Do you mind if I have a chip?" I asked, already taking a few from the edge of his greasy plate.

"No, help yourself."

"Yuk! Why are your chips so greasy and tasteless? In the mess each chip is cooked to loving perfection. Our food is absolutely divine, cooked with professional attention." Tim ignored me. Reaching across the table I lifted the salt and sprinkled the remaining stump. "That's better. Brings out what little taste there is. Don't you think so, Wes?" Wes Horton, sat opposite me, didn't answer. I finished and rubbed salt and grease from my fingers. They didn't have serviettes in the cookhouse. It was then, amidst their subdued conversation and at a moment I was guaranteed attention, that I struck. Picking up the salt cellar I pushed my chair back as if about to leave. They pretended to ignore me but out the corners of eyes they watched.

"Wes?" I called. "You look like you could do with some salt."

"No, it's okay, thanks."

"Sure you don't want some," he looked up, a puzzled expression crossed his face. I passed him the cellar. He took it and placed it beside his plate. "It's a salt cellar. Such a useful object. You never know when you might need one." In paralysis, his jaw locked and the muscles on the sides of his face twitched. His adam's apple bobbed up and down and his cheeks began to flush. He pushed a pile of marrowfat peas around his plate. The taste of revenge rippled through me and glands in the back of my mouth began to tingle and salivate. I had to suppress a blooming grin. Some of the bandsmen stiffened as if hit by a tiny electric shock. The scratching and scraping stopped and bodies mortified. Conversation ceased before heads bowed as if in prayer and the clanking of cutlery resumed. Their minuscule body language signified to Horton that I wasn't the only one who knew his sordid secret. His fork continued to slide blindly around his plate in pursuit of peas.

"Oh, well," I sighed. "I suppose I'd better go. Almost time for dinner." A few mumbled goodbye but most sat rigid. Outside it had begun to rain.

The response to my tactic came quicker than anticipated. I suspect that after my departure Horton had persuaded his faction that their behaviour was mean and that T/M Elwood was really a nice guy. Their surrender would have been encouraged by those who'd remained loyal to me but then this wasn't surprising as some of them had little secrets of which I was aware. Soon after they began apologising. All, that was, except for Leon; he was far too tight to say sorry.

In the spring we began rehearsals for the visit of Prince Charles. We rehearsed the marching manoeuvres for weeks, culminating in several dress rehearsals. The week before, we paraded on the square for an address by the CO. These addresses occurred annually and were often held before a major event. Most COs served two years at their rank before being posted to Staff College where, on completion of their course, they were promoted to a staff rank. Once the regiment and attached personnel such as the cooks, medics and REME were paraded, we were called to attention while the RSM reported to the CO. A large rostrum and microphone had been erected on which he now mounted. Most of his address, as usual, focused on the regiment's recent achievements: the squadron's live firing results from Canada, sporting achievements and our general reputation. Then he outlined our aims for the next few months and the significance of Charles's visit. He stressed the importance of our bearing and precision and outlined the objectives of the approaching rehearsals. He finished on a sombre topic. That week a spate of media publicity had focused on drugs and homosexuality in the military. One regiment, only just down the road, had seen two of its soldiers arrested for using marijuana. It was in all the papers.

"I needn't remind you, gentlemen, that the use of drugs is strictly forbidden, as is the practice of homosexuality. Of course, I know there are no quaars or druggies in my regiment, that goes without saying. However, we need to be cautious at all times. Aware that around us, in the bars and night clubs we visit, there are sick individuals waiting to prey on us. When we're drunk and having fun we're vulnerable. Be alert, gentlemen, and don't find yourselves in compromising positions." At the mention of 'quaars', grinning faces turned in my direction; I chuckled. For all the CO's education, his closeted public-school and life experiences, he hadn't a clue what his troops, or even officers, were really like. Only in the last weeks at Osnabrück, Ash had arrived at my flat with an officer mate. It was two o'clock in the morning and they were both fairly pissed. I didn't plan to entertain them and got straight back into bed. Ash sat himself on my bedroom floor whilst the officer perched at the end of my bed. Though I made light of it, I had to keep telling him to stop stroking my leg. The alcohol extenuated his camp mannerisms.

Weeks before Charles's arrival our accommodation was scrubbed out, vigorously polished and bumpered with electric polishers. Flowers had been cultivated in the regimental gardens, mostly daffodils and yellow tulips. The green foliage and yellow flowers provided our regimental colours. Outside RHQ a large garden contained daffodils and tulips in the shape of our regimental cap badge – a portcullis. The barrack buildings were all repainted. The regimental Provost Sgt presented his domain with a large brass plaque framed in wood which he secured to the front wall of his guardroom. The top was carved in the regimental crest and under this: 'Provost Sergeants of the Regiment'. The plaque was chronologically engraved with successive Provos. Provo Sgt Fuller's name appeared at the bottom of the list. Under the plaque, the veranda floor had recently been red-leaded. Every day, inmates bumpered it with ancient hand bumpers. Again, the Provo ordered the curb stones around the camp entrance painted in regimental colours. His prisoners, including Tpr Baden, the regimental rent boy, were sequestered for the task. So that we couldn't forget which barracks we were in, the RSM detailed all curb stones embellished in the regimental pattern. Eventually, even the large galvanised dustbins that stood outside our buildings were stripped in yellow and green.

The programme for the royal visit consisted of Charles inspecting the parade and taking the salute. This was followed by an 'all ranks' luncheon after which he was to visit the Officers' and Sgts' respective messes. Naturally, we had to rehearse his mess visit – silly little rehearsals at which we stood around sipping sherry in small groups each with prearranged conversations which we had earlier drawn from a hat. My group had to talk about the mess menu, another one football, and others the parade or holidays. With nothing left to chance our conversation was forced, false and boring.

"Isn't the menu for the luncheon interesting?"

"Yes, the cooks have been busy for weeks."

"It must have cost thousands of pounds." Then followed silence. We looked at each other with blank faces.

"It's not easy being a cook at a time like this."

"They've been busy for weeks."

"Isn't the menu interesting?"

The final rehearsal, in parade uniform, included a young officer impersonating Prince Charles. We had to address him in the correct manner and answer questions that someone had predicted Charles might ask.

Murray had been our bandmaster for almost eight years when he accepted a posting as Divisional Director of Music; this promoted him to the rank of lieutenant and, shortly afterwards, captain. I was sorry to see him leave us. Though we'd never seen eye to eye he was nonetheless an excellent bandmaster and a great personality. He was highly respected by other bands and even by the aloof staff bands and Household Division. He had been helpful lending money or giving us time off work. Above all he'd turned a blind eye to rumours and protected Carl and me from the SIB investigation. He left a massive hole in our band, one that was never filled. In an official capacity any number of new bandmasters could have replaced him. However, he'd exhibited qualities which KH either didn't foster or actively discouraged. He had a sharp sense of humour, could socialise with officers one day and arm wrestle with squaddies in the bar the next. He could be a drunken slob in the privacy of his mess or the band bar and the next morning be marching smartly in front of the band. He had a strong character and stood up to officers and soldiers who tried to mistreat us. We gave him the traditional farewell party both within the band and later in the WOs' and Sgts' Mess. On his final night in the mess I was tempted to tell him how much I'd miss him, to thank him for being a good boss. I refrained; he wasn't the sort of bloke you could say such things to and would have been embarrassed.

Our new BM, Phil Cottingham, was an ex-infantryman, and quite the opposite of Murray. Despite being thoroughly pleasant, he was a carbon copy of the perfect KH bandmaster. His sense of humour was dreadful. He lacked strength to confront factional conflicts and was deferential to both the RSM and baby officers. From the first day of his arrival he drew criticism.

He upset the band when he insisted we march at infantry as opposed to cavalry tempo. Though the difference is small, the cavalry pace of one hundred and twelve paces a minute allows for a distinctive and traditional cavalry swagger. Indeed, most cavalry bands march at a pace considerably slower than the official one hundred and twelve. Cavalrymen held the swagger close to their hearts. The BSM tried telling him that we always marched slower than infantry pace, as did all cavalry regiments. Phil insisted we marched at one hundred and twenty beats a minute. On marching band he set the pace by shouting the command in tempo: "Quick, march!" However, the bass drummer beat at a cavalry tempo. For weeks he argued and shouted at the SNCOs in private but between us the marching tempo was slowed to a noble, cavalry pace.

One of Phil's first engagements as bandmaster was a marching band display at a ball held by a college of Cambridge University. Booked to march onto their ancient quadrangle at 0300, we didn't leave barracks until midnight. Then we were to hide in an anteroom so our entrance would be a surprise. It was a cool summer morning which made a refreshing change from marching in the sun. Eventually, hidden in a recess of an old building, we formed ranks. The percussion set the beat with rolls and we marched into the spotlights. Startled students, dressed in evening dresses and suits, cleared a path for us. I actually witnessed one student's face turn from bewilderment to glee as he realised we were an army band. Suddenly, to the gay step of 'Colonel Bogey', they began skipping in and out of our ranks. One threw a glass of wine that splashed onto a red tunic. They stepped on our spurs causing us to stumble. In the middle of the counter, as Phil was in the centre of our ranks, someone shouted for him to march us off the quad. Proudly, he marched through our ranks with his head held high. Next they began tugging at our plumes, which whipped our heads backwards. A saxophonist's head jerked back and his instrument mouthpiece stabbed his face. A girl in a flowing dress giggled as she twirled amidst us and yanked another plume. Then a flash caught my eye and I noticed an upturned wine glass on top of the bass drummer's plume. Once out of sight and halted, we broke ranks.

"That was fucking humiliating," complained Tony. "We should have marched straight off the minute they began fucking us around."

"That's what we're paid for," replied Phil.

"Well, I have to question whether degrading the army is part of our job description," said Bungle in a serious voice.

"Wouldn't you be taking the piss out of an army band in their position?" I argued. "I mean, we're mere manuals by comparison. They're destined to be doctors, lawyers, teachers and academics. We're just the pawns of state; servants, the fodder for war."

"Leave out the Communist crap, Nick," snapped Tony.

"Well it's true. I mean, do you think that officers treat us any better than students? At least students don't hide their contempt."

"We've been paid. That's all that counts," stated Phil.

"True," I agreed. "In capitalism everything marketable becomes degraded and cheapened."

"Well I was ashamed," moaned Bungle. "Officers don't embarrass you like that."

"No, they do it formally and you're so used to it you don't even notice the degradation. We call them 'Sir', salute them, bang our feet to attention for them and provide entertainment for their meals. They take the piss out of us all the time."

"Oh, don't talk such rubbish," said Tony. "Officers are gentlemen!"

"And you're not, are you?"

"Not what?"

"You're not a gentleman. I mean we can't be, can we? We're just noncommissioned officers, the hoi polloi. I mean, do you really believe we play in officers' messes to provide musical entertainment?"

"Why else would we play at them?" asked Bungle.

"To remind them of their superiority. To make them feel smug.

Let's face it, they never listen to our music. They sit and chatter and basically ignore us, which in my books is as rude as running in and out of our ranks."

"Well it was embarrassing," stated Tony. "We should have marched off."

"Well, next time we do a mess we should walk out. They're just as embarrassing. Besides, officers or Cambridge students, they're all the same class. Some of the kids here will end up commanding squaddies."

All the way back to barracks we argued about the inequalities of class.

I was headhunted for an instructor post at JLR. The posting was a notoriously comfortable one that offered promotion to S/Sgt. Again it was my sexuality that kept me from accepting the post. It wasn't that I didn't trust myself around two hundred sixteen- and seventeen-year-olds, but that it would entail going into the closet. There were plenty of rumours about the 'gay' instructors who taught there and the sly advantages some of them took of young bodies. Mess Tin Order was a favourite JLR anomaly. Squads were given two minutes to run to their rooms and reappear naked except for a web belt from which hung mess tins covering the crotch and arse. One JLR officer even wove a tale about working for a sperm bank and paid juniors to masturbate into a test tube. As he required fresh samples, the boys had to wank in his room. With a swab he meticulously cleaned their dicks and checked their balls before they started and thoroughly squeezed out the final drops, claiming this was richest in spermatozoa. Before paying the flushed donor five pounds, he placed the sample in his fridge. Whilst such SNCOs and officers hid behind their rank, they were despised by soldiers. I didn't welcome having to supervise juniors showering or give them 'short arm inspections'. I didn't want to feign disinterest and look away from what I might find attractive and neither did I want to humiliate them. As for my regiment, its security, familiarity and my rank had finally made it a place to call home.

Life was satisfying but now I was alienated from close mates that I'd known for years. Very soon I began to notice that mess life and my rank were restricting. In the evenings the living-in members mostly frequented the bar. Their conversational abilities were as limited as their interests. Football, women, punch-ups and drinking were the main topics of conversation. Those of us who didn't drink ourselves into a stupor were held in contempt. One S/Sgt, a teetotaller, was regularly ridiculed by the hardened drinkers. They even went as far as to order the bar doors locked and not to be reopened until after he'd drunk a beer. The boozers' favourite pastime, which they could pursue whilst drinking, was watching pornographic films. These were a frequent feature in the evenings. Their comments were typical:

"Oh! Look at the fucking knockers on that!"

"Cor, wouldn't half like to fucking shag her."

"Shit, I'd love to pork that fucking pussy."

Their fat faces slavered and their beer bellies wobbled. Lesbian films always drew an extra crowd into the room. In conversation over the breakfast table the next morning one claimed he'd like to go to bed with two or three lesbians.

"But they wouldn't want to have sex with you if they're lesbian," I suggested. The Sgt/Major knotted his eyebrows in thought. "They wouldn't be lesbians if they wanted sex with you." He picked up a slice of toast and began spreading butter liberally.

"Yeah, but all they need to sort them out is a good fat cock, a fucking good ride from a man. That'll put them on the straight and narrow."

In the mess, I could tell by intuition who might be gay. Whenever the subject of sexuality arose their inclinations were betrayed by silence, stony faces and shifting eyes. Establishing any form of acknowledgement was beyond question, the risks were too great. Some SNCOs outside the band knew of my sexuality but it was never talked about. For the first time in years I started to divide my life between a gay identity and a fabricated straight one. At the mess table I sniggered at their pathetic jokes, sometimes racist, sometimes sexist and sometimes homophobic. I called them 'mate' and referred to women as birds or bicycles. When asked why I wasn't married my excuses were prepared.

As a SNCO I came to realise that military life is nothing but Boy Scouts for adults. I was expected to inspect soldiers' rooms and uniforms, and to supervise all sorts of degrading jobs. As a Bdsm and JNCO I hadn't been aware how petty much of army routine was. Having joined straight from school, army life had been the only life with which I was acquainted. The block jobs, areas, bulling of boots, brassoing of belts and spurs, the bumpering, cleaning, scrubbing, being shouted at, humiliated and the various forms of inspection had all become routine. I'd known nothing else for almost thirteen years. As a Sgt, I was expected to enforce and police such a lifestyle. When bandsmen complained that Lee Purvis was starting to smell, the BM suggested I hold a room inspection. An order was posted and the bandsmen scrubbed out their rooms and polished and bumpered everything that could shine. While they stood to attention at the ends of their beds, I looked in their lockers, ran my finger along the tops of their doors and scrutinised their communal toilets, showers and wash basins. All of the bandsmen were mates and most in their early twenties. It humiliated me to treat adults with such little respect. Lee, a close friend, wasn't a grot, he just had a problem with greasy skin and profuse sweating in hot weather. It didn't help that he was still in the throes of a hormone explosion. Shortly after the inspection he asked my advice. In a 'big brother' manner I suggested he shower more than once a day and use disinfectant in his wash-basin water. Several days later the skin on his face went brown and dry and began peeling.

"What on earth's wrong with your face, Lee?" I asked.

"I don't know. It suddenly started going like this last night."

"Have you been using disinfectant?"

"Yes. you told me to."

"Just how much?"

"I don't really know, maybe a capful."

"In the water?"

"No, I pour into onto my flannel and then press it to my face."

"So you're using it neat?"

"Yes. Isn't that what you meant?"

"Of course not, you fucking numbty. No wonder your face is all burnt. You're only supposed to use a few drops in your sink or bath!"

I had studied hard over the last few years, gained O-Levels and diplomas, and started Open University courses in social science and ancient Greek history. Feeling confident, I began writing letters to universities and colleges asking what the entry qualifications were for degree courses in music. Eventually prospectuses began arriving at mail call. I spent ages browsing through their colourful pages to discover that I was already qualified to apply for most humanities courses. For music degrees, however, they wanted keyboard skills which I only possessed to a basic level. The prospectuses captivated me. They were full of students learning, students socialising in the campus bars, students in political groups; even gay and lesbian societies were mentioned. Most prospectuses had sections on equal rights that banned discrimination on grounds of sexual orientation. I was tempted to apply straight away but decided to give myself time to contemplate my impulses; I didn't wait long.

In late May of 1987, I attempted to hand in my resignation. Visiting Phil's office I asked if I could speak with him. It was a massive office that we referred to as the hangar. It had originally been a four-man room but since his arrival he'd shifted our accommodation. To do this he had to kick four junior bandsmen out of their room and re-billet them on the ground floor. It was an action that upset the singlies since the ground floor was a squaddie domain. Phil invited me to sit in the armchair in front of his desk, a sign that he sensed I wasn't on a social visit. He had gone to great pains to ensure the armchair had exhausted springs. When I sat, my arse sank until it almost hit the floor. The arms rose up and engulfed me like some giant marshmallow. It was the sort of armchair found in the CO's or Adjutant's office, chairs which immediately made you inferior. Suddenly Phil was sitting above me.

"But you've got a good future in front of you," he implored. "You're next in line for S/Sgt and you'll easily make band BSM."

"Yes, I know that, Sir, but if I make BSM it might not be in this band. Tony Shaw is next in line and since we're the same age any BSM rank I'm likely to get will come with a posting. I don't particularly want to transfer to another band."

"He might be posted out. He might go off somewhere as an instructor."

"He might, but then he might not. Staying is a gamble. Besides, I'll have to leave anyway in eight years' time. My twenty-two years' service will be up. I want to go to university and I feel it's much easier to so now than in eight years' time."

"But you'll get a large lump sum of money and a pension. It would make student life much easier."

"No, Sir! If anything, a lump sum would remove my entitlement to a student grant. Besides, such a large sum will eventually disappear."

"Oh! Come on, Nick. You're an excellent musician and you do your job well; we all like you. I think you're making a big mistake. I know you want to study but you could do that through the Open University; couldn't you?"

"It's pointless trying to argue with me, Sir. I appreciate it but my mind's made up. To be honest there is one main reason why I want to leave. I suppose I'd best tell you, you'd find out eventually anyway... It's because I am gay."

"Are you serious?"

"Of course I am. No, it's not a ploy to get an instant discharge. I am serious."

"But I thought that was all a joke... God! I never suspected for one moment you were gay," he said in a tapering whisper. He seemed lost in reflection.

"Well, I'm sorry but it's true."

"It doesn't bother me. I've known a few gay bandsmen over the years. Look! Please think about this for a couple of days. Then, if you're sure you want to leave, I'll pass your letter to the CO."

"And what if I say I want to stay?"

"Then you stay. You can change your mind whenever you want. What you've told me won't go beyond these four walls."

"What, even though I've told you I'm gay?"

"If you decide to stay then as far as I'm concerned you told me no such thing."

"Well, that's really nice of you, Sir."

I gave much thought to handing in my resignation and eventually decided to wait until the end of the year. So, in preparation, I began applying to a variety of colleges and universities. It was the first step towards Civvie Street.

19

My next posting was to Paderborn, a garrison town near Osnabrück. We moved in the autumn of 1987 and it was such an easy move I barely recall it. Apart from packing my own possessions I touched no other boxes nor scrubbed out any rooms. Instead, my MFO were collected from my room and the mess staff detailed to clean it. My arrival in Blacker Barracks was just as effortless. My wooden crates were delivered to my room in the mess and the only boxes I lifted or dragged were my own. The bandsmen and JNCOs, on the other hand, had to drag our heavy crates packed with instruments and music up six flights of stairs. Due to forthcoming engagements, the band had been detailed as part of the advance party. Over the coming weeks I witnessed the alien barracks gradually turning into home. After a month, Blacker Barracks was ours. Over six hundred soldiers, their families, and all their equipment and belongings transported several hundred miles, and all I'd contributed was to drag a few boxes into my room. The WOs' and Sgts' Mess wasn't as grand as the one in Kanpur Barracks, Tidworth. My room was small, the smallest I had ever had. Over the years I'd collected several hundred music scores as well as hundreds of tapes and records. I couldn't get everything into my room so had to leave several boxes outside my door.

I soon discovered that the mess kitchen was crawling with big, well-fed cockroaches. Like all cockroaches, they were concealed during the day, but in the early mornings and at night they appeared everywhere. Next to the kitchen was a small anteroom which housed our night fridge, tea, coffee, biscuits, cutlery and china. The fridge was always stocked with portions of chicken, cheese, sandwiches and cakes. Plates of bones and half-eaten sandwiches bedecked the draining board and sugar was spilt around the working top. I was generally the first person up in the mornings and always made myself a cup of coffee in the kitchen. It crawled with roaches. You heard them scuttling away as the light went on. Hundreds of bony feet tapping over the metal draining board. Within seconds they vanished, hidden in the cracks of tiles, tucked away in tight little crevices in the skirting boards or hidden inside the perforations of metal racking. There they hid vaguely staring, their antennae busily bibbling as they sensed vibrations and chemicals. I became obsessed with them and began rushing into the kitchen to catch them unawares. If quick enough, I killed a few in the sink with scorching hot water. It only took a little poking to uncover their particular hiding places. Steam from a boiling kettle spout sent them dropping to the floor where they either ran or dragged themselves away – if I didn't tread on them first. A long strip of masking tape inverted on the wall behind the fridge always ensnared an army, all still alive and frantically trying to rip their limbs free of sticky adhesive. Some had torn limbs from their shiny bodies. A war with roaches was a pointless battle. There numbers never dwindled and the regular exercise I gave them sharpened their ability to evade me. Even after official fumigation they returned in the same numbers. But eradicating a squadron each morning was a therapeutic start to the day.

Soldiers like sinks in their bedroom. They don't have to scuttle out in the middle of the night to have a piss. My new bunk had a sink but was so small that I barely had any floor space. On seeing the size of it, Phil gave me the opportunity to move into the band accommodation where there was a large room vacant. The extra space it afforded far outweighed the small loss of privileges. With no washbasin I had to use the ablutions further down the corridor. I also had to walk a short distance to the mess; however, the band bar was almost opposite my room and my mates were all around me. I was the obvious SNCO to be detailed with the responsibility of the bandsmen's accommodation and living amongst them had an official capacity. Our barracks were the old German type with high ceilings, lofts and cellars, and broad spacious corridors that still contained rifle racks built into wall recesses. My new room was big enough to house all my possessions with ease.

Within days of arriving in Paderborn I had established a small gymnasium in the vacant attic above the mess. Here I hung my kick bag and placed my weights. In a corner I laid a blue army carpet on which I could do sit-ups. I found a Taekwon-do school in town. It was run by a Korean fifth dan named Yoo Tai Kim. It was a well-equipped school with padded floors, kick bags, mirrors and a separate weight-training facility adjacent to the dojang. Both the weight room and training hall had perspex windows at one end, behind which was a bar. It was hard training in a school and the sessions always comprised vigorous warm-ups, plenty of painful stretching and a lengthy period performing basic techniques. However, the school was open six days a week from lunch time until the late evening and I was able to supplement my class training with lone sessions on the bag or in front of the mirrors.

The excitement of Christmas was approaching and with it the regular Hallemünsterland concert. Christmas was the highlight of band life. We played in all the messes and generally gave a regimental concert. Drink always flowed freely, there was plenty to eat and everywhere there were jovial faces and colourful decorations. The final event before we began leave was the soldiers' and JNCOs' Christmas dinner. After a few years' experience, I learnt that the nature of these dinners necessitated certain defensive procedures. You never wore decent clothes and all but the most junior bandsmen wore old pullovers and jeans. Then you made sure you fixed your music stand higher than normal, in fact as high as it took to hide your face. It was the only time in band life that we performed a concert in civvies or that we fixed our stands at differing heights. Like the dinner at KH, the regimental Christmas dinner was a riot. It was the only time in military life where for a brief moment anarchy ensued. They pelted us with nuts, usually walnuts and brazils, sometimes with oranges or legs of turkey. We hid behind our stands whilst they hooted and laughed and swigged their cans of beer. All the while officers and SNCOs hovered between them serving meals, picking up plates and handing out cans of beer to eager hands. The deference and servitude of the officers and SNCOs was as traditional on this occasion as the usual saluting officers or standing up for the National Anthem. When the BM saw the cooks running to hide or officers scuttling out the doors, he cut the band off and we ran for the wings. Beer cans started to fly and all hell broke loose. Sometimes tables and chairs were overturned and on particularly raucous dinners the RP waited outside the exits. After dinner, our band bar opened and those who wanted got merrily pissed.

Shortly after returning from leave, on a dark evening when crunchy snow froze the barracks paths, I took out my old typewriter and drafted my letter of resignation. It had been months since I'd decided to terminate my service and my mates and colleagues had convinced themselves that I wouldn't carry it through. Dean Firmin, who'd recently been promoted to Sgt, kept telling me with a laugh, "You won't go; it's all a ploy." He was certain I was pushing for a future promotion to S/Sgt. Dean saw ploys and plans in most band and regimental intrigues. With one finger I tapped heavily at the stiff keys, aware of the magnitude of what I was doing. The letter would seal my decision and end a way of life that I'd been accustomed to since leaving school:

> Sir, 24324732, T/M N. Elwood, humbly requests
> permission to terminate his service henceforth.
> Your Loyal Servant. T/M N. Elwood

The next morning, I carried it to Phil's office with a heavy sense of awareness. This was it, the next and most important step to my new life. With a sigh I handed it to him.

"Well, here it is, Sir. Thanks for letting me wait."

"Well, at least I know you're serious. But if you decide to change your mind then my lips are sealed." In the corridor an immense joy surged through my body; I'd actually done it. The BM accepted my resignation, and the great and not so great wheels of military bureaucracy set in motion.

My final year of military life was strange. Annual events such as the spring parade, the passage of seasons, the anniversaries of Balaklava and Waterloo and the Cavalry Memorial Parade; everything that was for the last time was mentally noted. Like prison, the army pervades and controls every aspect of your life. It controlled my body language, my civvies and the nature of my social relations. It clothed everything, be it thought or deed, in uniformity. I had never used a National Insurance number, or had to arrange somewhere to live. I had always had ample food on my table regardless of how much money was in my pocket. I had never had to walk farther than fifty yards to a pub, decorate a room, vote or select what clothes I wore to go to work. I had never had to tell a hairdresser what sort of haircut I wanted or had to cook a meal. Cultural icons established in the UK over the last fourteen years were unknown to me. I had never watched 'Blake's Seven', 'Red Dwarf' or 'Dallas'. When the tabloids speculated about JR's death I had to ask who he was. Apart from pissing and shitting the army arranged everything. Most squaddies who joined as teenagers, boys, and stayed in for a long time, were wary of leaving. They had led a life of security, disposable income and convenience. Some stayed in rather than risk the responsibility of Civvie Street. I was both thrilled and frightened. The freedom of college was inspiriting yet the thought of leaving behind all familiar and casting myself adrift filled me with trepidation.

My friendship with Matt developed, especially as his room was next to mine in the band block. He was an accomplished flautist but was weak on theory, form and history. I gave him lessons. When not reading scores, he wrote harmony exercises or trained his ear with the help of a piano. At other times he practised conducting from a score, the music blaring out of his stereo system. Gradually, he became a friend and we spent most of our time together.

Even though Matt had a girlfriend and was engaged, gossip started amongst some bandsmen. We ignored their little comments and carried on our intimacies much as before. He was aware I was attracted to him and we discussed my feelings on several occasions. He had a warm personality; he was affectionate, inquiring, funny and passionate about music. Though not intentional, he was an incredible prick tease. His friendship verged on the homosexual, though he never actually crossed that line. On several occasions he showed me his dick by taking it out of his boxer shorts or flopping it out of his army trousers. One morning, while I sat on the edge of his bed, he guided my hand over his thigh and pushed it onto his erection – unfortunately, covered with bed clothes. When pissed, we childishly showed each other our dicks at the urinal. Everything appeared a preamble to something greater, but I knew it would never get there. Matt was a horny adolescent and straight. He wouldn't overstep the parameters of his sexuality. One evening he took my sleeping bag out of my locker, lay on my bed and covered himself and then had a wank. I sat with my back to him and followed the score to Richard Strauss's 'Festliches Praeludium'. Loud music hid his shufflings and panting. He wore a black T-shirt and when he had come wet patches covered his stomach, one side of his shoulder and chest. He was quite soaking and must have been particularly horny. Like an offering he proffered me outstretched fingers. Thick white spunk stickied them. Holding his wrist lightly I licked them clean. "Brothers," he whispered.

Matt lived in a room with Parks. One Sunday afternoon, on the phone in their room, I received a call from Ash's wife, Dawn.

"You know, it's all around the regiment. It's the talk of the Sgts' Mess."

"What is?"

"That you've seduced one of the husbands and that Matt is your toy boy."

"What a load of fucking rubbish! Who on earth told you that?"

"It's obvious. Matt is never out of your sight. You're always together. If you're not in his room then you're wandering around town with him. You know you shouldn't be socialising with lower ranks, especially not a new boy."

"I don't really think it's any of your business who I hang around with, Dawn. Besides, he's hardly a new boy; he's been in the band over six months. There's absolutely nothing going on between us."

"No! But you can't tell me that you don't fancy him?"

"Has Ash been talking to you?"

"He doesn't have to, darling; it really is so obvious."

"And who am I supposed to have fucking seduced?"

"Well rumour has it that you've had sex with Tim Bray."

"That's a load of fucking rumour. I haven't touched him. Who's been telling you all this fucking nonsense?"

"Look, I don't want you to get into any kind of trouble. You've only got a few months left and I care too much for you to spoil it."

"Well, you might do a lot better by believing me rather then listening to a lot of malicious gossip."

"It doesn't matter what I think. It's the rumours that are important."

Army wives are a force to be reckoned with. They were just as able to manipulate opinion as the men. I knew that behind my back gaggles of gossiping wives were busy hacking away, influencing and manipulating the opinions of their husbands. There was some truth in their allegations but they'd severely distorted the facts. I had indeed planned to seduce Tim given the chance. He'd made several blatant hints that he was up for it. On the bus, where I usually kept one seat among the SNCOs and one with the bandsmen, he asked me if I wanted to wank him off. I replied that I would, provided he did it to me. It was suggested with an air of humour, just enough to make it seem that we might be joking. Then he moved the jumper on his lap and I saw his erect dick sticking out. My eyes bulged as a sly grin broke across his face. But once the gossiping started his suggestions ceased.

One evening, when we were playing at yet another officers' mess, Ash and Edward Parks got drunk; both were Cpls. Phil was ill and the mess was conducted by Bungle, the BSM. In the anteroom we got changed, arranged our music and warmed up. Parks and a few others enacted a horse show, it was a common practice during the long wait before we performed. Cantering around the large room they jumped over coffee tables and chairs whilst someone gave a running commentary. Parks didn't perform well due to an injury he had sustained a few days earlier, when he'd jumped on top of his wife during sex. Dressed only in a cape and boots and spurs, his ankle hit his buttock causing a deep puncture from the spur. He needed several stitches.

We performed in the minstrels' gallery and were visible to the mess below. The band were in high spirits and bottles of beer were passed under our chairs. Bungle was a useless musician who'd gained his SNCO promotion after I'd sat his music exams for him. Concerts were regularly bodged by his incompetence and he was definitely a musical moron. When the Queen Mother appeared at a horse show he dropped his side drum. It crashed onto the floor along with his drum sticks. We began the National Anthem without a roll. All the significant thumps, crashes or rolls that composers had scored, he at one time or other managed to miss. Even when a march climaxed to an obvious percussion strike he could be trusted to either miss, pre-empt, or delay it. On the drum kit he was clumsy and stifled his beat. Inconsistent rhythms forced the tempo in one place and dragged it down in others.

Bungle's management skills were just as bad. At the same time as advertising proclaimed the professional army, Bungle was busy bungling engagements. We spent the summer season waiting for un-booked buses to arrive or having to send a driver away when Bungle had double-booked. In the early hours of morning we arrived at a strange barracks to find no accommodation arranged or no meals to eat – sometimes both. His shortcomings failed to embarrass him and were instead borne with a laugh. He hadn't a clue what he was doing when he conducted. His main task, mutually and tacitly agreed, was to indicate when to raise or lower our instruments and when to start and finish playing. In the duration between start and finish, the collective musicianship of the band controlled the performance while Bungle pointlessly gesticulated with both arms in tandem.

During the mess the band decided to play the wrong piece of music and not tell him.

"All he has to do is to drop the baton; we do the rest. It doesn't matter what we play," said Dean.

"He wouldn't even notice," added Ian.

Then Tony suggested the piece to play. As a SNCO he carried responsibility for the joke and we changed the music on our stands. Bungle lifted his baton expecting to thrash out 'Stars and Stripes Forever' and instead flailed theatrically to 'The Birdy Song'. He had to be told he'd conducted the wrong music and even then he didn't believe us. More beers were passed by the percussion section under chairs to the front row. Our clasp stable belts, which we wore under our blues tunics, were suitable bottle openers. During the 'Spanish Gypsy Dance', the sax and horn players suddenly produced the most ridiculous ball masks, with winged sides or jutting foreheads from which sprung manic clumps of hair that flopped around in time with the music. We almost broke down as bandsmen stopped playing to laugh. The pranking around became boisterous and we attracted suspicious glances from the mess below. I looked across at Bungle but he just grinned and waved his arms about, fully aware that his efforts lacked meaning. Beers passed under chairs were swigged behind the cover of our music stands. During 'Karma Chameleon', Parks began inserting ambulance calls which screeched above the mundane melody. They were short calls, simply 'wha whaa, wha whaa', but were enough to raise heads in the mess. Bungle motioned him to stop but his signals were indistinguishable from his meaningless conducting. Then Ashley began squawking on individual notes. Like Parks's siren, they were clearly audible. Bungle waved an arm and frowned but few noticed. More officers looked up. Parks played a siren and Ashley squawked raucously in response. Between them the bandsmen laughed and the clumps of hair bounced like the plumes of strutting cocks. Bungle became agitated and waved at them. Tony cast them an annoyed glare. Leaning back, I ordered them to stop. Parks let burst a lengthy, penetrating wail.

"Fucking stop it!" I shouted.

"Fuck off, Nicky!" said Ash, and he squawked up to the highest notes of his register. Bungle threw his baton at Parks and it hit him on the head. He looked up.

"Stop, now!"

Stealing from an officer's mess was legitimate. Jars of caviar, tins of halva, silver cutlery and salt and pepper sets were consider payment for our services. On the bus, Parks and Ash sat with two bottles of wine, glasses, and a lump of cheese. They laughed and joked as other bandsmen packed their equipment into luggage racks and made themselves comfortable. I walked down the aisle. Parks wore the mask that sprouted hair. He twitched his head in a spasmodic motion.

"You two very nearly got us into trouble tonight."

Parks flicked his head towards me and Ash cackled.

"It's no big deal, Nicky. They never noticed. They were too fucking busy partying."

"Take that stupid fucking mask off and wipe the grin off your face!"

Like a chicken, Parks craned his head sideways and focused on me with one eye which peered from behind the mask.

"Oh my, Gay Boy Nicky's getting all serious."

"Don't call me Nicky. Use my rank, you fucking little shit and get that mask off!"

He pulled it from his face.

"All right, keep your fucking hair on."

"I said, you two very nearly got us into trouble. Officers were looking up. Just because the BM isn't here doesn't mean you can rip the arse. It only takes one complaint and then Bungle's in the shit."

"We were only having a laugh," interrupted Ash.

"Yeah, go fuck yourself," added Parks.

Bungle, who was sat at the front of the bus, yelled: "Pack it in, now!"

"Fucking queer," snarled Parks. Bungle stood and walked towards us.

"Right, when we get back to barracks you're both on a charge. I'm not having you speak to a SNCO like that. You're both Cpls, you should know better."

The following day they paraded in the BM's office and were punished with extra duties. As was their prerogative, they refused punishment which meant going in front of the CO on appeal. Passing my room, Tony called in to tell me they'd told the BM I was gay. Parks claimed I was jealous since he shared his room with Matt who I was in love with; further, they intended telling the CO. Storming into Matt's room, I grabbed Parks by the neck and thrust him against the wall. He gasped as breath was knocked from his chest.

"You open your fucking big gob and I'll bloody kill you," I snarled, spraying spittle over his face. "Have you fucking got that?" Suddenly the door opened and Tony appeared. I looked around; Parks was still pinned against the wall by my hand.

"Nick. Could I have a word, please."

Calming down, I released him and followed Tony into the empty corridor.

"Don't worry," he said. "Everyone's behind you and everything's been sorted out."

"What do you mean?"

"Just that. Nothing's going to come of it. The RSM isn't even going to let them speak. "

Next morning I received a message from the RSM asking for a trumpeter to sound CO's Office at RHQ. At the same time Ash and Parks were detailed to attend the parade which was held outside the CO's office. That night in the mess the band SNCOs took me out for a drink. It was their way of assuring me of their solidarity. After a few pints Phil narrated the events in CO's office at which he'd been present.

"It was fucking funny, Nick. You should have seen it. The pair of them were stood outside his office smiling and smirking, as if they were on to a real winner. By the time the RSM had marched them in they were like two lost sheep. The CO fined them each a hundred and fifty pounds and ordered them out of his office. Ash managed to say 'But...' before the RSM screamed at him, 'Keep your fucking mouth shut, soldier!' Then, the CO added, 'Oh, and eight extra duties.' They were fucking gutted, it was written all over their faces. Your name is going to be fucking dirt now."

"But you've no worries with friends like us," said Dean raising his glass.

"And we all love you," said Tony affectionately.

In the early summer we travelled back to the UK for ten days. Mercer was being married on the first weekend and Matt on the second. To make the trip official the BM arranged a midweek concert at an RAF barracks.

Matt was married in Brighton. He had wanted me as best man but since his fiancée had been given an update on the intimacy of our relationship she began trying to distance us. She persuaded him to study with the bandmaster rather than me, and said he should spend more time in company other than mine. Caught between two influential voices Matt didn't know what to do, and I began seeing less of him. Several weeks before the wedding he asked me to relinquish the role of best man so they could ask someone whom they both knew.

At the party which followed the wedding Matt's parents thanked me for being a friend to their son. Matt, so they told me, admired me a great deal – but this I already knew. Then his mother asked if I'd make sure Peter, their youngest son, arrived home safely as they were spending the night in a hotel. It was late and both Lee and I had drunk enough. We found Peter stood in the corner of the bar, his glass of lager and lime almost empty. He too was ready to leave. We said our goodbyes and started walking back in the dark.

It was when Peter and I stopped for a piss that he suggested we had sex when we got home. To emphasise his offer, he waggled his cock around for me to see. A beam of moonlight illuminated it. Like all adolescent boys' cocks it was big and fat, accentuated by his boyish frame. Hurriedly, I put myself away, left him pissing and caught up with Lee.

"I don't fucking believe it!"

"Believe what?"

"He's just asked me to have sex with him."

"You're fucking joking?"

"No, really. He asked me if I'd have sex with him."

"My God! Not Matt's brother!" Peter appeared out of the bushes further down the road.

"What am I going to fucking do?"

"You can't. You fucking well can't do it with him."

"Why not, he wants it."

"You're not going to, are you?"

"What would you do in my shoes with a sixteen-year-old girl fucking gagging for it? Sweet sixteen and all that."

"Well, I suppose I'd want to do it, if she was sexy."

"Well he is sexy, he is very fucking sexy."

"But you can't."

"I know," I said reluctantly, "he's Matt's sodding brother."

"Exactly!" Then we stopped walking and turned to wait for Peter who was staggering towards us.

At his house we made ourselves coffee before going to our bedrooms. I was sleeping in Peter's room and Lee in Matt's. Peter was on the sofa in the front room. In his bedroom with the door closed, I snooped around. Boys' bedrooms are a turn-on; they are a private domain of sordid secrets. Under his pillow I found a stiff hanky and under his duvet small yellow trails marked nocturnal emissions. I browsed through his bookshelf, untidily stuffed with comic books, games, a tennis ball, some little plastic fantasy models and his school books. Next I rummaged through a drawer in which lay ironed and folded underwear. Mickey Mouse, Batman and an assortment of colours and patterns decorated his boxers. In one corner lay underpants, sexy white ones through which my fingers ran and probed. It was a typical boy's bedroom, from its untidiness and wall posters of pop icons to the heady scent of adolescent male hormones.

Downstairs I heard noises from the kitchen and opened the door to listen. The kitchen had been quite tidy when we left it; from it came a medley of noises: taps turned on, cutlery clinked on the draining board and footsteps shuffled in the hallway. Peter clumsily ambled around the front room before returning to the kitchen. I stripped to my boxers and got into bed. Picking up my book, I started reading. Any second now, I thought, and he'll make his move. At that very moment I heard footsteps on the stairs and a knock on my door followed; it opened. He'd taken off his shirt and was bare to the waist. His little nipples were dark brown and his trousers, undone at the belt, hung loosely from his hips. All that kept them up was the jut of his dick.

"I want to sleep in your bed, Nick," he whispered.

"Well you can't, can you?" I said in a subdued schoolmaster manner.

"Why not?"

"Because I'm in it, silly."

"Oh, come on, let me in," he implored. "You've got my duvet and it's not warm, and besides, it is my bed."

"You're drunk; you don't know what you're doing"

"I'm a bit pissed, but I can get a hard on – no problem." He stroked his crotch seductively.

"I am not doing anything!" I insisted.

"I promise I won't get horny, please, I just want to sleep next to you."

"Well, if you must. But I'm not doing anything. You're Matt's brother." He sucked in his waist and his jeans fell to his ankles where he stepped out of them. All the while he held my gaze. He turned off the main light and switched on the bedside reading lamp where he stood to remove his watch. I cast my eyes over his body, mesmerised by the play of light and shadow across his torso. In the lamp's close glare each hair on his forearm was illuminated and his chest a golden soft down. Smothered by white cotton, his dick and balls bulged heavily.

"And keep your pants on!" He jumped in beside me and tugged part of the duvet over his body. A busting hard on kept me awake. His sighs and agitated twisting and turning were a plea for sex that I painfully ignored. I could smell his horniness; it oozed from him and scented the bedding. It was the fresh smell of underarms, hot bollocks and viscous dribblings. Eventually, some hours later, I drifted into sleep with his chin nestled into the back of my neck, his hot breath gently huffing onto my shoulder and his damp erection against my thigh.

In the morning he got up and pulled on his trousers. I felt a sense of guilt in having slept with him, but he acted as if he'd just spent the night downstairs. In the kitchen we made breakfast. The smell woke Lee, and he came banging down the stairs, bounding into the front room with a broad grin on his face.

"Do you know what you asked Nick last night?"

Peter hid his shock well though I noticed him beginning to blush. "I've no idea; I was drunk."

"You asked him to have sex with you."

"Yeah! Okay," he laughed.

"No, you did, really. Don't you remember?"

Peter buried his face in the task of tying his trainer laces. "Didn't he, Nick? You heard him."

"He was drunk. He won't remember," I claimed.

"What's important," said Peter, looking up, "is did we do anything. I mean my bum feels normal."

"No, I'm afraid we didn't," I said to Peter. "I mean, if you'd come upstairs we might have got it together."

"Yeah, okay," said Lee, unconvinced. "But I heard you."

After the incident with Ash and Parks, and the malicious gossiping of wives with little better to do, I was angry. It took me months to forgive those who'd taken part. In November, the band SNCOs met in Phil's hangar to discuss the promotions required by my resignation. It had already been decided that we should promote a Cpl before I left. This gave me a perfect opportunity to exact my revenge on Ash. I'm quite ashamed of the manner in which I did this but being a bitch was part of our daily lives and a matter of survival. For the last time in my military life I expertly manipulated a band faction to my pathetic advantage. My influence was a reflection of my social status within the band. Ash, who until recently had been one of my best mates, was next in line for promotion. Band opinion favoured him as the next Sgt and he was well supported by most SNCOs. The meeting in the hangar was to discuss the strengths and weaknesses of nominees. Every mistake they'd made was debated and their strengths acknowledged. Ash's nomination was last on our agenda. Immediately, the panel began to smile and nod in approval.

Tony was first to praise him. "I think Ash would make an excellent choice."

"Me too," interrupted Phil.

"He's a good, reliable instrumentalist," continued Tony. "He's punctual and though he's made a few mistakes, I think he's our best choice."

There was a murmur of approval.

"Hear, hear," added Dean.

I waited before pitching my voice above the murmur.

"I really don't think Ash is the right man for the job," I said clearly. I paused, conscious of their shocked eyes that bore into me. "I know it's really unfortunate and perhaps unfair to mention, but we have to consider the behaviour of his wife in this matter."

"What do you mean?" asked Tony.

"Well, to put it bluntly, she's a fucking slag, nothing but a whore."

"Only last week she was caught giving one of the junior Bdsm a blow job. I'm sure most of you know who the flushed-faced recipient was. And he's not the only one to have been seduced by her. She's been caught with her knickers around her ankles at the Cpls' Mess party. Then she's been having an affair with a squaddie and only last Thursday she tried to get off with one of the Sgts at the 'Cpls versus SNCOs' games night. She's the talk of the regiment and most of you know it. I dread to think what she'd get up to with her iron-knickered ways in the mess. She's a reputational liability."

Tony rubbed his neck in thought. "But he's the best man for the job."

"I agree, he is," I continued, "but unfortunately he's married to her and it wouldn't be long before she made a big mistake and really dragged us through the dirt. She's hardly the sort of person we want in the mess."

"I think Nick's got a good point," said Phil from behind his huge desk. "This promotion does entail some consideration of the wife's behaviour. After all, she's being promoted to the mess as much as him and I must admit I have heard rumours."

Heads nodded in agreement; most would have agreed with whatever the BM said. It was ludicrous that the reputation of a wife could be considered during the selection process, even more shocking that I slated her on the grounds of her sexual adventures. Perhaps I acted out of jealousy, as the men she had sex with were really sexy. My vindictive oratory caused Ash to be passed over by Ian Moore and revenge felt sweet. Ash never did make Sgt.

It was a few days later that I received a letter from Essex University offering me an unconditional place to study history and philosophy. I was thrilled and proudly presented the letter to my mates. I had applied to a number of colleges but didn't expect to be accepted at a university. Within half an hour I telephoned the UK to confirm the offer. Now I could enjoy my last few months without worrying about my future.

My last military engagement was a Christmas concert in Paderborn cathedral. We rehearsed with the choir and finally, the night before the concert, top and tailed the programme. Phil wanted to listen to Handel's 'For Unto Us a Child Is Born' and passed his baton to Bungle.

"I'm not conducting, I'll fuck it up, give it to Nick, he'll do it. Won't you Nick?"

"No problem," I replied eagerly.

"Yes, perhaps that's a better idea," said Phil, extending the baton to me.

"On one condition. You let me do all of it."

"Agreed. Take it as a going away present," he said smiling. I took the baton from his outstretched hand. I was too excited to realise this would be the last time I would conduct the band. We had rehearsed the music to perfection and the cathedral choir were superb. The acoustic properties of the interior fortified our rendition while the choir exacted our best effort. When cut off, the final chord echoed around the solid walls into oblivion.

The following afternoon I cleaned my ceremonials for the last time and bulled my boots to a higher standard than such an occasion required. I hadn't used a floor-polish finish for years and had learnt how to bull with spit, polish and huff. Besides, I could quickly bull my toe caps to a deeper shine than floor polish produced. I scrubbed my white sword belt with washing powder, brassoed the ends of my gold lanyard, pressed my tights, polished my spurs and oiled them so they jingled. Dressed, I took my place for the last time on the bus to an engagement. As usual I kept two seats, one with the SNCOs at the front and the other in the back with the bandsmen. At the end of the concert we played the National Anthem. As was my custom, I poked the first two fingers of my right hand in a 'V'. It's possible to play most of the anthem using the fingers of the left hand and my gesture was a snub at the monarchy. Finally, after the percussion beat two, three pace rolls, we played our Regimental Quick March. I sat to attention, and for once, I supplicated myself to the regiment. I had met some wankers in my service. I'd often been given shitty jobs, shouted at, hounded and humiliated. I'd been taught to know my place in the hierarchical system and to be humble to officers barely out of their teens. But I'd had many worthwhile experiences. As much as the regiment pissed you off, it also protected and nurtured you whilst moulding you in its image. Finally, during the last bars of the Regimental March, I realised that the regiment itself was a living entity. It had its own character, expectations, idiosyncrasies and history. I felt pride at having become one of its dragoons and having performed my duties to the best of my ability. I even felt a pride at being a queer dragoon. The motto that 'If you ain't Cav – you ain't' rang true but with one exception, I wasn't just Cav, I was a 15th Dragoon, a Gay 15th Dragoon – and proud of it!

After the concert a crowd gathered to watch us packing our equipment back onto the bus. We always attracted onlookers when in jangly, shiny ceremonials. I felt an immense urge to be on my own, to reflect on the magnitude of my last concert. If I'd done so I'd probably have wept silently for the things, people and ways I was about to leave. However, I couldn't allow reflective thoughts to develop. I had to look strong in my convictions in the face of my comrades – if not to persuade them of my sincerity then to convince myself. I was the last to board the bus.

"Well, how does it feel, Nick?" asked Tony.

"You really want to know? It feels fucking great. I'M FREE," I shouted in exhilaration, throwing my forage cap down the aisle. "Free to be as gay as I want, why, I could even go all camp now."

"You are camp," suggested Ian. "You are the Queen."

Just as I had when I joined, I visited the medical centre for a medical, called in the MRO to collect documents and trundled my army equipment back to the RQMS' stores in a military suitcase and holdall. Some items I returned had originally been issued at training camp in Catterick. My holdall, which had travelled on ferries, aircraft, three-tonners and Landrovers, hardly looked used. My original combats, now faded and worn, would have been the pride of any recruit. They still had years of wear in their material. My best boots had never been bulled. Since the day I passed out as bandsman I had worn George boots in parade uniform. Instead I had worn the best boots on every exercise, BFT, and guard duty. The leather had surrendered and was soft and pliable. Years of service had been etched into their sides and the toe caps had been scuffed and cut. They were so accustomed and shaped to my feet that there was not another person in the world who could now wear them with comfort.

"They've done me well," I sighed as I passed them across the counter to the storeman.

"Any use to you? he asked inspecting them. "They're nowhere near worn out yet. We'll only throw them away. No use to anybody else."

"Yeah, sure, I could do with a buckshee pair," I replied, taking them back from him. "Any chance of me keeping a sleeping bag as well?"

"You're supposed to hand 'em in. But I could let you – at a price, of course."

"Such as?"

"Well, any chance of getting me a set of trumpet cords?"

"I'll see what I can do."

Once I'd handed in my military equipment I signed the necessary forms with my number, name and rank. The following morning, dressed in civvies, I handed the storeman an old pair of cords from our store. In return he allowed me to keep my extra-long sleeping bag. It was a bargain as army sleeping bags are made of duck down and very expensive.

Suddenly I was on the periphery of band life. The vacancy I was to leave had been allocated to Ian Moore who took charge of the fanfare trumpeters. A new clarinettist arrived from JLR and within days the insatiable Dawn had seduced him. The band rehearsed without me and on more than one occasion I stood silently in the corridor listening, regretting that I had to leave for new challenges. Every time I stopped to talk to passing acquaintances I was asked what it felt like to be on the verge of Civvie Street. I smiled, replying that it was a great feeling, but it wasn't. The final week passed and soon, with excitement and apprehension, it was time for my farewell parties; one in the mess and one with the band.

The mess gave me the standard bronze dragoon statuette for which my monthly mess fees had paid. If I'd served two years longer it would have been cast in silver. The band presented me with yet another statue and some record tokens. I made speeches in both bars. However, it was at the band bar that I was the most passionate. That evening I wore the same jacket in which I'd arrived fourteen years ago.

"Well, this is the big moment," I said as the laughing and talking subdued. "I really can't believe I'm actually stood here and that I've handed in my notice and am about to leave. I would be quite happy to stay here. I've had some brilliant experiences, some of the best experiences of my life. But I need to move on and do other things."

"Yeah, I can imagine," shouted Tony.

"Most of you know why I'm leaving and that the army can't give me what I really want."

"What, a sore arse?" grinned Tony. The few officers and squaddies present laughed out of conformity. They had no idea what the joke referred to. Phil, beer glass in hand, chuckled to himself. A big grin span across his face and he was content that for once there was something he was a part of. He rarely knew the band intrigues and now was party to one of the most ancient.

"Though having said that, it hasn't done me too badly," I continued. "I've spent fourteen years in this band and some of you – Tony, Bungle – have spent that time with me. Those years have seen our service in Bhurtpore, Polemedea, Bolton, Rawlpindi, Kanpur and finally Blacker Barracks. Fourteen years sharing the same accommodation, the same bar, the same building and barracks. It doesn't seem that long ago I walked through the gates wearing this very jacket – my 'teacher's jacket'." I held up an arm and the cuff tightened around my forearm. "I seem to have outgrown it," I laughed. "We've had our ups and downs but no matter what, I've been supported and looked after." I paused, aware of the sudden silence across the room. "Perhaps I'll never find a place again that's so familiar, so homely, but then I just have to go and find out. I'm not going to say much more, just in case I start blabbing. Wherever you go, as a band or civilians, I wish you luck... lots of luck." I felt a massive lump swelling in my throat and knew it was time to stop. "Thanks," I said, holding aloft my presentation.

"A toast for the Queen," shouted Ian Moore, his hand gripping his crotch. The bandsmen came to attention with their glasses or bottles held in their hands. The wives, squaddies and officers stood or sat confused, unfamiliar with either the ritual or its meaning.

"The Queen," they chanted, raising their drinks to their mouths.

In the quiet of my room that night I cried for everything good and bad I was about to leave behind. Eventually, I was lulled to sleep by the sound of someone being sick, retches piercing the silence. A familiar, reassuring song of the night.

I had arrived at my regiment a naive youngster who'd failed at school and wasn't very popular. Though I regret having spent so much time on military music, I don't regret joining the army. I was lucky enough to meet people who each had a share in creating my personality, my thinking, humour and self-confidence, and leading me towards independence. The nature of band life afforded me the time to study and train. In the macho environment of army life, I had been taught pride in my sexuality. I wasn't odd, there were gay soldiers and officers in every barracks. To most soldiers they're invisible and to the hierarchy they don't exist. The personal histories and service to the Crown of gays past and present has been blanked out and denied, but it has always existed and always will. It was in the closeted environment of military barracks, behind perimeter fences, barbed wire and sentries, that I came to accept my difference and was encouraged and nurtured in expressing pride. I met gays from proud, tough regiments, from amongst the macho ranks of squaddies, from the bands, medics and officers' messes. Whilst many of them might want to deny, rationalise and rename the activities they engaged in, they were undeniably consenting homosexual acts. For whatever reasons, those frightened, silent soldiers, whether discharged or still serving, play their part in maintaining the silence and in doing so deny and obliterate a history in which they participated.

I left the barracks in Paderborn on a bitterly cold winter evening. Hoarfrost covered the bare trees between the barrack blocks. The lights from tall street lamps made their ice-frosted boughs sparkle like a scene from a Russian fairy tale. With the warmth and familiarity afforded by fourteen years' service, I said goodbye to my mates. Some shook my hand, others hugged me. A few kissed me and at the back of the crowd Matt and Lee stood crying. Tears slid off Lee's greasy face. Matt kissed my cheek. His lips were cold.

Ian, the first adult I had a crush on, gave me a crushing hug. He was still a sexy-looking soldier. He kissed me and holding me in his embrace spoke words I have never forgotten and cherish as the greatest tribute a straight man can offer a gay: "You know," he said, "if one of my sons turns out gay, then I'll just think of you and it won't ever be a problem."

Then, choked and emotional, I stepped aboard the regimental bus bound for London. Ice covered the inside windows, I rubbed a patch clear with my hand but it was so cold it immediately frosted over. Through the window, the small band were partially blurred from view. The frost distorted some and obliterated others. As the bus pulled away I was denied final eye contact. Away from the curb we chugged over the icy road, past the NAAFI and empty cookhouse. On the pavement groups of squaddies huddled through the shiny cold. Their heads hung in the bitter wind like figures from a Dostoyevsky novel. Next, past the Regimental Headquarters illuminated by spotlights where the regimental gardens lay under the even snow on which no footprint had ever been placed. Only the barren rose bushes marked its borders. Then we turned towards the gate and passed 'C' Squadron barrack block. The rooms were lit up like portholes on a dark ship. Soldiers were lazing in their warm rooms occupied with a routine I was intimately familiar with: talking, joking, cleaning, bitching and bulling. Pausing at the guardroom, the sentry lifted the barrier with one arm. The other held his black, cold SMG. The condensation from his breath wafted thickly from his mouth. On the veranda, surrounded by his paraphernalia, stood the Provo Sgt. He looked as ornamental as his brass plaque, bass drum and brass tank shells. Even from a distance I could see the mirror-like finish on his bulled ammunition boots. Through my frosty window I watched the Guard Commander going through the initial routines of his duty. As the bus lurched out of camp, its cold engine spluttering, I swung around to glimpse the regimental sign proclaimed at every barracks in which I served. Through my window and in the dark, the green and yellow colours and portcullis were indistinguishable. However, in a flash of light from an approaching headlamp, it was momentarily illuminated. My regiment, mates and friends, my home and life were disappearing into the wintry distance. For the last time I passed the motto, *Forever Onwards*.

Glossary

Active Service: Deployment in a battle role. Service for the UN, though generally in a peace-keeping role, is also deemed active service. Dog tags are worn throughout deployment.

Areas: The term for the fatigue which cleans barrack footpaths and roads of litter and dog-ends. Regimental departments are each responsible for the cleanliness of an area.

Bandmaster: *(See BM)*

Bandsman (Bdsm): This can refer either to a military musician of any rank, or specifically to the rank of bandsman which is the equivalent to that of a private or trooper. In staff bands this rank is musician.

BAOR: British Army of the Rhine. Collective term for those troops stationed in Germany.

Barrack Dress: A uniform worn on routine duty in working hours. There are two forms of barrack dress. One, worn by working soldiers, consists of synthetic fibre trousers, boots, serge shirts and berets. In winter a pullover and stable belt are worn. The second variation, worn by bandsmen, storemen and clerks, consists of the same basic uniform but with cotton shirts (No2 dress), shoes and side hat.

BFT: Basic Fitness Test. A two-mile run which is divided into an eleven-minute forced march followed by the last mile in a personal best. For soldiers under thirty this has to be in under eleven minutes.

Block jobs: The daily routine of cleaning communal facilities.

Blues (Officially known as 'No1 dress'): A blue jacket with chain-mail epaulettes and high collar, worn with forage cap, sword belt and yellow or gold lanyards. Rank on blues are bordered against red felt and woven in gold braid. In the cavalry, Blues are worn with cavalry tights, George boots and spurs.

BM: Bandmaster. Within a line band he holds the rank of warrant officer first class, equal in status to that of the RSM. Bandmasters are trained at the RMSM Kneller Hall and are usually posted into another band rather than returning to their paternal one.

BSM: Band Sergeant Major. In a line band, this warrant officer class 2 rank is the furthest an individual may progress without completing a bandmaster's course. The BSM is usually responsible for the day-to-day running of the band and for discipline.

Buckshee: A military colloquialism for an item of clothing or equipment that is unsigned for and hence unaccounted for. A form of black market for floating items.

Bulling: Polishing boots until they develop a reflective shine.

Bumpering: The polishing of tiled floors with the use of floor polish and either hand bumpers or electric floor polishers.

Bunk: A single soldier's room.

Bunking: Skiving off work.

Brasso: A brand of metal polish. Brassoing is the term used to polish metal.

Charge: On breach of a military regulation soldiers are officially punished. This is known as a 'charge'.

Civvies (1): Civilians as opposed to the military. Often used derogatively.

Civvies (2): Civilian clothes.

Civvie Street: Forces slang for the civilian world.

CO: Commanding Officer. A lieutenant colonel in charge of a regiment.

Combats: A uniform usually worn in the field. Combats come in several camouflage patterns (temperate, desert and arctic) and consist of trousers and a smock. They are worn with boots and either berets or combat helmets.

Cpl: Corporal. A JNCO rank above lance-corporal and denoted by two chevrons.

Crash Out: The mobilisation of a regiment or garrison. These are called in order to test troop and regimental readiness for combat. Tanks are employed in the field and ammunition loaded onto the three-tonners. Crash Outs can be called off before deployment in the field or may last several days.

Dragoons: Formerly mounted cavalry who carried swords. Dragoons fall into two types – Dragoons and Dragoon Guards. The Dragoon Guards ride larger horses and carry heavier swords. (cf. *Lancers* and *Hussars*)

Dry-Knacking: Writing or copying music by hand.

Dualling: The illegal practice of bulling your boots with a layer of floor polish. Certain brands of polish give the boot a highly reflective shine but are not recommended in wet or damp weather as they cloud the toe cap.

Forage Cap: A peaked cap which forms part of No2 dress though it is often permitted to wear it with other forms of dress. Forage caps carry regimental colours, designs and cap badges.

Full Band: Though this can refer to the assembly of the whole band, it is also used to describe the practice or rehearsal of the band.

George boots: Cavalry boots which are of either ankle or calf height. Tights are worn over the shin or ankle leather and fixed under the boot by straps. George boots are normally worn with spurs. They form part of cavalry blues or reds dress.

Green Grollie: Army jargon for a military bus which was usually matt green in colour.

Guard Mount: These occur at 1800 and 2200. The standard format is a parade in which the guard are inspected. At the 2200 hrs parade Last Post is sounded.

Guardroom: Most barracks have their own guardroom which is normally located by the main gate. Guardrooms are run in working hours by the Regimental Police and at other times by a guard. Guardrooms have a jail facility for offenders and a large dormitory room for the guard.

Individual: Term used by bandsmen to denote practising your instrument on your own, or the timetabled period allowing for this practice.

JLR: Junior Leaders' Regiments. Institutes that train soldiers too young to train in an adult camp. The training, which begins at age sixteen, lasts about two years. Most corps have a JLR regiment.

JNCOs: The ranks below that of sergeant. In a cavalry regiment the JNCOs are L/Cpls (one chevron) and Cpls (two chevrons).

KH: Kneller Hall. The Royal Military School of Music (RMSM) in Whitton, Twickenham. This school trains both bandsmen and potential bandmasters. The bandsmen, who are lower ranks, are referred to as 'pupils' whilst the trainee bandmasters are called 'students'. A pupil's course lasts one year whilst a bandmaster's course lasts three.

Last Post: The guard parade held at 2200 hrs and at which the bugle or trumpet call of this name is sounded. There are both infantry and cavalry versions of this call.

L/Cpl: Lance-corporal. The lowest JNCO rank, above private or trooper and denoted by one chevron.

Line Band: Bands commanded by a WO1.

Mess: An area designated for the use of soldiers of a particular rank. For the Troopers and JNCOs this is the cookhouse though JNCOs frequently have their own bar. For SNCOs and officers a mess includes a bar, dining room and living accommodation. Though soldiers may frequent messes below their held rank they may not socialise in messes above them.

MFO: Military Forces Overseas. This term is also a name for the wooden and cardboard boxes that soldiers pack their belongings into when posted.

MO: Medical Officer. Usually one was resident in every barracks.

MP: Military Police. Distinguished by their bright red forage caps.

MRO: Manning and Records Office. The offices within corps which deal with manning and the updating of soldiers' service records.

MRS: Medical Reception Station. A small medical centre which may hold patients with minor illnesses.

NAAFI: Navy, Army and Airforce Institute. An establishment that provides barracks with the JNCO mess, the privates' bar, and also provides shopping facilities both on camp for soldiers and within the garrison for families.

NAAFI Break: A mid-morning break. So named as many soldiers visit the NAAFI canteen.

NBC: Nuclear, Chemical and Biological. Forms of warfare for which soldiers learn to protect themselves. The NBC suit, colloquially known as a Noddy Suit, is a carbon-based uniform worn with a gas mask.

Noddy Suit: Military colloquialism for an NBC suit.

No2 Dress: Parade uniform which generally consists of khaki trousers and jacket, cotton shirt, tie, best boots and a forage cap.

Office/Orders (1): Commanding officer's orders/office. The name given to the period when the CO holds meetings or interviews, often of a disciplinary nature.

Office/Orders (2): Trumpet calls for the above parades.

Pad: A married soldier or the military flats and houses they live in. Also refers to an army family. Pad can also denote a soldier's bed space.

PFA: Physical Fitness Test. A gymnasium test which assesses strength, endurance and suppleness.

Provost Sergeant (Provo): The SNCO in charge of the RP and guardroom. He also helps maintain discipline within the barracks.

PT: Physical Training. Physical exercises requiring no particular skill. Most are repetitious, e.g. sit-ups, press-ups, running, circuit training.

PTI: Physical Training Instructor. A soldier who is usually attached to a regiment from the Royal Corps of Physical Training.

RAC: Royal Armoured Corps. The RAC consists of the former mounted regiments of Hussars, Lancers, Dragoons and Dragoon Guards as well as the Tank Regiments and mounted Household Division. Today the RAC is employed on tanks.

RAMC: Royal Army Medical Corps.

Reds: Officially known as 'ceremonials', the felt red jackets are worn with similar embellishments as blues but with a ceremonial helmet instead of a forage cap.

Regimental Call. The trumpet call which identifies a regiment. It precedes trumpet calls such as Office, Guard Mount and Stables.

Reveille: The start of the date (0600), or the trumpet or bugle call which signifies this. In a military funeral it precedes Last Post. Infantry and cavalry regiments each have their own version.

RHQ: Regimental Headquarters. The administrative centre of a regiment. It contains the pay office, clerks' offices, CO's and RSM's offices.

RMSM: Royal Military School of Music. Situated in the house of the artist Godfrey Kneller (1646-1723) at Whitton near Twickenham. The RMSM is also referred to as Kneller Hall or KH.

RP: Regimental Police. NCOs drawn from the regiment who ensure discipline is maintained within the barracks, run the guardroom during working hours, and supervise prisoners. The usually wear RP insignia on their arms and white belts and forage caps. The RP come under the jurisdiction of the regimental provost sergeant.

RPs: Restricted Privileges. A term used to denote soldiers who have committed a trivial offence but have not been jailed. RPs are not allowed to leave the barracks, must wear uniform at all times, have to attend Guard Mount and Last Post in full No2 dress and are assigned off-duty fatigues.

RQMS: Regimental Quarter-Master Sergeant. The clothing and equipment stores.

RSM: Regimental Sergeant Major. The most senior of the warrant officers. The RSM is responsible for discipline within the regiment.

RTU: Returned to Unit. The official term for being sent back to your unit from some other location.

Scrim: Camouflage netting used to cover tents and combat helmets and in which twigs and foliage can be fixed.

Sergeant (Sgt): The first SNCO rank, denoted by three chevrons.

Shirt Sleeve Order: In the UK and BAOR the year is split in two and governed by slight variations of uniform. Shirt sleeve order consists of barrack dress minus the pullover. The opposite form of dress is 'pullover order'.

SIB: Special Investigation Branch. A non-uniformed branch of the Military Police (MP). They conduct military investigations.

Side Cap: A felt, triangular cap which sits on the top of the head. It is worn in barrack-dress uniform only and carries the regimental colours.

Singlie: An unmarried soldier or a married soldier who is unaccompanied and lives in barracks.

Slash: The act of adjusting the peak of a forage cap so that it is very narrow and slants downwards to rest on the bridge of the nose. Slashed peaks obscure the eyes. Slashing is a tradition in guard regiments and is forbidden in most other regiments.

SLR: Self-loading rifle.

SMG: Sub-machine gun.

SNCO: Senior Non-Commissioned Officer. The collective term for sergeants, staff sergeants and warrant officers. SNCOs have certain privileges such as their own mess and accommodation.

SOS: Band colloquialism for 'same old shit'.

Sprogg: A derogatory term for a new recruit or newly passed-out soldier.

Squaddie: In civilian use this may apply to anyone who is in the army. Amongst soldiers it is a term to denote lower-rank personnel and/or those with a field role such as the infantry. When used by bandsmen this term is often derogatory; e.g. 'that bandsman is a real squaddie'.

Stable Belt: A large, banded canvas belt that carries the regimental colours and a cap badge on the clasp. They are worn with denim trousers in summer and over jumpers in winter as part of 'barrack dress' order.

Stables: In cavalry regiments a trumpet call sounded for the start of the working day (0830). Some regiments employ the fanfare team for this call.

Staff Band: Bands commanded by a Director of Music who holds an officer rank. These bands are usually larger than line bands and have the luxury of instruments such as the bassoon or oboe – which are obsolete in most line bands.

Staff Sergeant (S/Sgt): The SNCO rank following sergeant. Signified by the chevrons above which is a crown.

Thunderbox: Temporary toilet. Often they lack any door partitions.

Three-tonner: A military lorry with a canvas canopy.

Trooper (Tpr): The lowest rank in the RAC. Outside the cavalry the equivalent rank is that of private.

Trumpet Major (T/M): A cavalry appointment. The T/M is usually a sergeant who wears four inverted chevrons above which are two miniature, crossed trumpets. He is responsible for the training and duties of the regimental trumpeters and fanfare team.

Webbing: The collective term for belts, cross belts and shoulder straps which when assembled are used to attach rucksacks, pouches and equipment. Webbing is usually worn with combats.

Warrant Officers (WO1, WO2): The two ranks beyond that of staff sergeant. WO rank is either second class or first class. WO1 hold positions such as the BM or RSM. They provide the chain of command between the officers and the lower ranks.

W/O: Wife of. This abbreviation was used to denoted the wives of non-commissioned soldiers only. Officers' wives were 'ladies'.

WRAC: Women's Royal Auxiliary Corps. The female branch of the army.

Also in the new GMP series:

Ulster Alien *by Stephen Birkett*
A poignant coming-out story set amidst the troubles of Northern Ireland.

Meet Matthew Woodhead - a sensitive child with his beloved best-friend Danny; an awkward teenager struggling to fit in with the gang; a young gay man on the brink of coming out. But in Northern Ireland everything is more complicated. Matthew's journey to adulthood takes place against a background of civil rights protests, terrorist bombings and the Save Ulster From Sodomy campaign. A world where young lives are destroyed by murder, and young minds by sectarian bigotry. Closely modelled on his own experience, Stephen Birkett portrays a world where the bonds of male friendship are strong, but a gay identity is that much harder to attain.

price - £9.95   ISBN : 1 902852 01 X

Teleny *by Oscar Wilde*
The only complete edition of this erotic tale.

First published in 1893, this outrageous novel of homosexual love has been attributed to Oscar Wilde with varying degrees of certainty. This edition, carefully prepared from original sources in the British Library archives, is the only one on sale annotated and unabridged. Ahead of its time in its celebration of uninhibited sensual passion between men.

"It is a bizarre book, alternating porn with florid purple passages, a hymn to sodomy with an angry attack on notions of the 'natural'" New Statesman.

price - £9.95   ISBN : 1 902852 00 1

Banged Up *by Jack Dickson*

Detective Jas Anderson, the hero of "Freeform" is imprisoned and fighting for his life in this new adventure.

Detective-Sergeant Jas Anderson, the violent anti-hero of Freeform, ended that story being expelled from the Glasgow police force. Banged Up starts with Jas being framed by his ex-colleagues, and remanded to Barlinnie prison. Soon he is forced to share a cell with Steve McStay, sentenced for Aggravated Assault on two gay men. In this all-male enviroment, inmates don't divide into gay and staight, rather into who fucks and who gets fucked. But resilient as ever, Jas forms an unlikely partnership with Steve in his fight survival.

price - £9.95 ISBN : 1 902852 04 4

Foolish Fire *by Guy Willard*

The first in a new trilogy of an all-american teenager's sexual adventures.

Guy willard is your all-American boy, a good-looking, popular teenager with only one hidden secret... a flaming desire for other boys. This first book in a trilogy of his sexual adventures is set at Freedom High School, where he inches his way out of the closet through a series of humerous and poignant episodes. From "Physical Education" to "Technically a Virgin", Guy's personal story is thoroughly true to life: always sexy, but very human.

price - £8.95 ISBN : 1 902852 02 8

Growing Pains *by Mike Seabrook*

The sequel to this author's most popular novel "out of bounds".

Mike Seabrook's many fans will remember Stephen Hill, the dashing young cricketer from Out of Bounds, his teacher and lover Graham, and his clever schoolfriend Richard. Two years after Stephen was forced to leave home, Graham dies in a plane crash, and Steven comes into an unexpected legacy, including a large country pub in Sussex. But as well as the strains this new fortune places on his relationship with friend Richard, the pair have to confront the homophobia of a group of the villagers, resentful of the changes Steven and Richard bring into their lives. Things finally come to a head when a young boy is brutally raped and left for dead.

price - £9.95   ISBN : 1 902852 05 2

The above books can be ordered through the outlet where this volume was purchased or direct from the publisher (enclose £1.95 p&p in the UK or £5 overseas) :

GMP Mail Order, 3 Broadbent Close London N6 5GG.

Cheques payable to 'MaleXpress Ltd.'

(or call 0800 45 45 66 for our catalogue)